FIELD MAN

THE SOUTHWEST CENTER SERIES

Joseph C. Wilder, Editor

Publication of this volume was made possible
in part by a grant from the
Amerind Foundation of Dragoon, Arizona

FIELD MAN

LIFE AS A DESERT ARCHAEOLOGIST

Julian D. Hayden

Edited by Bill Broyles
and Diane E. Boyer

THE UNIVERSITY OF
ARIZONA PRESS

TUCSON

THE UNIVERSITY OF
ARIZONA PRESS

© 2011 The Arizona Board of Regents
All rights reserved
First issued as a paperback edition 2011

www.uapress.arizona.edu

Library of Congress Cataloging-in-Publication Data
Hayden, Julian D., 1911–
Field man : life as a desert archaeologist / Julian D. Hayden ; edited by Bill Broyles and Diane
E. Boyer.
p. cm. — (The Southwest Center series)
Includes bibliographical references and index.
ISBN 978-0-8165-1571-4 (pbk. : alk. paper)
1. Hayden, Julian D., 1911– 2. Indians of North America—Southwest, New—Antiquities.
3. Archaeologists—Southwest, New—Biography. 4. Archaeologists—United States—
Biography. 5. Archaeology—Fieldwork—Southwest, New. 6. Deserts—Southwest, New.
7. Excavations (Archaeology)—Southwest, New. 8. Southwest, New—Antiquities.
I. Broyles, Bill. II. Boyer, Diane E. III. Title.
E78.S7H377   2011
979'.01—dc22   2010039353

Manufactured in the United States of America on acid-free, archival-quality paper
and processed chlorine free.

16 15 14 13 12 11   6 5 4 3 2

Well, Nan, I don't accomplish very much, considering how much I'd intended to do after Helen died. But I do have a good time, with her help in the background. I really seem to enjoy life, in a relaxed, non-pressured way, and I laugh and tell stories where'er I go, and I think maybe I do as much good that away as I might were I to be all solemn and serious and writing learned tomes. The students I know seem to enjoy me and flock around for my tales (or is it my tequila?) and they hear about the early days of Southwest archaeology, which they can't hear from their profs and I suspect it's worthwhile. And now I go to bed.

Love, Julian

—From a letter from Julian Hayden to his sister Nan,
   October 23, 1980

Contents

Foreword

J. Jefferson Reid

All the world's a stage,
And all the men and women merely players;
They have their exits and their entrances;
And one man in his time plays many parts,
His acts being seven ages . . .

—William Shakespeare, *As You Like It*, Act 2, Scene 7

There are as many ways to draw inspiration from the bard as there are portraits of Julian Dodge Hayden. Family members who knew him at life's different ages, friends who crossed at points along the stage, and fellow archaeologists—students and professionals who learned from or argued with him—all have stories, anecdotes, pieces of a complex and complicated man who played many parts in his time.

Julian's memoir reminds me of crusty Ed Tom Bell, the old-time Texas sheriff and central character in Cormac McCarthy's novel *No Country for Old Men* (2005). That title would have been appropriate for this collection of Julian's thoughts and stories. Julian's country, especially the Sierra Pinacate, was "no country for old men," and much of that country no longer exists, much less in the form Julian lived it. Crusty old men and their country are no more.

Bernard "Bunny" Fontana calls Julian the last of the real "desert rats" and provides a biographical sketch of this rare animal to introduce Hayden's last book, *The Sierra Pinacate* (1998). Gayle Hartmann (1998) rightly dubs him "a curmudgeon, but a curmudgeon of the Arizona Style, like his friend Barry Goldwater." Raymond Thompson (1998) provides a pithy portrait of the archaeologist as field man: "Julian Hayden was a rugged individual, tall, wiry, tough, almost formidable, and strong from years of hard work and field research in a forbidding desert region. He could have been the model for A. V. Kidder's 'hairy-chested archaeologist'. . . last of a group of independent archaeologists who contributed in a colorful and substantial way to the development of archaeology in the desert Southwest." Chris Downum (1998) draws on Hayden's Pueblo Grande field notes to provide a personal testimonial of Hayden's keen powers of observation and cultural inference. Stephanie Whittlesey and I (1998) struggled to squeeze Julian into the philosophical mold of American Pragmatism, which is not as absurd an exercise as it might appear because he wrote a concise thought-piece qua advertisement for the local newspaper that commented on contemporary issues as well as provided helpful hints for maintaining a healthy septic system. It remained, however, for Bill Broyles and Diane Boyer to extract and edit Julian Hayden's personal thoughts and remembrances.

Herein lies the result of their hard work and loving care—Julian Hayden's own story as only he should tell it.

His is not a story of archaeological discovery or the mysteries of the prehistoric past, though insights into the Hayden contribution to both topics are one of the rewards of this narrative. The uniqueness of these reflections, however, is that they profile a person and personality of the twentieth-century Southwest, especially Arizona and northern Mexico in the decades surrounding World War II. Julian Hayden was born in 1911, a year before Arizona statehood. He died two years before the end of the twentieth century. In so many ways he reflects a bygone Arizona that changed much too quickly from a hot, dusty, myth-enhancing outpost of cactus, cowboys, and cultures—Mexican, Indian, and European-American—to an undifferentiated amalgam of houses, malls, and cars. By November 2010, there were over one million people in southern Arizona.

Julian Hayden maintained a lifelong love of Mexico, its many peoples, and the Spanish language. Chuck Bowden (1998) writes: "He is Don Julian down here [Mexico], the old one who wanders the *despoblado*. In the Sonoran cafes he flirts with the waitresses. In the ranches he trades *dichos* with the vaqueros."

Bowden goes on to paint a portrait of the Julian Hayden revealed in the pages that follow. "He is seventy-five years old and has the moves of an old lion. The tall, lanky body has the carriage of a man who has used his muscles. The close cropped silver hair glows against the tanned skin and chest hair flares from the top of his shirt. He speaks in a monotone and at first the words seem like the product of some foreign language. Then the rhythms become apparent and whole sentences appear—sentences stated in a courtly turn of phrase. The smile comes easily and often and has the look of a grin on a Cheshire cat. He wears old clothes. He likes old things."

Hayden drove a '52 Chevrolet coupe until he could drive no more. He was, as the reader will discover, unapologetic in his seeming anachronisms. He had few regrets, or perhaps, like others of his generation, he regarded missteps and misdemeanors as too private for popular consumption and none of your damn business! He reveals only the merest hint of his lifelong romanticism and the mystical realism that was the leitmotif of his later years. Bear in mind that this narrative is an extemporaneous oral composition expressed in the closing ages of a long and eventful life. The last words in this tale say it all: "Oh, this field man's had a king's life."

This field man is remembered for far more than being a relic of a bygone time and place, at least in the archaeological community of the Southwest, where his substantial contributions underscore the essential necessity of competent field skills in piecing together the stories of the past. He got his start with his father Irwin Hayden, a Harvard-trained archaeologist, on several museum-sponsored expeditions to Utah and Arizona, and both men were members of the legendary crew that excavated Snaketown in the winter of 1934–1935. It was this excavation that provided the critical evidence to complete the delineation of the Hohokam culture sequence, especially the ceramic chronology based on Julian's excavation of Mound 29. Equally remarkable yet rarely acknowledged is Julian's pivotal role in preserving the Pima Indian creation narrative. In the evenings of March 1935, after a full day working at Snaketown, Julian transcribed and thus preserved William Smith Allison's English translation of Juan Smith's Pima narrative, edited by Don Bahr in *The Short, Swift Time of Gods on Earth: The Hohokam Chronicles* (1994). Julian would exercise his powers of ethnographic observation to record

O'odham (Papago) pottery making and the winter Vikita ceremony as he reinforced the absolute need for archaeologists to understand living cultures and their adjustment to local environments.

From 1936 to 1940, Julian worked at Pueblo Grande, a Classic period site shadowed today by airplanes landing at and leaving from Phoenix Sky Harbor Airport from the east. Julian's meticulous excavation and recording of the Pueblo Grande mound provide archaeologists with the most complete record of mound use in the Arizona desert. Interpreted and reported by Chris Downum and Todd Bostwick (2003), Pueblo Grande stands out as the best excavated mound by the best field archaeologist ever to explore the prehistoric past of the Sonoran Desert. Also early in 1940 Julian directed the excavations at the Classic period University Indian Ruin in Tucson (Hayden 1957).

In 1942 Julian took over as crew chief during the second season of excavations at Ventana Cave, a happenstance find that would become famous for charting the prehistoric cultural sequence of southern Arizona from the end of the Ice Age to the Desert branch of the Hohokam (Haury 1950). Looking back on Ventana Cave many years later, Julian believed he had unearthed crude tools of the Malpais culture in the basal level of the cave, and Stephanie Whittlesey and I took him at his word in labeling the cave layers in *The Archaeology of Ancient Arizona* (1997:50). We also in that book gave serious attention to his most controversial contribution to our understanding of the past—his concept of a Malpais culture being earlier than the well-established Clovis culture.

Julian began exploring the Sierra Pinacate of northwestern Sonora, Mexico, in the late 1950s to find crude tools, trails, sleeping circles, and stone cairns mingled with the surface debris of historical and contemporary passersby (Hayden 1998). The only difference in these surface artifacts was in the amount of desert varnish they exhibited, which led Julian into researching the processes and conditions that contributed to the formation of desert varnish. The crude tools of stone and shell, trails, and circles would make up the fragile evidence for the Malpais culture, while desert varnish would provide the dating necessary to place the Malpais in time. Julian spent the rest of his archaeological life gathering evidence of artifacts and associations in the Pinacate, studying the forbidding landscape, and thinking and rethinking the Malpais model. Michael Heilen's (2004) analysis best captures Julian's thinking on the Malpais in its most complete and final form. It remains, of course, for other researchers to take up where Julian left off. He would be pleased to see his pioneering work inspiring younger archaeologists and overjoyed if it continued to create controversy in the archaeological community.

References

Bahr, Donald, Juan Smith, William Smith Allison, and Julian Hayden. *The Short, Swift Time of Gods on Earth: The Hohokam Chronicles*. Berkeley: University of California Press, 1994.

Bowden, Charles. "Going to the Black Rock." In *The Sierra Pinacate*, by Julian D. Hayden, 2–8. Tucson: University of Arizona Press, 1998.

Downum, Christian E. "The Observer: Julian Hayden at Pueblo Grande." *Kiva* 64, no. 2 (1998): 245–274.

Downum, Christian E., and Todd W. Bostwick. "The Platform Mound." In *Centuries of Decline during the Hohokam Classic Period at Pueblo Grande*, edited by D. R. Abbott, 166–200. Tucson: University of Arizona Press, 2003.

Fontana, Bernard L. "The Making of a Field Archaeologist." In *The Sierra Pinacate*, by Julian D. Hayden, x–xv. Tucson: University of Arizona Press, 1998.

Hartmann, Gayle Harrison. "Julian Hayden, AAHS, and the Pinacates: An Anecdotal Reminiscence." *Kiva* 64, no. 2 (1998): 103–114.

Haury, Emil W. *The Stratigraphy and Archaeology of Ventana Cave.* Tucson: University of Arizona Press, 1950.

Hayden, Julian D. *Excavations, 1940, at University Indian Ruin*, Southwestern Monuments Technical Series, vol. 5. Globe: Southwestern Monuments Association, 1957.

Hayden, Julian D. *The Sierra Pinacate.* Tucson: University of Arizona Press, 1998.

Heilen, Michael P. "Julian Hayden's Malpais Model: A Pre-Clovis Claim from the American Southwest." *Kiva* 69, no. 3 (2004): 305–331.

Reid, J. Jefferson, and Stephanie M. Whittlesey. *The Archaeology of Ancient Arizona.* Tucson: University of Arizona Press, 1997.

Reid, J. Jefferson, and Stephanie M. Whittlesey. "A Search for the Philosophical Julian: American Pragmatism and Southwestern Archaeology." *Kiva* 64, no. 2 (1998): 275–286.

Thompson, Raymond H. "Julian Dodge Hayden, 1911–1998." *Kiva* 64, no. 2 (1998): 289–293.

Further Reading

Heilen, Michael P. "Julian Dodge Hayden and the Sierra Pinacate: Pioneering Archaeology of the Western Papaguería." In *Fragile Patterns: The Archaeology of Western Papaguería*, edited by Jeffrey H. Altschul and Adrianne G. Rankin, 63–75. Tucson: Statistical Research Press, 2008.

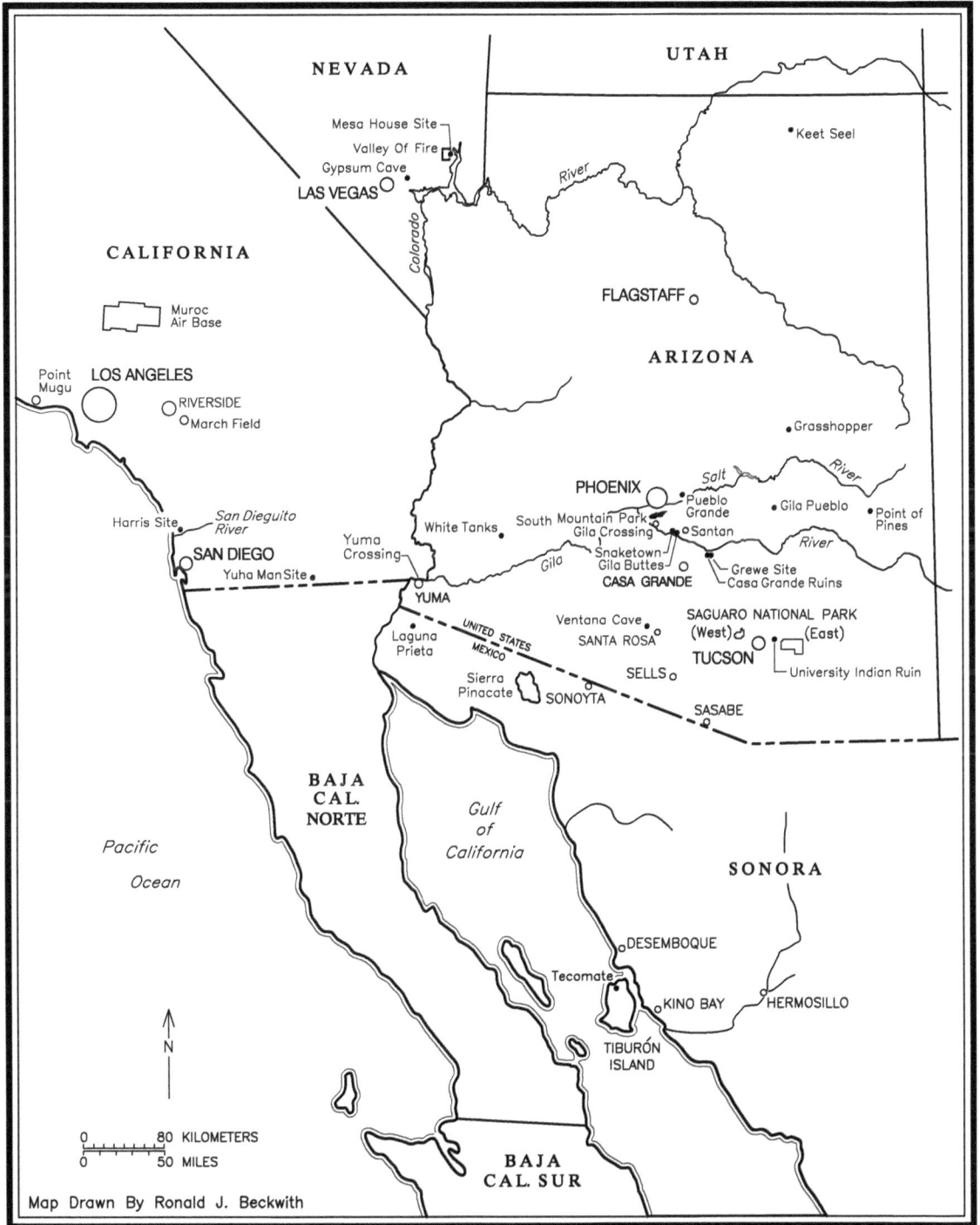

The southwestern United States and northwestern Mexico, showing places discussed in the text. (Map by Ronald J. Beckwith)

FIELD MAN

1. Heritage

My father, Irwin Hayden, got his master's in archaeology from Harvard in 1909 and was protégé of F. W. Putnam and destined to take over Peabody Museum, but he was also a bit thorny at times. Evidently some words were said at graduation over I don't know what, and the next day he drove to Montana where he took a job in a sawmill. My father, I think, always had a hidden desire to have been a mountain man. I think that's another reason he went to Montana instead of continuing with his anthropological work. One of his uncles had gone to Montana, oh, way back in the 1870s, I guess. Eventually he came back to New England, but stories came down to the family, and it was I think the Dakotas, which is even worse than Montana.

Some of my Hayden ancestors went up to Nova Scotia in the 1700s, before the Revolutionary War. I don't know much about Nova Scotia. I've never been there. My father used to go up there every summer when he was a little boy. Up to Haydentown, which is now Osbourne. He had relatives up there; they were all seafaring men: fishermen and sailors on the big ships. I remember he told me one time that there was a legend in his family about a remote ancestor who, in the days of clipper ships, was hauling tea from Canton, China. He was a captain at sixteen or seventeen. When they left Boston Harbor, he was on the poop deck and somehow slipped and fell badly. The fall rolled his nose over to one side, and of course it stayed there. Coming out of Canton Harbor he fell again and knocked it back the other way. And when they came into Boston Harbor, he took a final tumble and put it right in the middle of his face where it stayed till he died. It's one of those little stories they tell.

But my father had a model Gloucester fishing boat, the sailing vessel used by the Gloucester [Massachusetts] fishermen. It was handmade by one of his ancestors. The whole thing was a scale model, probably about three feet long. Its planks were an eighth of an inch wide, you know, and laid up. Oh, that was a beautiful thing sailing on the lake up in Phoenix. He brought it over one time to sail it on Encanto Lake there. I guess he took it to his first cousin, Thomas Hayden, who was assistant chief engineer of the Water Users Association. Thomas was a well-known man in his time, too. He was born in Nova Scotia. And he lived in Phoenix, where he came out for the TB [tuberculosis]. They had to carry him off the train, but in time he recovered. He was a pretty good man, too, but a man with a short fuse, as I remember. If you didn't understand what he said the first time, he became furious, which made life a little difficult to live with him. But he wound down. He died after the war.

My brother Perry went up. He was planning to live up there. He cleared the cemetery with the last surviving Hayden, last close Hayden, in Nova Scotia, cousin Lee. But they were a different physical type, they were short and broad, like my father.

Irwin Hayden in 1907.

*From "Notes on a Letter from Irwin Hayden
to Professor F. W. Putnam, April 10, 1908,"
by Julian Hayden, July 1989*

There is a clear affection shown [between Dad and F. W. Putnam], respect and friendship. Putnam was as near God as any man Dad ever knew, I believe. He always spoke of him with the utmost appreciation. And, in fact, the finest compliment Dad ever paid me, I think, was when he wrote in the margin of a typescript of a report I'd sent him, that "Professor Putnam would have approved of this."

Re: the exchange with Tozzer: Dad described it many times to us, saying that he'd stood beside Dr. Tozzer on the steps after the ceremony [graduation] and Tozzer had asked, as he drew on his white gloves (always a symbol of la-di-da-ism to Dad), "Do you intend to make anthropology your career, Mr. Hayden?" Dad, probably excited and therefore touchy, retorted, "No! I'm going to make a living at it!" And he went home and brooded over that, and left for Montana almost immediately. . . . I might also remark that Dr. Tozzer had married a wealthy woman from a Hawaiian missionary family which had made fortunes in pineapple, etc., and the graduate students resented this, as he was almost the same age as Dad, who was poor as a church mouse!

You never met him, I guess, no. Five ten, five eleven, but my father had a fifty-odd-inch chest. Powerful brute, hands like a bear. My brother did too, but he got height from my mother, who was six foot, so he was almost as tall as I am.

The Haydens settled near Boston first, Braintree I believe, and when the Revolution came some of them went up to Nova Scotia. The ones that went to Nova Scotia lost everything they had in Boston. So they set out to be privateersmen. They fought the British at sea. So my father used to say that one of the early acts of the First Continental Congress was a vote to indemnify them for their losses during the war in Boston property. But I never saw a copy of it and I'd like to have. That's the way it was in those days, of course.

I'd like to go back there but not enough to go.

I was born in Hamilton, Montana, January 1911. We had an old cow in Montana named Bluebell. She was blue and a good milker. I remember her for several reasons. One, she got in the corn patch one day and my mother, Mary Dodge Hayden, went out to run her out and she wouldn't budge. My mother did something most uncharacteristic of her. She was wearing tennis shoes, and she hauled off and aimed to kick at Bluebell's midsection, but Bluebell stepped at just the wrong time and my mother broke her toe on Bluebell's hip. So she never tried that again.

I also remember Bluebell because when I was but about five years old, I guess, I was out with my father and some men. I don't know what they were doing, talking about something maybe, and my father was bragging on Bluebell.

"You know," he said, "she's got the most beautiful tits."

And I spoke up and I said, "Ma's are prettier." I was considerably older before I realized what that silence meant.

Then when my father went off to Europe to fight in the war in early 1917, the family moved to Winthrop, Massachusetts, for a couple of years. That's where my father's mother, Rosanna "Rose" Etherington, lived. When he returned from the war, rather than return to Montana, where he had held various jobs, none too difficult or rewarding, he accepted a newspaper job in Riverside, California.

We had a little two-acre farm in Riverside, California. My father bought that with a house in 1919. He always loved farming. We had had a farm in Montana, too, a small one, where I was born. In Riverside we had a few rabbits, two or three goats, a couple cows, and two acres of Sudan grass plus a truck garden. My mother was a gardener, and she raised her own berries and fruits and everything, New England style. She canned all the fruit and vegetables.

Eventually my father built a rabbitry. It was the first one, and the biggest one, in Southern California. I think we had 300 breeding does, a pretty good-sized rabbitry. I worked on that rabbitry through the latter part of grade school, what you call seventh and eighth grade now, and all through high school. Taking care of those rabbits, I worked out their genetics and bred them and fed them and cleaned them, and every Saturday I'd butcher several score of them and clean them and deliver them to the butcher shops. Kept me busy. Kept me out of mischief.

That flourished for a while until about the time I got out of high school, when the rabbit mania hit Southern California and everybody had rabbits in the back yard, so the price of hay tripled overnight, and it broke us. That was the end of that.

Julian Hayden, age five, at right, with younger sister Nan, Hamilton, Montana, 1916.

Mary Dodge Hayden in 1908.

The Hayden home in Hamilton, Montana, ca. 1915.

Mary Dodge Hayden in a Metz automobile, about 1914–1917. Julian is to the left; the baby is either Nan or Perry Hayden.

I had damned little time. That's why I never learned how to dance or even how to talk to girls or anything else, 'cause I never had time for it. Of course, I'm glad to say I can these days, but I couldn't have then. No, it was good training. You learned how to work. And on a small farm like that, you damn well worked. Somebody had to do it.

*Julian with Abraham
the rabbit in Riverside,
California, 1921.*

My father was secretary of the Chamber of Commerce at that time, which occupied his time, so I took care of the animals. I was a pretty good milker, too. And I could talk goat-talk, also. I could bleat at the goats and they'd hightail it over to the milking stand to take their turns and run up and run down again. We got along fine. We had Saanen and Toggenburg goats. And Nubian. They were all dairy goats.

My father ran for mayor of Riverside, but he got beat by about 200 votes, because his opponent was a Ku Kluxer . . . at that time the Ku Klux Klan was in ascendancy in Southern California, and I mean that, too. Mr. Edward Dighton, the competitor, his opponent, covered the town with dodgers the night before election, referring to my father and referring particularly to me as that slope-headed kid that kept tormenting the neighborhood widow woman who lived next door. So, my father lost the election by about 200 votes. Best thing that ever happened to him. You know "slope-headed"? I'd never been called that before and not very often since.

Pretty near out of high school, I was sixteen. And I don't think my father knew what in the hell he was going to do with me, because during my senior year I got interested in motorcycles. I think if my father had been as wise as I think I am, he would have said,

"Well, son, if you want to know about motorcycles, by God, you just go down and you take auto shop. And learn about motorcycles and internal combustion engines."

Well, he didn't do that. He didn't say much of anything. So my grades went to hell and I damned near didn't graduate, although I was a straight A student, always have been, for no reason at all except that I've read so much, I guess. It confused everybody in the high school and we had various problems. So somehow, I think, my father came down to my graduation [from Riverside Polytechnic High School], which I certainly didn't deserve. I had several Ds in my senior year. And it was . . . hell, I was only, I was beginning my senior year at the age of fifteen, what the hell do you expect? Everybody else was two or three years older than I was. That's why I never go to high school reunions. I was a little punk with a . . . with the glasses and the knee britches, you know? Anyway, that's the way those things go.

I was in ROTC, which was nice because they finally let me become a second lieutenant in charge of supplies, and I was on the rifle team, and I was good. I was a good rifleman, not an expert, but sharpshooter. That gave me a little self-satisfaction.

Anyway, when I got out of school, Dad got me a job with Johnson Construction Company running a big pipeline into Riverside. So I went down into a ditch with a Mexican crew and worked as a laborer, shoveling sand into a cement mixer. And I enjoyed it. It was hard work and good for me. Except I didn't know how to work for somebody else, so pretty soon I got fired.

So I went and got myself a job with a Gunite outfit, spraying concrete. That lasted a while, and I did fine. Then I got fired from that for a good reason, because I wanted to go home one day when my father was waiting for me, which he shouldn't have done. He shouldn't even have shown up, you know. But he did. So the next morning I was out of work. After all, the machine's going all the time, so I learned that. Then I went to work for LA Construction, and I never lost another job. I shifted around a little, for fun, and wanted to get a motorcycle, but I never got fired again. That's how I got into construction. I started out as a wheelbarrow man, working the mixer.

In those days we didn't have pumps or ready-mix or anything else. I was the best wheelbarrow man in Southern California. And I'm still proud of it. A competing company had a wheelbarrow man who they said was better than LA Construction had. So they sent him over to March Field to compete with me. We got in line in front of the mixer. He was a big black man named Paddlefoot Johnson, Paddlefoot something or another. He stood around and watched me and said, "Hell," he said, "I ain't crazy, I'm going back to LA. That guy, he ain't got no sense." And he was right. I should have taken a half wheelbarrow-full, like everybody else, but no, by God, I wanted it slopping. Why the hell work if I'm not going to work?

We went up scaffolding and over planks. And you wheeled all that concrete to pour solid concrete walls, every damn bit of it. A big Indian on the uphill side used a hook to help pull it up. I'll never forget one time we needed another wheelbarrow-full on the other side of the big opening in a hangar wall . . . up about twelve feet. So there was a plank laid across this opening, and I started to cross it. A twelve-inch plank. A full wheelbarrow has about three or four hundred pounds of concrete in it. I got halfway across and somebody said, "Slim! That blonde is looking at you!" And I lost my balance—almost lost the wheelbarrow and me too, but I didn't fall. I didn't spill a drop, either. Never forgot that.

And when you were working on the mixer, you shoveled various grades and sizes of gravel into the hopper; somebody else shoveled sand; and the mixer man operated the batch. He was crusted with cement from head to foot. It was hard work. When you shovel inch-and-a-half rock with a Number Two Iowa scoop, you know you've been somewhere. I've still got a couple of them out in the shop. I always carry them with me on the archaeological jobs, those scoops. I can't get anybody to use them. I can't see any point in using a long-handled shovel, when you can move four times as much by bending over and making one sweep. I still feel that way about it. They don't make them like that any more. That's the way we were raised.

These were the steel-wheeled wheelbarrows. Wheel probably an inch or an inch and a half wide. We didn't have rubber, hell no. One time I loaded twelve sacks of cement—they were sacks then, not paper, cloth, ninety-four pounders—twelve sacks into a standard wheelbarrow, with the wheel in the rock and dirt, just on a bet. It's one reason I went to March Field, see, and indirectly one reason I went to Mesa House. I used to walk real tall, so I'd carry—you can believe this or not, I don't care, though I can't do it now, damn it—but I'd pick up five sacks. I'd take out five at one time and put them in the truck. Put one on each shoulder, one over my head across the two of them, and one in each hand. That's 480-some, 490-some pounds. I did that several times.

My father weighed 135 pounds when he was sixteen, and he was working in a grocery store. His father, Perez M. Hayden, had died; he had to support the family. And he could unload a 300-pound hogshead of sugar from a dray to the store floor, and he could also reload it. And he weighed 135 pounds.

My father was very much interested in geology. He had a minor in it. One of his instructors at Harvard, Dr. Eggleston, lived in Riverside, and every Thanksgiving he and his wife would come for dinner. Then he and my father would take a walk down the Santa Ana River bottoms to look at the cut banks and discuss geology . . . and I'd tag along. I've always been interested, and I had a couple of years of geology at junior college. The junior college prof, C. S. Bacon, was not much older than I was, and we were great friends. I've always loved it. Still do.

We took field trips at Riverside Junior College. Good field trips. I'm particularly interested in faults and fault zones, and things like that. Still am. Come by it natural. My father was a good geologist. He knew Gregory and Chamberlin and Salisbury, all those people who were extant around the turn of the century. I don't think he'd approve of geology now because they've changed so many things, but not much he can do about that.

Hell, yes, I would have been a field man. I wouldn't be a laboratory man at all. No way. Not any more than necessary. Not any more than I am now. They're both necessary, but I'd rather be out in the field. I found geology to be a great help because, although I don't remember much geology, I know where to go to find out what I need to know, which is the real value of a college education, what little I had of it, two years. If you know where to go, why, you've got it made, I think.

Neither of my parents were musical, but they wanted me to be. When I was ten years old I took piano lessons from one of Edmund Jaeger's sisters for about four or five years. They were old German spinsters, his sisters, and he was a bachelor. They were characters. I think that if I hadn't taken piano lessons from her, I might have known something about music: she would not permit memorization. No way. And, as a result, I've never been able to memorize any music at all, although I could have if I'd been started that way. And that took most of the pleasure out of it. But I took piano lessons for years under her, and then I took them again in junior college, from a Mills College pianist who was teaching. She was the most frustrated little woman you ever saw, because I had a good touch and I could span ten keys with no trouble, but I couldn't remember two notes from one day to the next. She'd get so frustrated she'd pretty near cry.

So naturally I never bought a piano. I used to play the ocarina, though. The potato horn. A little thing like a sweet potato with a nozzle on it, and you blow in the nozzle, and you've got eight or ten holes, and they come in various keys. You can buy them in any music shop, or could. I had one in the key of C, I think. When I was a kid, I'd get up and take a stepladder, sit out in the middle of a field in the moonlight, and do my best to remember some Mexican folk songs. Nice thing for a guy when he's lonesome and doesn't know anybody—you sit out there and play the potato horn. I've done a lot of that.

So after high school, I kicked around a few years, then started junior college in Riverside in the fall of 1931. Professor Jaeger, Edmund Jaeger, he didn't like me. When I went to Riverside he was teaching biology. He didn't like me and I didn't like him, just period, that's all there was to it. He disliked me to the extent that when my sister took biology some years later he gave her a B although she was doing A work, just because she was my sister. And she was real angry with him, but he made it stick.

He was a good naturalist, I have to give him credit for that. For some reason the thing that sticks in my mind about him was he used to put skim milk in his bicycle tires so he wouldn't have to inflate them. I don't how he got it in, but he filled them up. And one day he was bicycling toward school and the front tire exploded and covered him with rotten skim milk; he had to go home and change his clothes and take a bath. I chuckled over that . . . still chuckle over it. You ever hear of such a thing? Now you have. Yeah, that sour milk clabbered on him.

I never paid any attention to him. I don't think he made much fuss on campus. A bunch of us football players, or pseudo-football players, used to eat lunch on a big balcony outside his office. We'd get to telling stories and he didn't like that. I remember one time I was all alone, everybody was doing something else. He came out, and I was leaning over the balcony edge, and we struck up a conversation, or tried to. So he got off on the subject of whited sepulchers, which I thought was somewhat unusual, until I realized he was probably talking about me. So then I was noncommunicative, and he finally gave up and went away. I think he'd heard me swearing or something once. Whited sepulcher. That's pretty good. There aren't many of us who qualify for that, you know. But that's the way he was. Some of the boys who went on field trips with him had other remarks, which I will not repeat because he was a pretty good naturalist.

You've read his books, of course, yeah. He was in the Pinacate since I started. Did you know that? He must have been ninety-odd. Somebody brought him over to the dunes just west of the mountain there, and they traveled around for a couple days. So I was told. I'm not putting him down a damn bit. No, he was good. I make a real separation between his work and him.

Philosophy? I took philosophy in junior college under a wonderful old man, Harry L. Boardman, who changed his denomination three times, I think. He'd been a minister, three different denominations. He was criticized for it, but he was an honest man. He was in his seventies. A couple of times when he was ill I took his classes, once for a week. Not that I knew how to teach anything, but I had a lot of fun. I could abstract what I read. And I enjoyed it. A puzzle.

Then one day I was sitting in the library working on something and I thought, "What in the hell has this got to do with the real world?" And, I've never read any philosophy since, which probably says something to you, I don't know what. Damn little theory. And theory goes along with philosophy. If I can't lay hands on it I can't do much with it.

I tried to play football in college. Hell, I was big and strong and young. The two coaches had come over from the Trojans to take the football team out of the bottom of the conference to the top of it. And they did it in one year. In football camp, just before school started, they glommed on to me. I weighed one hundred and ninety pounds, but I was not an athlete. I was slow moving. I never learned coordination and speed at all. I'd only done heavy work, you know—it makes a difference. I never played games when I was a kid; we were always busy, too much to do.

So I was on the third string. I was fodder for the big boys. We had some professionals. I remember one man, named Shell, Walt Shell. He was in his eleventh year playing junior college football. And another man on the team, I've forgotten his name, Red something, he was a ninth year. He came over here to the University of Arizona after that and died of rheumatic fever over here. But there were professional football players in those days in junior colleges.

So the two coaches won the conference the first year they were there. And they sure beat the hell out of a bunch of scrubs, too. I don't know how many permanent injuries came out of the second and third teams. I got my neck popped and went home with a concussion and one eye out and nose bleeding. The next day I went in and said, "Here's your gear, to hell with you." And I never went back. I realized, this is ridiculous, just to make a couple of coaches a reputation. And they made it, too, became famous coaches: Jess Hill and Jess Mortensen. And I'm not criticizing them, either. That was the system. It was the way it was done. And I guarantee nobody criticized me for quitting, either, because I was too big. Not that I was a fighting man, but they didn't know that.

Did I play football in high school, too? Oh, hell no. I was just a snotty-nosed, bespectacled, knee-britched, squirt in high school, about three years younger than everybody else, so I didn't fit in anywhere. You asked me, and I told you. I didn't start school until I was eight years old, and then I went into the third grade. I skipped a couple of grades after that—they didn't know what to do with me, just because we had a big library at home and I read from the time I was three years old, that's all. No smarts connected, I was just a better reader than some of the teachers. That makes a difference.

My major in junior college? I didn't have any. Just signed up. I didn't give a damn about graduating or anything else. I just wanted to take the courses I wanted to take. And I did. So they graduated me, because I carried twenty-six units, two years, straight As all the way through. And they didn't know what to do with me. And I was older, and I knew what I wanted. Greek, Latin, geology, philosophy, English.

My father was editor of the *Ravalli Republican*, up in Hamilton, Montana, when he dropped everything and went off to the Marines in World War I. In Hamilton he was also secretary of the Chamber of Commerce and secretary of the light and power company, but he was bored stiff; there wasn't anybody to talk to in that valley. They were

Irwin Hayden in his U.S. Marines uniform, 1918.

all working folks, cowmen and farmers, very few college people . . . and Dad had been to Harvard with a capital *H*, so what do you do?

He joined the Marines. Three kids, a decent subsistence farm, he was overage and he had bad eyes. But he pestered Smedley Butler until Smedley Butler wired or called Missoula recruitment office and said, "If the damn fool wants in that bad, take him!" Smedley Butler was a general, commandant of the Marine Corps, a very famous man in those days.

My father wanted to be a Marine, that's all, so he went to the top. Didn't want to be a damn Army grunt, a "doughboy" they called them then. He was going to be a Marine; that's where the men were. So he became eventually a supply sergeant and went to France. He got his sharpshooter's badge in the fishtail winds on Mare Island in San Francisco Harbor. A sharpshooter's badge on that firing range was something to be proud of. It was the equivalent of an expert anywhere else. Yeah, he bragged about that till he died, and he'd show it to you at the drop of a hat, too.

So he went to France. The Marines landed. My father's ship disembarked at Brest on the coast of France, and Dad had a little time off, so he wandered over to the flood-plains on the River Loire, covered with flint nodules. He was an expert field man. He knew his business. He picked one nodule out a hundred yards away as being manmade. He brought back this honey flint tool from the Dordogne, Paleolithic, well over 35,000

Dear ones;

Herewith, Julian, is a statement on the coup-de-poing. . . .

In November, 1948, I, Supply and Police Sergeant, "G" Company, 11th Regiment, U.S. Marine Corps, was walking across a part of what I took to be the flood plain of the river Cher, a tributary of the Loire River. I was on an errand. The terrain was a pene-plain, virtually flat. The ground was covered with innumerable fragments of flint imbedded in the soil, closely approaching the "desert seal" of our southwestern deserts in Arizona and Old Mexico.

As I walked, my thoughts were far from archaeological matters. I did, however, as was and is my habit, keep my face toward the ground, my eyes searching the surface, with no conscious awareness of what I saw.

If the artifact referred to is at hand, let it be grasped in the right hand, as its maker seems to have intended it to be. One will observe that a small part of the artifact appears between the base of one's thumb and index finger; a portion about the size of the knuckle of one's thumb. This portion of the object has not been chipped.

It was this part of the artifact which protruded above the surface of the soil, amidst uncounted pieces of flint. It was directly in my path. Suddenly, without thought, I found myself on my knees, opened pocket-knife in hand, prying this piece of flint up and out from its resting place of who can say how long a time? When I stood up I had in my hand this beautiful example of a flint artifact, which, I suspect, I have correctly classified as a coup-de-poing, or "blow of the fist." . . .

I find myself, in 1966, still amazed that my somewhat trained eye had spotted a very small portion of it, there in the midst of tens of thousands of other flints.

The Phillips Printery, 4016 Orange St., Tel. 1499. The House of Fine Printing......

Riverside Bindery, 3556 Ninth St. Tel.3158. Books Bound, Re-bound, paper ruled.....

TEN CENTS PER COPY   FIVE DOLLARS PER YEAR

HAYDEN'S

Volume V. Number 16. 120th Issue.   A WEEKLY PAPER

Riverside, California,
April 22, 1936.

Dear Folks:

Nah-da-gum-kur-ly is a phonetic spelling of a Pima phrase meaning " crazy old man ". It does not mean " crazy " in the sense of insane. I first heard it after it became known in camp that Julian and Helen were married. The Pimas would look at me and say, gleefully, in their soft, slow way: Nah-da-gum-kur-ly. " That means the way the father feels when he finds out that his son is going to marry a nice girl, ", a Pima explained.

It is interesting and I think significant, the way one's friends congratulate one on becoming a grandparent. Can it be that there is even yet a spark of virility in our people, that prompts them to take delight in the birth of children ? We are not ancestor worshippers and we may eventually be conquered by ancestor worshippers, but it seems that we do, after all, have a hearty and wholesome interest in progeny.

The top portion of a 1936 copy of Irwin Hayden's Hayden's Weekly, *which he printed for several years in the 1930s. While Hayden invariably discussed politics, he often mentions family matters; in this issue he begins with comments on having become a grandparent after the birth of Julian and Helen's first child. Irwin Hayden worked intermittently for decades as a newspaper columnist and commentator, often for the* Riverside Enterprise *and the* Riverside News, *with columns that included "Hayden's Corner," "Highways and Byways," and "An Archeologist Afield." He also did a brief series in the* Arizona Republican *entitled "Hunting the Ho-ho-kam," on his work at Casa Grande.*

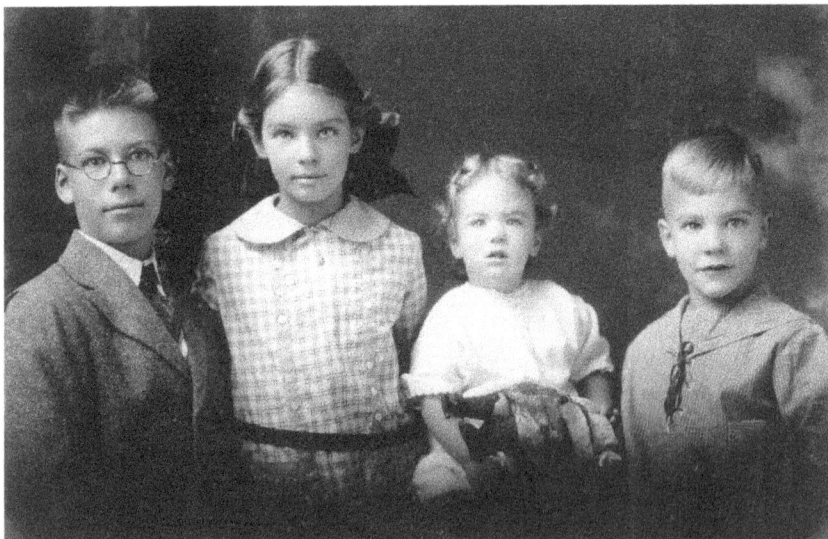

Irwin and Mary Hayden's children, ca. 1923, in Riverside, California. From left to right: Julian, Nan, Jessie, and Perry (Perez).

years old and probably a good deal more. Eventually I inherited it; that's why I keep it on the table here.

Anyway, he was in the Fifth Marines, Company G. And the Fifth Marines were about to go into action, I forget whether it was Belleau Wood or Chateau Thierry. And Dad's company was detached and put on guard duty at Gierres. And he never heard a shot fired. It like to broke his heart, plagued him all his life. He had nothing to do with it, couldn't help it. But the Fifth Marines went into action, and not very many of them came out.

So that probably had an effect on us kids, too. Who knows? But from then on, I'll tell you, when my father got mad about something, he stiffened his knees the way a Marine sergeant learned to do, and everybody got out of his way. I don't care if it was City Hall, or county supervisors, or the chief of police, they moved when Old Man Hayden was on the rampage.

In Riverside he'd gone on hard times, so when things got very bad, he undertook to report the county supervisors meetings and the city council meetings verbatim. He was an expert shorthand man. We didn't have machines in those days. He'd take them down verbatim, and he had an A. B. Dick mimeograph machine. And he'd mimeograph these sheets out with his comments, which were pretty pungent sometimes. Charged a dime apiece for them, and he made beans on it. Oh, lord, how the politicians hated to see that paper come out once a week. They used to buy them up so other people wouldn't see them.

Finally he got on the subject of cleaning up the weeds along the highways, and they said, "Hayden, by God, if you feel so strongly about it, here's a spray truck and here's a crew of men, chain gang, go out and clean them." So he did. That shut him up for a while. But he sure cleaned the highways down in Indio; they wanted him way away from the county seat. I've still got a few of those issues. I don't know if anybody ever kept a complete file. They were interesting.

2. Early Field Work

How did I get to Mesa House, Nevada? Did you ever read *Jurgen* by James Branch Cabell? He's out of style and nobody's ever heard of him now. He was one of my gods, and during the war I worked with an Irishman from upstate New York who could recite *Jurgen* from the first page to the last. Well, as Jurgen said, one thing leads to another, see. After my father got crosswise with himself and quit Harvard in 1909, he didn't have anything to do with archaeology for twenty years, when he returned to archaeology and took me along to work in Nevada with the Southwest Museum in Los Angeles.

Late 1928 or '29, his old college buddy M. R. Harrington, who had worked for the Heye Foundation in New York in the intervening years, came out to Los Angeles to work as curator of archaeology for the Southwest Museum. Harrington and my father had excavated in Madisonville, Ohio, and upstate New York, and Long Island; they'd done a lot of work. They knew each other and had kept in touch.

Our family was on hard times then, and Harrington asked my father if he'd like to go with him to Nevada and excavate Mesa House, which Harrington had spotted when he was excavating the Lost City in Nevada for the Heye Foundation in earlier years. My father said yes, and he took me along as a laborer. I'd been working at March Field, working for the LA Construction Company, rebuilding it. Heavy work. And I was seventeen or eighteen years old, and we weren't eating the sorts of things a young fellow needed to do heavy work. I was beginning to get a little "puny," as my Southern friends say, although I never said anything about it.

Anyway, I went along. M. R. Harrington had married the sister of Arthur Parker, the state archaeologist in New York; she was half Seneca and half Scotch, a good combination. So, Endeka Harrington was a cook. And I ate for about four months. I grew up on that job, physically, really. The first couple days up on the mesa they handed me a damn trowel and a whisk broom. Hell, I'd been loading 94-pound sacks of cement, hauling them out of a boxcar and putting them on a truck, and I was the best wheelbarrow man in March Field and all that sort of thing. This was sissy stuff, but I found an arrowhead, so that was that. I was hooked. You know how that can go. Does that answer how I got to Mesa House?

But I damned near didn't get to Mesa House, because while I was working March Field I bought a motorcycle, an old high-wheeler. Fifteen dollars. Nineteen twenty-six Harley, FCA 61. I can give you the serial number if you want. And the first time I got on it, I went around a corner too fast and went into a ditch and got thrown over a rose hedge. I got skinned up and the front wheel got broken, but that just made me sort of mad, so I learned how to ride it. I became a hill climber and a road racer, in a small way.

At the 1929 Pecos Conference, from left to right: Charles Amsden, M. R. Harrington, Irwin Hayden, Art Woodward, Frederick W. Hodge.

Anyhow, I went over to San Bernardino before we went to Nevada, and I got picked up for not having a taillight or some damned thing. When I got back to Riverside, I had to go to court. Judge hit me for thirty days' suspension of license, which is pretty rough, but I don't think he liked my father very well. Anyhow, I just went ahead with my business. I also had a little Chevrolet strip-down coupe at the time, and I even took my father to the movies one night, by a back road. The day before we were to leave for Nevada, my father was downtown. He was rather a politician, too, a very well-known man. And some police officer said, "How'd your son get along without his car?" And my father said, "Without his car?" "Yes. We took his license away for thirty days. How did he like it?" My father said, "I didn't know that."

So he came home, and he hauled me in. I was working, chopping weeds or milking goats or some damn thing. We had a produce subsistence farm. He said, "Did you drive that car without a license?"

I said, "Yeah, I sure did."

And he said, "You know that was against the law?"

I said, "Yes, sir."

"Well," he said, "I think I'll put a stop to that."

And he called a judge in the Superior Court who was a good friend of his, Judge Freeman. And he said, "I tell you I want this boy set up in the state reform school until he's twenty-one. He's incorrigible." The judge argued with him, but my father by that time had made his brag and he never backed off a brag, so it didn't look very healthy.

Julian on his 1926 Harley motorcycle, 1929, probably in Riverside, California.

And I was listening, of course. Just then M. R. Harrington came in the door. Harrington intervened, and so I went to Nevada. That's how close I came to spending three years in Ione, the state reform school.

Anyway, we went to Nevada, and we had a young fellow on the job named James Scrugham, who was the son of the governor. He was about seventeen, and he was "with it," as you would say nowadays, I guess. He'd grown up with Basque sheepherders, and he could speak Basque pretty well. He could drink and he could dance. He was quite a guy, and we got along fine. And we worked like hell, too. We made a good team. Yeah. I remember one night he knew some buddies over at the Moapa Ranch. So we went over there, he and I. First time I ever tasted whiskey. Ours was a teetotal household. Somebody had brought a gallon of bootleg from Searchlight. It was jet black—you couldn't see through the glass jar. I had some of it, and I thought it tasted pretty good, so I must have drunk half a canteen-cup full of it. Jim did the same thing, but he was used to it. It was interesting to me that the more I drank, not knowing what it was going to do, the more engrossed I became in the classified ads in the Las Vegas paper, whereas Jim, he was just cutting the rug, man. He was dancing with the cowboys, and they were having a wonderful time. I couldn't quite understand that; it didn't affect me that way.

Well, we came home, though I don't know how we got home. That was Jim's business, he was driving. I don't even know what we were driving. Borrowed the company car, I guess. And in the night, I paid the penalty. The next morning I dug the floor of the tent up and put in fresh sand. And my father told me, "You know," he said, "the mark

Jim Scrugham and Julian at Mesa House, Nevada, 1929.

of a man is that he can hold his liquor." And he rubbed that business of a man being a man into my face until by God I pretty near rebelled and changed my sex. Wished I could, anyway. I had my full height by then, went up to 195 when I got my full weight and working, you know, muscle and so forth. I was eighteen. Just turned eighteen. So it was very interesting.

Jim and I used to like to hike at night in the moonlight. It was high country, the sky was clear, there was no Las Vegas or nothing to speak of, and we went over to the Valley of Fire several times. It's that red sandstone, a national park now, or monument [Valley of Fire State Park]. Even in the moonlight, the undersides of the clouds would be red, blood red, reflection. We used to track coyotes in the washes as we walked over. We'd walk several miles, ten, fifteen miles, what the hell. When you're eighteen, that doesn't make any difference, does it?

It was beautiful country at Mesa House, lots of petroglyphs. We always used to go to Atlatl Rock, a big petroglyph of Basketmakers throwing an atlatl. This was before the advent of bows, to kill deer and what not. It's where I first learned about atlatls. Then we went up on a high butte, isolated butte, and I found a beautiful pink chert atlatl dart point. Well, I went down and showed it to Mr. Harrington, and M. R. said, "Thank you." And I said, "But I found it." "Yes," he said, "but you're on my payroll." So that's when I learned that expedition members turn everything in. Very interesting.

A man named Lewis Hicks showed up one day. He was a much older man—I mean he was probably seventy, sixty-five, older than God—driving a big Pierce-Arrow. He was an engineer of some sort. He wanted to be shown around, so Harrington detailed me to go with him over to the Lost City across the valley through the sand dunes. And Mr. Hicks kept getting stuck, and I kept having to dig him out, and I got tired of it. I finally said to him, "Mr. Hicks, you know, with due respect, I believe I can drive the rest of the way without getting stuck." He said, "You think you can?" And I said, "Yes sir." And I did. He'd driven all over the world, but he didn't have that touch. We saw Lost City, and I drove back, and we didn't get stuck. I don't think I'd driven the desert that much, no, not particularly, except some can, some can't, I guess, as the old man with prostate trouble said.

I had never studied archaeology per se and never have since, either, as far as that goes. But my father had a good library of Bureau of American Ethnology publications, *Journal of American Folklore* and all that sort of thing that he'd brought from Harvard.

And I read. My seat in fifth and sixth grade, in grade school, was right next to a big rack of books. When I finished my lesson I could read. Man, I read every day. I got more education that way than I did any other way, I think. Travel was always one of my favorites. From the time I was certainly not over five years old, I remember Stanley's *In Darkest Africa*. I can still see whole pages of it, with the woodcuts and the text adjoining. I can still see those natives marching across the pages. I read *Green Mansions*, too. I have a visual memory. My mother taught me to read when I was a little over three years old, three and a half, maybe, which is not precocious, but it came in damned handy, anyway. I was raised in a book-loving family, which I think is important to anybody.

Gwyneth Harrington Xavier and I used to talk about that. She was a renegade from a Boston Back Bay family, became an ethnologist, an archaeologist, and a famous woman. And her father, who was a banker, used to stride up and down in front of the fireplace with his hands behind his back under his coattails and say, "Oh, what in the

The Mesa House crew in 1929. From left to right, Endeka Harrington, Bertha Parker, Wilma (Billie) Parker, Jim Scrugham, M. R. Harrington, Julian.

world? What have I done to have two renegade children inflicted upon me?" Her brother was even more so than she. He was an OSS man in Algeria and a blood member of the Riff tribe. So, you see what I mean. She and I used to talk about it, since she was raised in the same way. She'd read something about Africa when she was three and a half, too. That's what changes a man's life. And a woman's life. You know that.

We put in about four months up there at Mesa House, I think. It had its side effects. Harrington's and Endeka's niece was Bertha Parker Pallan, Arthur Parker's daughter. Her mother had divorced Parker, and they'd come to the coast, Bertha with her little daughter Billie. The ex-Mrs. Parker and Bertha eventually wound up in Hollywood. They traveled with Ringling Brothers, Barnum & Bailey in the Pocahontas spectacle and all that sort of thing when the girl was up in her teens. They were interesting people.

Bertha came along on this expedition and learned how to cook. She finally did most of the cooking, and that's where she and I became acquainted. We became very good friends, and I thought the world of her. I met her grandparents, Grandfather and Grandmother Tahamont, who were marvelous, pure-blood Abenaki people. I've still got a souvenir that Mrs. Tahamont gave me. That was all interesting for a young kid like me, eighteen or so.

Mesa House was the first time I actually *did* archaeology. I'd never even seen it before or even read about it. I never really paid any attention to that end of it, no. I don't recall that my father taught me anything about it. He really didn't have to. Mesa House was a shallow site. The techniques were different in those days, too. We used stratigraphy, of course, in the trash areas. That's simple enough; anybody can do that. As far as taking out bones, that's just a matter of being handy.

I learned it mostly by doing it on my own. And from Harrington and Jim Scrugham, who didn't know anything more about it than I did, but we were reasonably intelligent, handy kids. We'd always worked with our hands, you know, we weren't city kids. My father was a good man with a trowel. We used to disagree once in a while because I could feel something that he couldn't, and he'd tell me off. So I had to respond in some form that usually cost me a little, but sometimes I was right, too. And sometimes I wasn't, in which case I profited.

That all added to my experience. I've since then developed a tremendous sympathy for any father who has a teenage son working on the same job. Not that I ever had any trouble with my sons at all. I didn't. But, after all, I knew how to cope, because my father didn't. We had some problems.

But I always had an ace in the hole. I could have gone up to Humboldt, Nevada, to work for Mittry Brothers on the construction of a big naval munitions storage station up there. I'd worked for Mittry and they liked me. They would have put me through engineering school, I suppose, if I'd continued with them, which accounts for me sitting here. So I didn't much care if my father and I couldn't make it. Why, I could move up north to Nevada and go to work again. And a he-man would, instead of using a trowel, you know. But we made it out.

That job lasted about four months. I remember we stopped in Las Vegas on the way over. Jim and I went downtown walking around; I don't know how many job offers we got. The streets were packed with men coming in for Boulder Dam, although it was before Boulder really got rolling. All were looking for work, on Boulder Dam but nowhere else.

Man would come up to us and say, "You fellows working?"

"Yes, sir, we have a job."

"God blankety-blank it." And he couldn't find anybody to go out and do some work around town on construction or whatever, you know. It was interesting. Everybody wanted to go to the dam. And Vegas. . . . I'd never been in Vegas before and damned seldom since, but it was a small town, then. With the gambling joints and bars and all the rest of it, it was an interesting place. We didn't get into it, since we were with M. R. Harrington and party, but it was interesting. Indians and all the rest of it, you know, I'd never seen that before.

So we came back to Riverside, and my father wrote the report on Mesa House. I illustrated it, because I had some facility and because I had taken a correspondence course in illustration from the National Art Institute. My mother was a professional artist, trained at Boston Normal Art School, which later became known as Massachusetts Art Institute. She painted until she died. So, I come by that legitimately. No, my mother never taught me to paint. I don't know how. I never have painted.

It was mostly a cartooning course. I paid for that for years, five dollars a month. I think it was a hundred fifteen dollars, which was a fortune in 1927, '28, you know. I used to get my way paid into the movies because I'd draw. In those days there were a lot of animated ads that came on the screen before the movie did. They were very simple, really. And the projectionist at one of the local theaters and I teamed up. We'd go out in the sun and put a piece of poster board up on the wall in the sun, and I'd have a cartoon drawn out in light blue, which wouldn't register on the film. Then he'd take a frame or two frames, and I'd add another half inch to the line. So I'd hold the

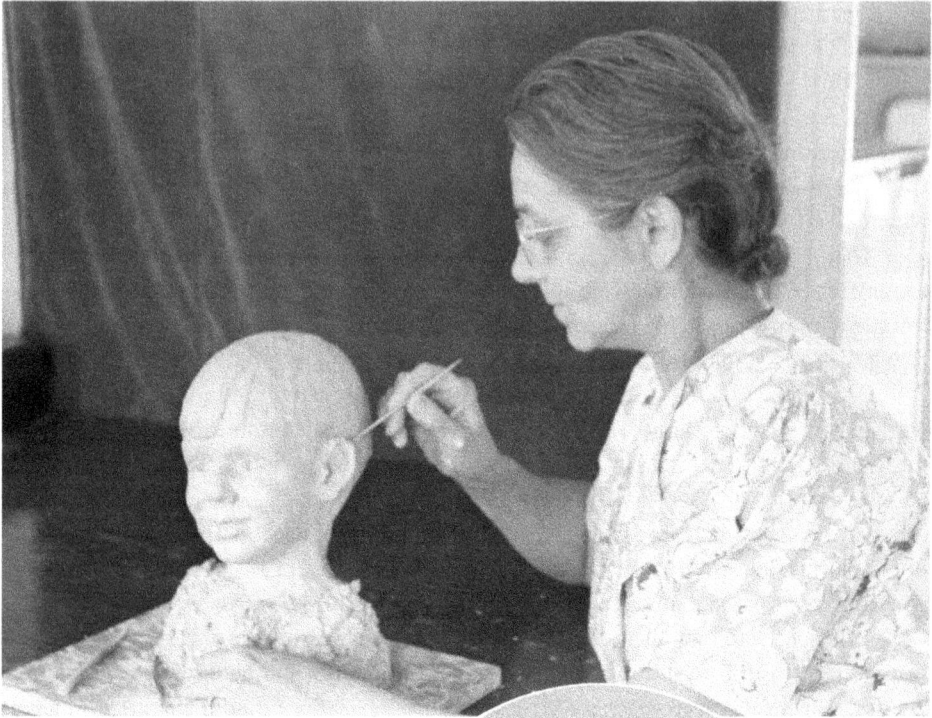

Mary Dodge Hayden working on a sculpture, ca. 1940; the model was her grandson, Julian D. Hayden Jr.

Mary Dodge Hayden's 1928 sketch of her son Julian, age seventeen.

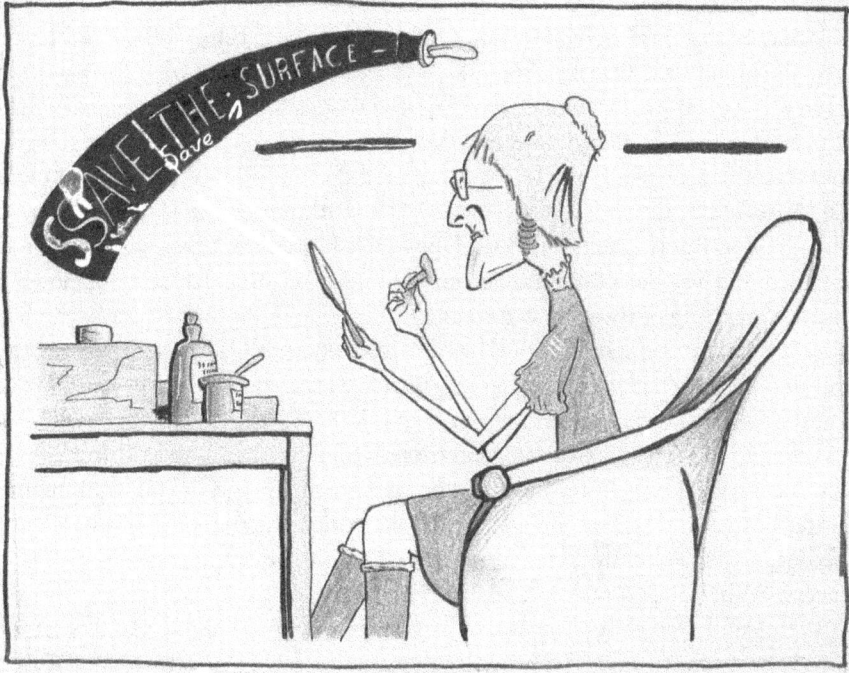

"Save the Surface," Julian's cartoon of a primping spinster, made as a paint company advertisement.

pencil and go *wssshts* here and there around and outline the thing, making animated cartoons.

Still I've got one of the cartoons hanging on the bulletin board in my bedroom. A paint company ad of a spinster primping in front of a mirror. Kid stuff, simple stuff, but it worked. That's how I learned to draw. A little bit. That's how come I illustrated that report on Mesa House. Just standard archaeological, pen-and-ink [drawings] of maps and artifacts and pottery. Can't do it now, my hand isn't steady enough. But I did it for a good many years.

On toward the last of Mesa House, Gypsum Cave came up, so Jim and I went over, and we worked about a week, I guess. We had water and carried everything. We did the assessment work on the cave and made a mining claim of it for the museum. The following year the museum went up there and excavated the cave. Ground sloth manure and so forth. Fascinating place. Selenite crystals six feet high, which were later destroyed by vandals. Spectacular place, high up overlooking the Colorado River valley, the river itself was down below. Colder than hell, windy, no water: we'd come out of there with a half-inch of pulverized sheep manure on us from head to foot. We wore masks, of course. After work we'd scrub each other down with burlap sacks, drink a beer, and go to bed. Good experience.

Mr. Harrington was a very gentle man, big man, tall as I am, much heavier. He had a speech impediment, so he stuttered. He was very slow-moving and slow-talking. He went from Columbia University to Cuba and excavated caves for years. That's where he learned his precise Castilian Spanish. I think that was before he worked for Heye Foundation, but I don't know. Very quiet fellow. And a good storyteller. For Heye, he'd worked all through the Ozarks, Arkansas, and all those cave and rock shelter sites.

He was a great practical joker, too. And the stories of their practical jokes that the Heye Foundation crew played on each other could fill a book. I played very few practical jokes. And I was usually the one that suffered. Jackie Snow and I roomed together in the Ware Hotel in Coolidge when we were working on the Grewe Site at Casa Grande. Milton Snow, "Jackie" Snow. Happy Jack Horizon Chaser was what he liked to be called. He was our photographer, an old buddy of mine. Jackie came down with the flu or something of the sort, so he was bedridden for a day or so. I guess the second evening my father decided to take a hand in it, so he got Old Dad Throckmorton, a laborer of ours, who had graduated from pharmaceutical college in Missouri. He came west and became a muleskinner down in Death Valley.

Well, Old Dad and Jackie were good friends. So my father took Dad Throckmorton to Mr. Davis's local drugstore, and he borrowed a bedpan and enema equipment and hot water bottles and thermometers, the whole works. The two of them marched into the bedroom, our bedroom. I wasn't there. And Jackie looked up, and his eyes got big as saucers. "What do you want?"

"Well," Old Dad said, "You know, Jackie, we're worried about you. You come sit down. We're going to give you a 'xamination." And Jackie—he jumped out of bed, grabbed the stuff, and tried to burst the screen out of the window in the second story to throw it all out in the street. And then he fled. He blamed me for it, and I very nearly had to roost with the chickens out behind the hotel that night because he thought I'd put everybody up to it.

Another time my father built an alidade. He didn't have money enough in the budget to buy an alidade. My father loved to survey maps with one, so he made one out of a steel carpenter's square and a Montgomery Ward builder's level. He had the local blacksmith put it together. The highway department crew surveying the Florence-Picacho cutoff headquartered in our hotel, and they were rawhiding him about it, saying that wouldn't work. But it did work. One night the place was packed with tourists, highway engineers, and all of us, of course, so the highway department started picking on him. Arthur Woodward was there, too. He didn't help any.

My father had made a case for it, so he sent Jackie upstairs to bring the instrument case down. Father set it on the counter. And I'm looking at it. Next thing you know everybody was just hanging on his every word. He slowly opened the door of the case, reached in, and pulled out a big bologna sausage with a red ribbon around it. Father stopped, looked at it, looked around very quickly, put it back in the box, and picked up the box. We didn't see him again until the next day. We'd been home, I guess, a month after the end of the job, and the postman delivered a letter: Sergeant Bologna, no street address. Came all the way to Riverside, California. Sergeant Bologna, Riverside, California. So Art Woodward must have gone to a good deal of trouble to set that up. I don't think Dad ever quite forgave Art for that.

We had some other practical jokes, too. Jackie was troweling in the cremation area one day. We had a lot of company—I think Hodge was there, and Neil Judd and Odd Halseth and oh, a lot of bigshots. Jackie was troweling a trench toward a cremation, and he spied something and he said, "It's white!" And he let out a squall. "It's shiny! It's green! It's blue!" Everybody dashed over, you know. And he flipped it out, and it was the side wall of a spittoon, or a chamberpot, I forget which. So he went away for a while and talked to himself. It certainly wasn't I who planted it. Certainly not.

M. R. Harrington was a good man, a good teacher. He was very kind to me, so I called him Uncle Raymond, Tío Ramón, after I left Mesa House and we became even better acquainted, Tío Ramón. Good man. My father published a report on Mesa House, one of those standard reports of the time. That was his first real project getting back into archaeology.

After making the drawings and illustrations for the Mesa House report, I went to work for Mittry Brothers, Basich Brothers at March Field, paving. In those days the concrete was mixed in a central plant, brought out in dump trucks, and dumped on the street, and a crew of men with heavy rakes and shovels pulled that concrete out and leveled it. You worked in the concrete. I was the only Anglo on the crew. They were all Mexicans from Highgrove and so forth. We got better pay than anybody else. We got sixty cents an hour instead of fifty cents, which was good pay in those days, damn good pay, for a young fellow. People were raising families on it and buying houses and cars.

I lasted there until a man named Dr. Charles Van Bergen, a retired blood specialist from the East and an Egyptologist by avocation, decided he wanted to become patron of an expedition in the Southwest. He went to the Southwest Museum, but got there at noon one day when Dr. Scherer, the director, was out at lunch. Dr. Van Bergen wasn't accustomed to waiting for people to come back from lunch, so he went over to the LA County Museum and ran into Arthur Woodward. Woodward glommed on to him, and they formed the Van Bergen–Los Angeles County Museum archaeological expedition. They worked on the coast, first, and then worked at Canterbury Ranch up near Ventura. They worked in a cave, worked at Point Mugu, went up to Avila, and so forth.

Well, they hired me as foreman. Me! By this time I would have been—it would have been summer of 1929—I was eighteen. Well, hell, I didn't know the damned business of being a foreman from a goose head. Anyhow, we worked here and there, and eventually it became clear they better have someone older and more experienced. So Art sent out a man named Kelemen, Alex Kelemen. I'll never forget the SOB. He'd been fired from the LA County Museum for stealing lightbulbs. But he had something that Art liked, for Art was a scalawag, too, in his own way.

Kelemen was a World War I veteran, in the Hungarian army. He was a rascal. So anyway, he became foreman, but before he became foreman, before he was hired, we needed a photographer. We'd already hired Dad Throckmorton, gimpy old fellow who had driven a twenty-mule team out of Death Valley in the borax days, before the earthquake. He was an old character, but not a photographer.

So, I called Jackie Snow, my old motorcycle buddy and much older than I. We used to ride all over the Mojave Desert every weekend. We'd carry bedrolls strapped to the handlebars, and we'd go to the old mines and into the mountain ranges, in the old days, when there were no roads. It was wonderful. Late twenties, '29. He was a hell of a photographer. So I called him. He was cleaning windows for the school district and very despondent. I think probably he would have killed himself if he'd not been rescued. So I hired him. Me. Eighteen years old. And he came up and went to work until he retired as photographer for the Navajo tribe. I think I did my good deed or whatever.

Art Woodward and Alex Kelemen on the Van Bergen–LA County Museum Expedition, at Avila, California, in the fall of 1929. (Photograph by Milton Snow)

Jackie was spastic-paralytic, by the way. A remarkable man, he'd overcome his paralysis by sheer doggedness. He shaved every day with a straight razor in the dark. It was a matter of self-discipline. And he was spastic, flipping in all directions, you know how it is. Uncontrollable. Somehow he did it.

We went on up to Avila and Morro Bay. My God, that was rich archaeology, but Art Woodward was a collector. He wanted to fill showcases; he didn't give a damn about the information. Eventually, one of the local landowners caught Mr. Kelemen selling the specimens, magnificent steatite bowls with the bead inlays around the rim and all that. He threw us off the property, quite properly. Kelemen had already stolen my wallet. I had to go into town one time for a week or so because I had a fever, but when I came back, the wallet was empty. "Oh," he said, "The gypsies came by." Gypsies came by, sure they did.

"End of a hard day at Avila," 1929. Left to right: John "Old Dad" Throckmorton, Milton Snow, Julian, Alex Kelemen.

Milton Snow and Alex Kelemen working at Point Mugu, California, 1929.

We were working on the coast, up at Point Mugu, on a big shell midden. We had a camp beside the lagoon there, and every evening we'd go across the lagoon in a canoe and go swimming in the ocean and wash off. It was a nice place. We were up there a large part of the winter.

One morning I said I was going to quit. They were angry. They were madder than hell at me because they had their eyes on me; I think they were going to start moving me up. I didn't pay any attention to that: I had a motorcycle, and I could get a job with Basich working on street projects if I wanted, what the hell did I care? But they were mad.

In 1930, my father and I came over to the Grewe Site and Casa Grande and worked there. But along in April my father and I got in a little jangle over something, and I said, "Oh, to hell with it," and I quit. After all, a young fellow I knew was going back to Michigan, so I rode with him. And that was that. I rode in his car. China Baby Conrad, I'll never forget him.

I went east and worked at the motorboat factory and went to jail and worked on the ships, and so forth, seeing the country. Good experience. Jail? I just happened to be passenger in a car that was struck by another car and flipped. I wasn't hurt, but my driver was killed, died, so they kept me in jail as a witness. The deputies there were most kind—I had dinner with one family, worked in another's garden. The other man, the driver of the other car, was an employee of the political boss of the county, so that was that. The officers took up a collection among themselves, of three dollars, and with this I went to Newport News. The police were very good to me. Very nice people.

No, I shouldn't have said anything about jail, because it conveys the wrong impression, which is all right, too. That's where I learned about parrots. I had to stay there—I had to sleep there, in the county jail. Fine. Henrico County, Virginia, I'll never forget it. When they let me out, I still was wearing my clothes that I had on during the accident, and I must have looked pretty rough.

One evening I went for a walk, and I walked by a city park. A bunch of little girls playing ring around the rosies and things and parents, women, standing around. And I wasn't thinking, and I said to a pleasant-looking woman, "What is this?" She turned on me like a tiger, she said, "You can't pick me up, you nasty creature!" Man, I took off. I walked away with some rapidity. I was somewhat embarrassed. Coming back toward the jail, passing by a vine-covered cottage, in the street, somebody said, "Hello!"

So I stopped. "Hello!" So I walked up the walk.

"Come in!" Stuck my head around the vines, and a parrot said, "You son of a bitch, get out of here!"

So the next night I didn't go on a walk. I can still hear that damned parrot laughing at me.

Horace E. Dodge had started a motorboat factory at Newport News. The first production-line motorboat factory in the world. I heard about it, so when I got out of the "can," I went over to American Foundry, I think is the name. They built freight cars. I heard they had a contract to build a bunch of hopper cars, so I went over, and they said, "What can you do?"

And I said, "I'm a riveter."

Letter from Irwin Hayden to Arthur Woodward,
April 6, 1930.

Everything is going well. Julian made an ass of himself one day and I fired him. Then we talked the thing over and we decided that after all there were other folks to be considered and so he is still on the job and doing just as well as can be expected. . . .

And to Dr. Van Bergen, the day before:

You remember Conrad, "China Baby." He leaves tomorrow for Michigan and New York. Julian is going with him. I am very glad that he is. Conrad is a prince. Julian goes in good company. Will go to New York with him and then to Boston and New Hampshire, to visit his grandmothers and aunts, etc. It will do him a world of good. I think he may go to college in the East. Hope so.

I figured I could sure as hell learn how to rivet in three days. They weren't going to open for several weeks, and gee, I was broke. All I had was three dollars a policeman gave me, for which I've always loved him. So I left my camera and my leather jacket as security for my room, which was fifty cents a night, or something like that, and I hit the road for Newport News.

I got down to Newport News and I got a room in a hotel for a dollar a night and bought a bar of chocolate and a *Saturday Evening Post*. And I went out in the lobby. A bunch of fellows there talking about the motorboat factory, which needed hardware fitters. I wasn't sure what a hardware fitter was, but I figured I could find out. The next day I went over to the factory, and they were hiring. And I sat in the office until noon, watching and listening, and a man would come in, "What can you do?"

"I can do anything."

"Sorry."

"What can you do?"

"Well, I tune engines."

"Ah, when can you go to work?" And so forth. So I went up.

"What can you do?"

I said, "I'm a hardware fitter."

"Where'd you work?"

"Fisher Body Pontiac."

"Where are your tools?"

"The hotel."

"Seven o'clock in the morning."

"Yessir."

So I go down to the hardware store. I got the owner, and I said "Mister, you don't know me and I don't know you, but I got a job, if I can show up in the morning with the tools I need, but I don't even know what tools I need. I'm gonna be a hardware fitter and I think I put trim on motorboats. If it would help any, I used to be a Boy Scout and all the rest of that stuff, too." Well, he was a Boy Scout himself at one time.

"Well," he said, "I think you need a pair of pliers and a ratchet drill and whatnot."

So I walked out with it and I went down at seven o'clock and I stayed until they closed the damn factory. It was perfectly sensible. If I hadn't been smart enough to make it in three days, which is your usual break-in time, why I'd go to somewhere else and say, "Yes, I worked at Horace E. Dodge Motorboat Factory," and by that time I'd know how. That's the way we operate. The way you learn, too. And nobody there knew any more about hardware fitting than I did. They were all North Carolina hill-country villagers who had been brought down because they'd work for nothing, see.

I think it lasted till August or so. Beautiful motorboats. Then it all shut down. So I hitchhiked up to New York, walked around the docks, and learned the ropes. I bought myself a little anchor patch and sewed it to a good go-to-hell sea-going cap, you know, with a bill. And I got a trench coat. I looked pretty damned sharp.

But there weren't any jobs, so I came back to Newport News, and a little three-island, well-deck tanker was in the dock there. Somewhere I heard about it—you know how guys out of work are always talking. So I went over to it. I had my trench coat on, a necktie on, and my goddamn anchor, you know. I walked right by the guard at noon when everybody was coming back from lunch. Everybody was showing their passes, but he didn't ask me for mine. I didn't even have a pass. I went over to the ship, found it.

I didn't even know which end was which, never been on one, never seen one before, hardly. And I said to some deckhand, "Where's the captain?"

"Over there."

So I got up and I said, "Sir, I don't know much about ships, but I can work."

He said, "Where's your referral?"

"I don't got a referral."

"How'd you get in the yard?"

"I walked in."

"You walked by that guard? Well, by God, you got a job."

So I worked on that ship until the captain hit the busboy, and the busboy pressed charges. We were tied up at Everett, Massachusetts, at that time. And the captain, in order to avoid the law, made a midnight departure with a pier-head crew. When I went down the next morning to the ship, along with all the other fellows that'd stayed in town, we had no ship. So we went down to the maritime commissioner and told our stories. They put us on a bus to New York. That was fun. There was a hell of a storm. It

Julian in his "go-to-hell sea-going cap" with the anchor patch, 1930.

took the ship sixty hours to go from Boston to New York instead of about twenty. It's just as well we didn't sail on her, I might have gotten seasick, you know? They couldn't get us out on it because the captain had to stick around and go to a hearing, so they put us on other tankers, and I stayed on a tanker through Christmas, and then I came home.

I missed a seven-months' round-the-world voyage on the *Java Arrow* for Standard of New Jersey, and that irritated me, so I hit the highway instead. It was good experience. Sounds like more than it is, which is often the case, when old coots get to telling stories, you know?

I went back to Los Angeles after I got back from the East and in 1931 did some work for M. R. Harrington around the Mission San Fernando, helping to restore it. I was just working on the grounds helping him out. And I worked with him for a few weeks at a place called Casa Adobe, a Spanish hacienda that belonged to the Southwest Museum in Highland Park there. His niece [Bertha Parker] and I were going together at the time, so it was sort of a family affair.

Then I went back to construction for a while to save up a little money. I worked for the USDA, and the sugar beet harvest, one thing and another. I had no trouble getting work. Never did have. I spent the summer teaching handicrafts to Boy Scouts and church groups in summer camps, which is not only fun, but fairly profitable. The second year we cleaned house at LA County Fair. Every piece we sent in got a blue ribbon. I was teaching leather, silver, copper, beads. I correspond regularly with a man who won first prize for a leather wallet. He's a retired mechanical engineer from General Electric who lives in Taos, now. We correspond a dozen times a year. He was just a solemn, Germanic kid with owl eyes, and we're still good friends. That's a long time ago, 1933.

We're talking about getting jobs and hard times, and a number of young folks remember hearing their parents talking about it. They don't know, but their parents never got over it. People never forget it; they don't forget hard times. I was raised in hard times. That's why I hate like hell to go to a restaurant and spend five dollars for a piece of meat when I can feed the family for a week on it. It just galls me, galls my Scotch soul, and it's not a Scotch soul: it's a hard times soul. I can buy two beers if I want to, but I sometimes buy just one, because I remember in the early years when my wife Helen and I and Charlie Steen used to come up to Pueblo Grande from Casa Grande [in ca. 1935]. He was an archaeologist and ranger. He'd come in with his arms full of four bottles of beer. We'd have beer, and it was the only beer we ever saw. That's what you call running short of cash.

That's why sometimes, when you get me talking about the old days, I sort of seem to harp on it, but I'm just talking about what affected us most deeply. And I was very fortunate, because I never was out of a job. I don't know why, except I was big and willing. When I used to go up to a construction job, there might be twenty, thirty men outside the gate. And the gate was locked, too. All wanted to get in.

Foreman would come up, "What can you do?"

I'd say, "I'm the best goddamned wheelbarrow man in Southern California, and I can prove it."

Helen Hayden and Charlie Steen after a swim at Roosevelt Lake, June 1935, during the Haydens' honeymoon trip. The Haydens' Model T "Sophie" is behind them. (Photograph by Julian Hayden)

"You? You're just a water-headed kid," you know, but by God, he'd open the gate. And these family men would be outside. Once in a while I'd feel badly about it, but not very often.

And I kept my jobs. Eventually you get known in the business, and then you're all right. I don't know what I'd have done if I had had three or four children with a house I was losing and had to have work. I might have had a different attitude toward it. I'm sure I would have. But I watched the breadlines in New York. You could get a cup of coffee and a doughnut for a nickel, if you had a nickel; if you didn't have, you'd go somewhere else and stand in a line that reached for blocks. In the wintertime.

A lot of those men were family men, and that's why my sister-in-law [Isabelle Pendleton Schiff] became a communist when she got out of college. She believed that they offered the only hope there was, at that time. Can't blame her a bit. I saw the same thing that she saw, but she saw more than I did because she was working for family welfare in New York City. It was a traumatic experience.

I came to Arizona for the first time in 1929 for archaeological work in Casa Grande with Los Angeles County. It was the Van Bergen–Los Angeles County Expedition, financed by Dr. Van Bergen for the LA County Museum. I came back several times.

Then in December 1933 I went to Keet Seel up in northern Arizona, the cliff dwellings, and worked there for four or five months for the Civil Works Administration as an archaeologist. That fall [1934] my father and I came over to Snaketown and worked the entire winter, until we closed it when it got hot.

3. Sandstone Country

What took me to Keet Seel? Partly because my father and I were the only two available field men. It was December 1933 and a Civil Works Administration [CWA] project. I've written this up in the *Kiva* [1978] and also in *Camera, Spade and Pen.* In order to make work for the unemployed, the National Park Service created a number of projects, and the Keet Seel cliff dwelling up in Navajo National Monument was one of them, administered out of the Museum of Northern Arizona. So my father and I were offered a job there. My father was archaeologist and I was cataloguer. Though my father left early, I stayed until it was done, working for Hosteen John Wetherill, which was a rare experience, for he was one of the legendary men. Not many people could work for him. After all, he only had one short lifetime. And he was a real pioneer. Hosteen John was known everywhere. There aren't many people alive now who worked for him. I'm one of them.

Now, he was a practical joker. A German girl came up to camp in March, colder than hell. I've forgotten her name, but she was young, tall, and a strapping blonde, a regular Brunhilde. She peeled off from the rest of the party at Marsh Pass where our base camp was and walked into camp. She promptly told Bill Young the packer, "I want to go to Keet Seel."

"Well," he said, "it's late in the day. Can't do it."

"Well," she said, "I'm going." She insisted. So Bill put her up on old Jimmy, a twenty-four-year-old white mule who was wiser than most people.

She didn't have any bedroll; she didn't have any clothing except what she had on, just a shift, bare-legged. What she had on under that, of course, I don't know, but she had no jacket or anything. Jimmy took her up canyon about three miles and stuck his head in a clump of Gambel oak and that was it. And when she gave up, he brought her back to camp at Marsh Pass.

So Bill had to put her up. He was an old fellow, an old packer. Bill put her up in his bedroll. "Now, girlie," he said, "don't worry, you're just as safe in that bedroll as you would be in God's pocket." Well, the next morning he again put her up on Jimmy, and Jimmy brought her to our camp. Her arrival caused a considerable commotion, because none of us men had been out of camp since the first of January, you know. There hadn't been a woman in there but one, and she was director of education for the state school department, and she was no beauty.

The wind was blowing, and this girl's legs were blue. Hosteen John had Milt take her through the ruin, so Milt got teased. Hosteen John had a green umbrella tent, several yards away from our brown umbrella tent, in which my father and I slept, one on each side of the center pole. That evening she got tired, and Hosteen took her out and

Julian at Keet Seel, Navajo National Monument, Arizona, 1934.

showed her where to sleep. He was going to bunk with Milt, I think. So after a while, I thought, "Shoot, I better go to bed." And Dad had already left the minute she showed up, he left camp. He didn't hold to women in camp at all. He holed up somewhere up the canyon until bedtime; he didn't even come in for dinner.

So I barged into my tent, and there she was just peeling off and getting into my bed, my bedroll, but here was Dad snoring on the other side of the tent pole. And I stopped, of course, startled, and she said, "Oh, am I in the right tent?" Her English was understandable, and I said, "No." So I backed out and she got dressed, and I took her over and put her in Hosteen's tent. I didn't tell Dad. No way.

The next morning I got Hosteen and stepped off to the side and I said, "Damn it, Hosteen John, you damn near blew the whole thing here. If my father had waked and found that happening . . . How in the hell come did you do that?"

And he said, "Julian, didn't you know I was color-blind?" And I never told my father, he never knew it to this day. That scoundrel. So she went back the next morning, and Dad came back to camp. Officially. Oh, my. And Hosteen was color-blind.

Nakai Yazzi was a Mexican-Navajo half-breed. He was born at Fort Sumner during the exile and had a Mexican father. And he was a little bit nuts. So by 1910 he had become a shaman, a medicine man, and a bad one. Not a good one, but a bad one. And he had people terrified of him, but he made the mistake of getting mixed up with Old Man Whiskers, who was a war chief who lived down at the mouth of Keet Seel canyon. They got into a feud, so he witched Whiskers's wife and sister. And I think his wife died of it. So the Navajo was going to take care of him.

They called a meeting, and they agreed that he was a bad man, and they were going to tie him to the four horses and whip the horses, which is the way they took care of evil medicine men in those days. But Hosteen John and his brother-in-law, Charlie Day, interceded and talked the Navajos into letting him go. He was in their care, provided they sent him up to Canton, South Dakota, to the insane asylum. And provided he lifted the curse on Whiskers's sister, which he did. So he went up to the asylum.

Sometime in the very late twenties he escaped, and he walked all the way back to Tsegi Canyon. And he went around to the various people and he said, "I'm back." And they were terrified of him, so he walked away with gunnysacks full of turquoise and blankets, and pretty soon he was a very wealthy man, by the time he got up there. He announced in the spring that he was going to bring his sheep up to Keet Seel National Monument, and it had never been grazed. Oh, it was a lush place. That simply couldn't happen. It wasn't fenced, you know.

So Hosteen sent one of his Navajos down to Kayenta for his Halloween mask. He came back. I climbed up in the Turkey Cave, it had remarkable acoustics, you could whisper up there above the camp and it would be a shout down in the camp. And I put a tarp over my shoulders, and I put the mask on and Hosteen's stocking cap, and I hid down behind a wall. And after a while this big strapping young Navajo, a great friend of Bill Young the packer, rode up to visit with Bill. And they went in the tent. And I dropped a stone. And I dropped another one. The Navajo came out looking. So I bobbed around just a little bit like I had a sore paw, you know, and I let it be known that I had a sore paw.

Finally he burst out, jumped on his horse, and went down, stopped at the high point to look back, and so I cut up a little more, and away he went. Well, that night, we learned, the little people attacked Nakai Yazzi. They shot all his joints with rheumatic fever, and he was incapacitated for a while, so he never came up. It did what it was supposed to do: it stunned him.

Until about a week later here came a whole convoy of old men, some of them in their eighties. Some of them had ridden for scores of miles. They were friends of John's, and they gathered us all together that morning, and they told Hosteen John, "Somebody in your crew has got a bad heart. And we're going to sing over you. And exorcise it." So we all lined up, and they sang over us and put corn pollen on us. That exorcised the evil heart, the evil spirit, that one of us had, whoever it was. Hosteen John and I just looked at each other; we hadn't told anybody, of course. I felt a little badly about it, myself. And I think he felt a little shamefaced too, but it was necessary. Those old men had gone to a lot of work, and hardship, in order to express their love for him, you know? Nakai Yazzi never came back. So the place was ungrazed, I guess, for a good many years.

Hosteen was a character. He owned La Osa Guest Ranch down at Sasabe, but hard times got him. So before we went up to Keet Seel, he'd closed the place and driven all his horses and mules up to Kayenta. That's how come we were riding some of the mules that he'd had for so many years, like Whalebone. Both he and Jimmy, you know, were oldtimers.

And then, just before we went up there, Harrison Forman, the great explorer and traveler, and one of Calvert Whiskey's men of the year pictured in all the men's magazines, showed up. And he wanted to go to Keet Seel. He had a whole bevy of dowagers with him, and he was guiding them.

Hosteen put him up on little Julie, an awfully nice little lady mule. She had a pump-tail trot, as the muleskinners said, which would jar your eyeteeth. But anyway, Forman was up on Julie, and he'd spur on the side away from the women, so she'd buck and pitch. Then he'd control her, and the women would say, "Oh, he's a centaur, you know, oh, what a horseman, what a marvelous man Mr. Forman is!" All in awe.

John finally said, "You know, Mr. Forman, little Julie's got a good memory, and she'll not forget this treatment."

"Ah," says Forman, "I can take care of it."

So they went up canyon. And Forman stopped at Lookout Point, over the canyon about fifty, sixty, a hundred feet, you know. He had a big old Graflex, the kind you look down through the top of. He hung the reins over the horn, got that camera all set, and Julie pitched him into the canyon and broke his arm.

She laughed and laughed and laughed, she stood up there above him and hee-hawed. You could hear her all the way down to Kayenta. Hosteen said, "Mr. Forman, I told you." That's one reason I love mules. They've got more sense than a damned horse does. And they got a sense of humor. I like mules.

Our daughter Serena was a horsewoman from the time she was five years old, and it was nothing but horses at dinnertime. She'd get on me for not talking horses, and I said, "Serena, when you talk about an animal with good sense, you're going to talk about mules. I'll talk mules, but I ain't gonna talk about horses." She'd get very mad at me.

I rode mules, but never owned one, hell no. I would if I could, but we were never in that situation. You've always got to remember they're smarter than you are. Smarter than I am, anyway.

Milt Wetherill was John Wetherill's nephew, Milt being the son of Winslow Wetherill, John's younger brother. Richard, John's older brother, was killed as a young man by Navajos, if I recall. Somebody shot him, anyway [at Chaco Canyon in 1910]. I don't know what kind of a guy Milt was. Hell, I knew him too well. Or else I didn't know him at all, whichever you like. I camped with him for five months, and we wrote off and on after that, pretty much till he died. He was Navajo, really. He spoke Navajo, was raised Navajo. He knew everything there was to know about Navajo country. He made a wonderful ranger for Navajo National Monument, Betatakin, and Keet Seel and might have become custodian after his Uncle John left the post, but the BIA [Bureau of Indian Affairs] came in and they canned him because he didn't have a degree.

My friend Jackie Snow was the official photographer for all of the Park Service work in northern Arizona. He'd gone up in the world since the old days, too, you see. He came up with Milt Wetherill on muleback to photograph Keet Seel. That's how he got there, and that's how my father and I got there. When he came up to Keet Seel, Milt Wetherill and I took him up the canyon across from Keet Seel to where you look down on the site. It was six hundred feet high. Somehow we got him up there, and he stood out on the point with his camera and his head under the black cloth, jerking and twitching and his hands flying uncontrollably, and we knew just damn well that we were going to have to pick him off the crag down below. But by God, he got some beautiful pictures. I don't know how he did it. He was one of the good men. We had a number of good men. And we had some bastards, too, of course. That always happens.

Milt Wetherill (bottom) and Julian climbing up a crevice to access a viewpoint above Keet Seel, where Milton "Jackie" Snow wished to take a photograph, 1934. Note large-format camera and tripod at right center. (Photograph by Milton Snow)

How come I didn't get hooked on the archaeology of the Four Corners area? As much as anything because I worked at Keet Seel. That cured me. I come from these deserts down here where everything is clean and in the sun and in the breeze, but up there. . . . Why hell, at Keet Seel, when it came time for abandonment, those folks used the farthest room as a toilet, and they filled each one as they came along. When they had to use the last one, they abandoned the site. As I said one time in a *Kiva* [1978a] article, we had a cold wet season and all the aromatic esters were released. I have had no use for pueblos since.

I've got no use for them. I don't like ghetto dwellers, and I never have anyway. As far as I'm concerned, that's what Puebloans are, as compared to our nomadic desert people. That's why I don't like pueblo architecture. I don't like anything about it. It doesn't even interest me; there's no challenge.

4. Pima and Papago

The Grewe Site, eh? That's a famous site in my book. It will never be erased from my punkin head, I can tell you that.

I was working for the Los Angeles County Museum, the Van Bergen expedition. Van Bergen agreed to finance an expedition, which was the word in those days, and it was an expedition because we were coming to the wilds of Arizona or to the wilds of Malibu or wherever it might be. It was very often self-sustaining, you know, tents and all the rest of it. So it started out. We worked on the coast all fall. I was hired right away, because young men were very scarce at the time. When we'd done what Art Woodward wanted done on the coast, he got his collections, which was all he wanted, really. He was not much of a hand for notes and publications, which is too bad.

The Gila Pueblo survey group down at Casa Grande National Monument collected potsherds and decided that one of the small compounds north-northeast of the big ruins would be worth investigating, although the pottery was pretty late. So we decided to come over and work at Compound F. We got there on the last day of December, 1929. We found some very interesting late material. My father was hired as the archaeologist, which at least gave us a competent man in the field. And we had Alex Kelemen, who after a while, we realized was spending his spare time over east of Casa Grande National Monument, east of the railroad, working on a patch of land that was going to be put into cotton. It became known as the Grewe Site eventually, and he was bringing out all this beautiful early pottery. That got Art Woodward excited, and Gila Pueblo was also interested in it. So we dropped Compound F and went over to the Grewe Site.

We had, I think, five months or so many months in which to clear five acres of land which was going into cotton at the end of that time. My father brought in a mule-drawn scraper, a fresno, and that's where I learned about Johnson bars. Do you know what a Johnson bar is? When you're walking along beside the fresno, you pull a rope on this bar, and the thing tumbles over and spreads the dirt. Sometimes it's called a tumble bug or a fresno. A Johnson bar is a long handle that comes up on one side of the scraper when it's in operating position, just cutting a little bit of dirt, cutting into the soil and filling up. When it's filled you pull the bar back to quit digging, and go on to where you'll dump it. Then you pull the rope, and the thing will flip over and empty itself, and then you come back. I think everybody who has ever run a fresno has served his time, has passed his initiation. As sure as the dickens, he'd be right alongside that Johnson bar when that Johnson bar hit a rut or a boulder and flip by itself. That Johnson bar would hit him right under the jaw hinge and knock him galley-west, ass-over-teakettle, just like that. Forked-end up. So I got a sore jaw, and I learned how. I never got hit again.

Julian, Odd Halseth, Frank Pinkley, and Irwin Hayden at the Grewe Site, Arizona, 1930.

A fresno in use at the Snaketown ballcourt, Arizona, ca. 1935.

We cleared the greasewood, the creosote bush. It was all desert. We scraped off the wind-deposited fill, sheet-flood-deposited fill above the old ground surface, so that we didn't have to spend three-quarters of our time removing sterile earth. That worked fine. We got pit houses; we worked on trash mounds; we found cremations. And we found what we called ceremonial areas, for lack of a better term, where within a limited area, people had burned and damaged just great quantities of beautiful shellwork, carved shells, bracelets, finger rings, and hair ornaments, I suppose, like bodkins with mountain sheep made out of deer leg bone. And you know the upper end of the joint has two little humps in a deer bone. If you carve it right you can make a beautiful mountain sheep out of it. These had mountain sheep standing on the tips of these and the shafts were carved with entwined rattlesnakes, about a foot long, depending on the size of the deer.

And beautiful pottery, effigy pots, and whole parades of what we called incense burners—thick-bodied, shallow, cylindrical bowls with legs and a tail and a head, looked like guanacos or llamas. That made headlines all over the world. I'll show you a copy of the 1930 *Illustrated London News*, which I have over here on the table, which I've had ever since that time. It had a feature on that and photographs of these things.

Along in May 1930, or thereabouts, I got crosswise somehow with my father, and I left. But they worked on until summer got too hot, and then they went back up to Cornfield Canyon [Desha Canyon] on Navajo Mountain for the summer, before coming back down to Compound F and finishing it.

This comes to mind because of the recent newspaper story that a developer is going to put not only that five acres but a lot of other acreage there right across the street from

Julian Hayden, Pueblo Grande, Arizona, about 1937.

Casa Grande National Monument into condominiums and a shopping center and God knows what. Right over that incredibly rich area. This first came up about a year ago, and the Park Service got concerned, but it's private property, so they can't say anything.

The developer decided he'd better call a contract archaeologist to make a survey, and Mary Lou Heuett of Cultural and Environmental Services Incorporated went up from Tucson and surveyed the place. She and I talked it all over, because I had a lot of notes on it, still have. She recommended that the whole thing be excavated or preserved, preferably, as part of Casa Grande, but there's not much money in the federal budget for that sort of thing. Now the man has sold half the land to somebody else, so that there are two developers to cope with, and the price is up in the millions now, where it was not worth too damn much before, maybe a few thousand an acre. It will probably be plowed up and dug up and nothing done about it. Nobody can make the man excavate if he doesn't want to. So that's what the Grewe Site is.

It contains Gila Butte, Santa Cruz, and Sacaton pottery from about 700 to 1050 AD, something like that. Flared-rim bowls, incised exteriors, lots of zoomorphic paintings on the bowls, decorations. Lots of shell, lots of everything. It's a shame, but what are you going to do? People who do the excavation on the site, the trenching, and dig the basements and the swimming pools and so forth, will find they have a treasure trove and will make some money off of it. So will the developer.

It wasn't included in the original Casa Grande Site, because nobody knew anything about it at that time. Casa Grande is one of the oldest of the Southwest monuments, you know, 1918. Frank Pinkley was the first custodian. I think he was paid a dollar a year. I've forgotten what he did for a living, but his father and mother owned the trading post at Blackwater around the turn of the century and the latter part of the 1800s, 1890 perhaps. Fewkes worked there, Jess Fewkes, and Mindeleff, and oh my, everybody talked about it. They visited Casa Grande of course, excited by all the Spanish travelers who had come through.

There was lots of speculation about Casa Grande. That maze pattern on the interior wall of the second story used to bring visitors from all over the world, because it was a sure sign that the Phoenicians had visited Casa Grande around about two thousand years ago. It's the old Cretan maze, which we know now around here as the Pima man in the maze, I'itoi. We had a lot of company while we were working at Compound F. People had come to see the maze and had come to see the Masonic symbol shell carving in a showcase, which was proof that the Phoenicians were Masons, also, you see. Masons made tours, practically religious tours, to Casa Grande to see that square and compass. This aggravated my father no end because he knew better, and he didn't mind saying so.

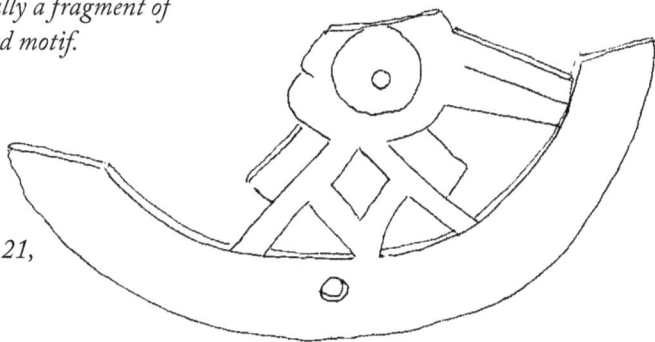

The "Masonic symbol" shell carving found at Casa Grande. This is actually a fragment of a shell pendant, with a bird motif. (Sketch by Steve Hayden, after a photograph in Casa Grande: the Greatest Valley Pueblo of Arizona, *by Edna Townsley Pinkley [March 21, 1927])*

So Art Woodward got interested in the maze. Casa Grande ruin is a multi storied structure which was partly filled with debris, wall slump, and collapsed walls, and so forth, up to above the roof of the first story. A man of ordinary height could stand on top of that debris. This carving would be just about at his waist level, where if he wanted to stand there with a jackknife in hand, he could carve himself a nice pattern into that polished limy-adobe plaster, which was still beautifully preserved. Some people left their names that way.

Art Woodward was a historian, a good one, and he could track down mysteries like that and find the answers. He loved to do it. So he went back to the records and discovered that sometime in the eighties, if I recall correctly, an immigrant train came through from the East. They stopped at Casa Grande, of course, and they admired the ruins. Several of the people kept journals, and one of them was a classics scholar from the Mediterranean, who had lived in Crete, visited Knossos, the Minoan remains, and all that. He was a classics scholar. He commented at length on the ruins of course, but he didn't say anything about carving a Minoan maze, a Cretan maze, on the wall. Yet it wasn't until after that time that anybody ever mentioned it. They never mentioned it prior to that time. Shortly afterward you began to hear talk about it. So Woodward believed, and probably correctly, that this man, whose name I've forgotten, was responsible for it.

To wind that one up, a man named Dr. Barry Fell, who's a world authority on echinoderms, starfish, Harvard University, is a little too enthusiastic about early man in the New World. He has it in his head that the Phoenicians were here two thousand years ago, coming through southern Arizona on their way to the coast and having navigational schools in Folsom, Nevada, and God knows what. He's written a number of books about it, some of which I've collected because I find them interesting. And he has pretty near a chapter on the Cretan maze. So I read that, and I wrote him a letter. I complimented him on his extremely interesting text, and well presented, and then I went ahead and explained Woodward's reasoning about the Cretan maze.

It doesn't show up in the baskets until after 1880—that's when it becomes popular. I had a snapper in there, too, on something else. He believed that Frank Russell's transcription of the Pima Creation Myth (with all of the songs presented in linguistic form, I forget the terminology, "syllabified," in Piman, with the translation in English underneath each word), Dr. Fell decided that those songs were actually the hymn to the great god Ba'al, of the Phoenicians. And that the priests who accompanied the Phoenicians across southern Arizona had taught the Piman medicine men the hymns of the great god Ba'al; they'd been converted, at least that far, and those songs had come down unchanged, syllable to syllable, until Frank Russell recorded them. So I went on to say that I thought that was very interesting, too, but as an archaeologist, pseudo-archaeologist at least, I knew nothing about linguistics, but I had heard of linguistic drift. And it seemed strange to me that these things should have come down orally for two thousand years without a single letter out of place.

When the next edition came out, he eliminated it and the Cretan maze too. He didn't answer me, of course, but indirectly he did. So that was fun. But [as for] the Masonic emblem, the square and compass. . . . We found at the Grewe Site a shell carving, carved out of thin shell, of the very common Hohokam motif of a long-billed bird eating a rattlesnake. Or eating an egg, or whatever it might be. They eat several things,

Charles "China Baby" Conrad at his home, Linda Vista Ranch, Portal, Arizona, June 1935. (Photograph by Julian Hayden)

fish also, sometimes. And by golly, you could duplicate those breaks on this complete carving that we found, and you had the square and compass that's in the showcase. So they took it out of the showcase, and the Masons were furious.

People have a good time. We had help on Compound F. A German fellow from Michigan came out for his health. He was a handsome fellow, blue-eyed and blonde, going around in brief shorts to get all the sun he could; I think he had lung trouble. He'd come over and help us at Compound F. When company came, tourists—and there were lots of tourists—he'd move aside and put a Navajo blanket over his shoulders and crouch on a foundation and glare at people. Once in a while he'd say, "Ugh." And by golly, every once in a while a party of tourists would take one look at him and hear him say, "Ugh," and they'd turn around and go away. So we used to tease him. We called him China Baby Conrad. One of the gang planted a little china baby doll on China Baby who, unsuspectingly, dug it up. From then on he was known as China Baby. C. B. Conrad, which were his initials, too. China Baby was a nice guy.

Anyway, that's the Grewe Site. Woodward had promised Van Bergen a good publication on glossy paper with photographs and everything else. All that ever came out of it was a mimeographed brochure called "The Grewe Site." Hardly any sketches were in it, just a very brief thing, really nothing at all. I've held that against Art Woodward ever since. He had told my father when he hired him that he was going to make his fortune and his name on Van Bergen—"the old man" as he put it—even if it broke the old man.

The silver cigarette box Julian made for Harold and Winifred Gladwin.

Well, he did; he broke the old man's heart and he broke the old man's pocketbook, too. And that's all we got out of it, except some showcases full of stuff.

Then, when I found the Pima Creation Myth, which talked about the people from the East, who were Pimans, coming in and running out the Hohokam priests and chiefs, but leaving the common folk because they were all the same people—that states it as far as I'm concerned. Still it isn't totally accepted, but I haven't heard any better explanations. But Casa Grande is where we first got an inkling of all that, so it really turned out to be a rather important place. We'd like to see a lot more work done there, but I guess it won't be done.

There's nothing below what we found. It's all on caliche and limy adobe with nothing in the adobe. No, there's no question about it being the bottom when you reach it. It's good limy adobe, not the hard rock that we have here, but a material you can dig and mix with a little sand to make darned good adobe, if you want to. After all, Casa Grande is still standing.

When I was working at Snaketown, I was silversmithing. I went over to the coast and got my tools and set up in a tent. Did quite a bit of work for Harold Gladwin, who was the patron of the expedition, you know. I made him a cigarette case for the table.

Winifred Gladwin I never knew very well. She was pleasant enough. She never bothered me, and she was hospitable when Helen and I stayed at Gila Pueblo for a week or so on our honeymoon trip, collecting designs. She was the very soul of hospitality, a sweetheart that way. The only thing that ever really caught my eye was that Ted Sayles, one of the archaeologists, grew a mustache between the time she'd last seen him and the time she came down for dinner. She said, "Ted, I don't like that mustache. Take it off." And he said, "Yes, ma'am." I had one, too, so I stared at her hard, but she didn't look at me. If she had, I'd have left. But then they'd known each other for a long time.

I was born with a mustache. No, when I got out of junior college I very nearly went to Stanford, because I had heard that only seniors could wear mustaches, and I wanted to by God find out whether that was so or not. But I didn't, luckily. I was going up to become a geologist, provided I could keep my mustache and find a job.

To most people Kirk Bryan was a god. And damn near to me. After Haury asked me if I'd come and dig Ventana Cave, and I consented, he invited me down to Ventana Cave to meet him and Kirk Bryan. I came via Tucson and picked up Gwyneth Harrington. We drove on out to Ventana Cave, and Gwyneth surprised Emil and Kirk Bryan. Emil knew her very well, of course, but I don't know whether Bryan knew her. Any rate, it worked out well, and we spent a very delightful evening together around the campfire. The next morning we climbed the butte and went all over the top of it. Bryan told us this and that. He knew what he was talking about; he made sense. He was a very personable man. I liked him very much. He was a tall man, that's all I remember. He could deal with the academics as well as the men—he could deal with Haury and me with no trouble. I was a working blue-collar stiff, and Haury was an academic from the word go. My father worshipped him [Bryan], and when my father liked anybody, he was probably pretty good. My father read his reports. I've got his *The Papago Country, Arizona* and anything of his I can get hold of. Boy you know they're worth their weight in gold.

Matter of fact my copy of that paper came indirectly from Forrest Shreve. I knew his daughter Margaret, Peggy Conn. She worked for Malcolm Rogers by the way. Oh hell, Shreve was a character; he was wonderful. He's the great one, rightly so. His daughter worshipped him, too; she was a student of Cummings's, of Haury's, and then of Malcolm's. She worked for Malcolm Rogers for years.

How did I get signed on to the Ventana dig? Emil Haury set up a project with the Indian CCC [Civilian Conservation Corps] to employ Indians doing archaeological work on the reservation in 1941. The Bureau of Indian Affairs needed projects, and Emil saw a chance to get some work done. He set out to excavate Batki, which is a Papago village between Sells and Quijotoa over toward the foot of the Quijotoa Mountains. That was a village that had been visited by Father Kino, and it was still visible. So Haury and the Indian crew went over there to work. In the burned-out houses they came across some Apache arrowheads. That ended the project right there. Apaches had attacked the village after Kino was there and had been beaten off. Papagos were killed and Apaches were killed, and the houses were burned, of course, by the Papago afterward, so everybody stayed away from the place. The old men went and said, "No, no more digging, because the spirits of the Apaches will come back to afflict us."

Then Haury went up in the top of the Quijotoas and excavated a bat cave. He had to pack the guano out on horseback hoping to find some archaeology, but there wasn't any. The Papago made a little money from the sale of the guano. They got about ready to quit, when somebody pointed out Ventana Cave. Haury went over and looked at it, and there seemed to be a chance there was some depth to it, so he decided to excavate.

One of the graduate students did the work, Wilfred Bailey. He was a social anthropologist working on his degree. In all due respect, he knew nothing about cave excavation. They dug the upper half of the cave and found the bones of extinct animals and all that sort of thing, which was quite interesting. But it wasn't until they found what looked like a Clovis point in his back dirt that people began to prick up their ears, because nothing like that had ever been found in this country before. The season ended with that.

I had played out of the CCC in May of 1941 and went on annual leave for a while. By that time I was silversmithing in Phoenix and had a shop there. I was working for Lord & Taylor in New York, manufacturing for them. But I'm an archaeologist, so Haury arranged for me to start the Ventana Cave job.

And the war came along, of course, in 1941. The Indians lived at home. I really can't speak with much authority on the Indian CCC because Ventana's the only real contact I had with them. But my trucks came out of the Indian CCC at Sells, tools and so forth, and employees. And, of course, the CCC paid them. I noticed one thing about the Indian CCCs. My foreman, Juan Xavier, a Papago, and I drove up the road to Anegam, a village up north of Santa Rosa. There was a big crew of men out there working in an arroyo, under the bridge highways. I said, "Is that CCC work?" And Juan said, "No, it certainly isn't. We don't like Washington. This is all village work. All these men come from the village. We do our own work. We don't depend on Washington, except, of course, when excavation of the cave comes along. That's special stuff."

When we found that we had humans associated with extinct fauna, then it became obvious that something would have to be done. I think I was paid by some fund that Haury had to excavate the cave. But I know later on that some patron [Mr. and Mrs. Wetmore Hodges] forked over enough money to enable me to write the final report, or a large part of it. I worked there for four months, and I wrote my section of the report on it.

At the start of the season the next year, we got a grant, not only from BIA-CCC, but also from [Mr. and Mrs. Hodges]. I don't know what happened to Wilfred Bailey. Maybe he'd moved on. They had to find somebody to supervise the dig, and I was the only one available. Field men were very scarce in those days. And if Haury had had a university student who had cave experience, he'd have done it, or if Bailey had been available, he would have done it. But, none were available, and I'd worked in caves myself before, Gypsum Cave and here and there. So, they offered me the job and I took it, because the Pueblo Grande job had ended.

That's how come I dug Ventana Cave, and I'm glad I did. I had enough geological experience and enough cave experience and enough experience with different soils, that I could do it properly. I don't think I missed very much. I made the isometric details in the publication that clarifies the whole thing, and I wrote the notes, on the geology of the cave, the structure of the cave, of which I'm pretty damned proud. I was on the site at Ventana from the first of January into sometime in late April 1942.

The family moved into Santa Rosa schoolhouse for the season. Ruth Underhill, the famous anthropologist who worked with the Papago so long, had quarters there also, so we got slightly acquainted with her. Helen made friends with the young Papago girls. Gwyneth Harrington, who later became Gwyneth Xavier, had been working with the Indian Arts and Crafts Board earlier. Her driver and interpreter was Juan Xavier, out of Choulic village. She and Juan Xavier and I had gone to Tiburón Island the year before, so we were old friends. Then Juan Xavier became my foreman at Ventana Cave. That's how one thing always leads to another, as *Jurgen* says.

We didn't try to collect soil samples and charcoal samples and everything as we went, because we didn't know. In the 1970s Jane Rosenthal was sitting here at lunch one day with Helen and me, and she said, "You know, as much as I think of Dr. Haury and think of you, Julian, I'm going to say I don't understand why you weren't foresighted enough to collect charcoal samples for C-14." And Helen and I stared at her and at each other, and finally one of us, Helen maybe, said, "Do you remember when Ventana Cave was dug?"

"Well, certainly," she said. "In 1942."

"Do you remember when C-14 technique was discovered?" And she thought a minute and she turned bright red. It was in the fifties.

We didn't know about saving charcoal samples unless they were large enough to look for tree rings. So I told her, "You know, you should be complimenting us, both of us, because we left a study block," an untouched block right in the middle of the stratigraphy. Years later, in the '60s, I returned and got charcoal and bone samples by which we dated the cave deposits. She got the point.

The study block was hard, cemented with carbonates. So it was reasonably safe to leave, but it's all gone now. People have chopped it out and kicked it around and torn it up. I was told the other day that there wasn't anything left of it. But we got what information we could from it. You might ask if we got pollen, not from the lower levels, certainly, because of the carbonates, and pollen apparently doesn't survive. In the upper levels, I don't think we checked for pollen in those days. That's forty, fifty years ago. Now we'd have done flotation and all kinds of things and learned a lot more. There's lots of technical things now that we didn't have then. I think we did a good job of recovery, and I make no bones about being proud of the stratigraphic work we did.

The book, *Ventana Cave*, had been criticized, but I never knew a report that wasn't criticized. Jess Jennings up in the University of Utah excavated Danger Cave and wrote it up. I dug out a copy for Malcolm Rogers when he was living here, working on his San Dieguito report, but he was upset because he couldn't make head or tail of it. He couldn't place the artifacts in the fill, in the stratigraphy, which is a fault of the author. But he could have at Ventana Cave. We could place them.

And, if you have to, you could always go back to the field notes. I've still got copies of all of them, by the way. They're exhaustive; they're detailed. I'm proud of them. So those things have to be considered. My idea of an excavation is one in which Joe Blow can come back twenty years from now and replace every object in its stratigraphic position to reconstruct the whole thing. Of course that's physically impossible to do, it's impractical to do, but we do the best we can. That's why I'm a good note taker, if I do say so.

I took pictures of the Children's Shrine before that sometime. The pictures don't show everything, or else everything was not there. There used to be seats made of flagstone on either side of the ellipse there in the central ring. At some point when I was there and also in the early twenties, there was at least one and possibly two ollas of seashells standing in the entrances to the ellipse. They were taken away by the Papagos for fear the white man would steal them.

That's what Ray Cawker told me, who was taken there as a little boy. He told me that in '64–'65, Snaketown II. He was a man who had a great reverence for the old

The Children's Shrine near Ventana Cave, Arizona, October 21, 1953. (Photograph by Julian Hayden)

shrines, and he had cleaned up the Shrine to Siuuku up in the pass in the Gila Buttes. When Helen and I saw it in 1965, it had all been cleaned up, and the pathways were outlined in white pebbles, neatly swept. Ray was the man who had taken on the task of preserving that shrine, which I thought was nice. When Helen and I became engaged, in '35, we had gone up to the shrine and made our offerings, and then we went back thirty years later and did it again.

At the party that the Pima workmen gave us at the end of Snaketown II, at the San Tan schoolhouse, a great big ceremony, the Pimas put on a great feed and had singing and everything else. Then each one of the staff members had to make a little talk. Since I was up there only once a week, they had forgotten me. But Helen and I went up for it, and they made room at the tables. They hurried out and scrounged a nice Pima tray basket for us as a gift, and then I had my turn at the mike.

So, I told them about going to this Shrine to Siuuku, in '35, and our wishes for the prosperity of the Pimas and for ours and so forth. I told them we had just gone there and renewed our wishes. I heard later that the young folks were looking at each other, "What's that white man talking about? What's that word, Siuuku? What's that shrine? What does that mean?" They don't know. They don't know. They all had radios. We thought that was sad. The old people knew instantly.

Along in the spring of '42, we were working at Ventana, and along in the afternoon a pigeon, a domestic pigeon, flew into the cave. I later found out it was a Silver King pigeon, a domesticated, highly bred pigeon. The pigeon flew into the cave and walked around among us all. We couldn't touch it, but it wasn't afraid of us. It kept its distance,

Helen Hayden at Siuuku shrine, in the pass between the two hills of Gila Buttes, east of Snaketown, Arizona, March 24, 1935. This photograph was taken two days after the Haydens were married, probably by Milton "Jackie" Snow.

and this continued all afternoon until we packed up and went in for the evening. I wondered if it would be there in the morning.

Antonio Wilbur, a medicine man riding with me, said yes, he thought it would be. I didn't ask him any more. The next day, the next morning, the pigeon was there, waiting for us—so we thought. It circulated among us, until about ten o'clock in the morning, when I looked down, and there was dust on the highway, and a man came scrambling up the trail, and he said, "Is Juan Xavier here?" And I said yes. "Well," he said, "tell him that his daughter died yesterday morning at St. John's Hospital." "Okay." So I went over to Juan, and I said, "Juan, I've got bad news. Your daughter passed away yesterday morning, and that's the message."

He said, "Thank you," and did not change his expression. He called his son and they left. The weekend before, this was on a Tuesday, I think, he had gone to the hospital at Gila Crossing. His daughter was in the last stages of tuberculosis, in that last flush, as they say. Rosy cheeks, bright-eyed, you'd think she was just ready to get up and go dancing. The nurses had curled her hair and made her up, and Juan came back feeling cheerful.

So, later I asked Antonio about all this. I said, "Juan didn't show any sign of emotion." He said, "No. His daughter had come to see him." And that's the way it was. The bird was a symbol of death in his family.

He had an uncle who got up one morning for breakfast and walked out on the porch under the ramada at Choulic, stretched in the sun, and was shot dead by a man who had left the country many, many years before and had been forgotten about. But while he was eating breakfast, his wife and his children saw him turn into a bird. His wife knew what was going to happen, but she couldn't say anything, of course.

Another time, a cousin, a nephew, I don't know which, went on roundup, and he went galloping into the yard one day and said, in effect, "Ma, fix me something to eat. Gotta go." So she fixed him something to eat. And while he was eating, the feathers grew, and he turned into a bird. She didn't say anything, and he got up, leapt on his horse, and ran into a gate that should have been open, breaking his neck. So that's the story, and I find it difficult to tell. It's a very moving story, obviously. And I have more like that which I don't think I'll tell you now. That's enough. *Bastante.*

Pia Machita was headman out at Hickiwan, which is a village in the conservative part of the reservation out northwest of Ventana Cave. He was chief of the Hickiwan district. Before the war a body of men came up to see him, and they said, "We have been sent by Washington to install privies for all of your people."

Pia Machita said, "Washington sent you?"

"Yes." This was WPA days, you know.

"But," he said, "that arroyo has served this village for thousands of years. And it's good for another thousand. Now Washington, those people there are so stupid as to send you out here to spend money and labor and all the rest to put up privies for us! Get out of here! And don't ever come back!" So they got out.

And not much later the U.S. marshals came out and said, "We have to register all of your young men."

And I was registering men out there on the side while I was working at Ventana. I handled also food rationing and all that sort of thing, too. It was one of those things I had to do, nights or weekends. But I didn't get out to Hickiwan. That was the word, the young men had to register. Pia Machita told his men, he said, "No way. We're not going to register you. We're not going to do anything Washington says, if they haven't got any more sense than to send people out to dig privies."

So then the marshals came out, and they arrested him. Somebody showed some good judgment. They sent him to San Pedro, California, to the prison there at Terminal Island. He was an old man, and somebody put him outside gardening, which made sense. And when the marshal took him over, they detoured around through some other cities that the old man had never seen and never dreamed of. He had a pretty good eye, though.

From San Pedro they sent him to Atlanta's federal pen. And they toured way up through the north through the industrial areas and the farmlands, took a long time. They got him to Atlanta. There again they put him in the garden. Eventually let him out. And he came home, and he called his young men together, and he said, "I have climbed the mountain and I have seen the bear," in effect. "We have never had a school here," he said. "You men get out and build a school right away." He got the point. I thought that was very nice.

Never trust an Indian if he gives you a nickname deadpan. At Snaketown II, in 1964–65, I had charge of the backhoe. I bought it for the university for the project, took it up there, took my operator up, and broke the Indian operator in on it. The Indian operator was named Fred Marietta. And we had an instant antipathy; I didn't like him and he didn't like me, for whatever reason.

Well, he found out rather shortly that my nickname at Snaketown I, back in the thirties, was Bitacoi Viappwuh. *Bitacoi* means the black beetle that stands on its head all the time. We call him Pinacate beetle, or stinkbug, too. And *Viappwuh* is "young man." So I was "young man black beetle who stands on his head," because I always used a Number Two Iowa scoop, a short-handled scoop shovel, and I could keep four or five Pimas using conventional shovels just working their hearts out trying to keep up with me. So somehow Fred found out about that, and instead of calling me something in Pima, he said "little stinker" in Pima. What the devil could I say? I can't speak his lingo. I had to take it and like it.

Another time I had an employee named Rudy Vergara. He was a very, very tough man. He was pachuco. And he'd been through the wars, as a pachuco. I don't think I have to explain pachucos. Like the hippies, zoot suiters, whatever you like, of the late war and postwar era. They had their own language, which changed every day. The old people could never understand it, which is one reason the pachucos were resented. One day Rudy got mad at me on the job, I don't know why, I don't remember. He started discussing me in front of the other men, and I recognized one word, which was a fighting word. I knew I couldn't talk back to him because I didn't speak pachuco. And I didn't want to fight him. I didn't know what to do.

So I swelled up like a poisoned skunk and moved in on him and glared at him, and I said in my nastiest tone, looking him right in the eye, you know, [an unintelligible Pima phrase]. And he stared at me and his jaw dropped and his eyes popped, and he didn't know what to say because he was then in the same fix I'd been in. I was speaking Pima. About all the Pima I knew, but he didn't know that. And we turned and went about our business. What I said to him was, "Is there any water in your canteen?" And, of course the last bit was simply "Dog woman," which was not a polite thing, but he didn't know that. But he gathered by the tone that I was being impolite, shall we say.

Once we were working up at Keet Seel. We were out on the stabilization of that ruin in 1934. I grew a pretty good beard. Pretty near five months' growth. It was sort of streaky and wiggly, but still, by God, it was mine. The Navajos called me Dághá Niłchxon. "What does that mean?" I asked.

"Oh, that means 'brown beard.'" Then I found out that it meant "dirty beard, dirty whiskers." Never did know. I've been spooky around Navajos ever since.

Erik Reed, whom I mentioned earlier, was a small man with a very sharp face and red hair. Pimas called him Vishag Ee-pik. I didn't find out till after the job was over just what that meant. It means "hawk urine." "Oh, why do you call him that?"

They answered, "Because he's too sharp." I guess hawk urine must be considerably acid, I don't know. It's all I could ever get out of them. And I never told Erik. He had heard the name and thought it was a term of great respect. What do you do? [In tune with typical Native American humor, both Julian's and Erik's nicknames were far earthier than Julian had been led to believe. Dághá Niłchxon is more accurately translated as "stinky beard," and is more indicative of pubic than facial hair. And Erik's nickname, Vishag Ee-pik, means "chickenhawk penis."]

5. The Right Woman

How did I meet Helen? All started in Flagstaff in the spring of 1934, when I came out of Keet Seel after five months there. At Coltons' [Harold and Mary-Russell] house I met Fisher Motz and his wife Pen. Fish had been job engineer at Wupatki, CWA [Civil Works Administration] project, as was Keet Seel, and we were both under supervision of Museum of Northern Arizona, Dr. Colton's institution. Well, Pen was a tall, big-boned girl, very pregnant, and I paid her no more attention than politeness required. I was anxious to meet Happy Jack Snow, my old buddy, and go get a Mexican meal on the south side of the tracks and whatever. Didn't see them again.

Then at Snaketown, Fish was job engineer again, working for Gladwin. And just by the way, Fish had been on Ansel Hall expeditions to Rainbow Bridge and loved Navajo country and archaeology. He'd heard of Gladwin's Snaketown job and wrote asking for work as a cartographer, etc. (graduate architect, he was). Gladwin asked what he wanted in way of pay. Fish, being timid and uncertain, said, "Would fifty dollars a month be too much, with found [food and lodging]?" Gladwin said okay. Gladwin paid Dad and me and the others one hundred dollars a month and found!

Fish was from somewhere in Pennsylvania, but he married Pen, a girl who was a cousin of Helen's. Anyhow, Helen had gone through Smith College, as her sisters did, too, and they wanted her to go ahead and get a doctorate in medieval English literature. That was her specialty, but instead she had to go to work at the Carnegie Library for thirty cents an hour, which was standard in 1930, as you know. She was lucky to have a job at all. Then she developed an intermittent fever of some kind, and the doctor said, "Well, it might be a good idea to go to dry country." So she remembered that her cousin Pen was married to Motz, and Pen invited her out. Pen and Fisher had just had a baby girl, so this would relieve Pen, and it would work out very nicely. So Helen came out.

I was cutting wood one afternoon, and here she showed up in Motz's Model A. She got out looking like a million dollars with black silk stockings on, a black coat with a fur collar, and some high-falutin' eastern-stylish cap on her head, frizzy hair, dark, high cheekbones. She said to me, "Is Fisher Motz here?" and hell, I wasn't even polite enough to guide her to the tent. I said, "They're up there at the end," and kept on cutting wood. I don't think I'd ever encountered a city girl from the East before, and I didn't think anything about it. I went in for coffee with Mrs. Jones [the cook] after Fish and Helen had left, and I remarked, "Well, that's a city girl for sure, wouldn't be worth shooting on a ranch, would she!" Mrs. Jones agreed heartily, being an old mining camp cook her own self.

So eventually Helen and I met, perhaps at her house. Fish and Pen and she telling stories about their childhoods, and Helen reading out loud a love letter from her

*Fisher Motz repairing
the Snaketown office tent
after a storm, March
1935. (Photograph by
Julian Hayden)*

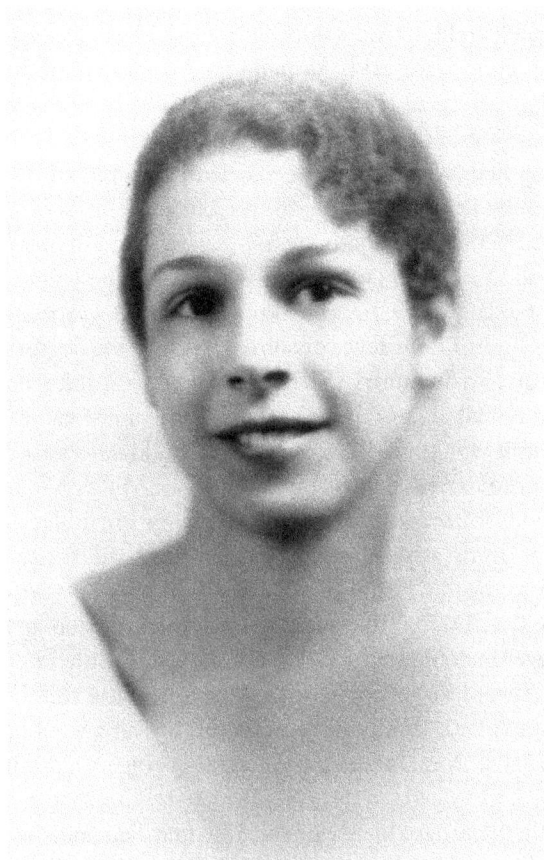

*Helen Botler Pendleton in
1930.*

Ted Sayles, Irwin Hayden, and Mrs. Jones at Snaketown, Arizona, fall 1934. (Photograph by Julian Hayden)

fiancé back East, all of them laughing themselves sick at his extravagant language of love. I was amazed and thought that these Easterners surely had odd ways. I suppose Helen came out to camp for dinner now and then; I do remember Dad and her arguing language and history at a great rate, and she fairly enchanted Dad, who couldn't stop talking about her. I'd been back to Riverside once, in October, and brought back the old Edison phonograph, with records, which Dad and I used to play. Sometime in the spring I took it to Chandler for the Motzes and Helen to use. Their cook, Emma, referred to it as Hayden's bouquet, which I thought a bit ridiculous.

Hans Steinke and Strangler Lewis were wrestling in Phoenix one night. My father liked to watch them and so did I, so he said, "Let's invite Helen."

I said, "Well, if you want to."

We ate before we picked her up, in Chandler, and carefully didn't put any onions on our hamburgers, lest we give offense. Saw Lewis and Steinke in an exhibition match, with several other staged matches before, including Gorgeous George, wonderful show, pepper in eyes, slugging, jumping, etc., crowd went wild, and we did enjoy it. On the way back we stopped for hamburgers, and Helen put everything on, which tickled Dad and me. I'll never forget her when we picked her up. She was dogged out to the guards, the "skunk" coat, of course, and a hat which looked like a Number Two Iowa gravel scoop flat on her head, had three strips of stainless steel on the bill of it, which projected over her bangs, which themselves stuck straight out and frizzy. I remember distinctly being astonished and thinking, "Well, maybe we're not exactly things of beauty either!"

Then I didn't see her again for a while. Later we went into Phoenix to visit my father's first cousin, Thomas Hayden. There was a piano there, and we stopped to pick

Helen up; the Motzes were there, too. I was playing the piano, which I could do then, and she was a good singer, Helen was, so we were singing.

When it was time to go home, I told my father, "You go on home; I'll bring her home." And I did, and we drove toward Chandler. Nice moonlight night, broken clouds, rain squalls here and there—and the [Model] T had no top. I said, "How about a drive to the Gila Buttes?" Okay! So we did, didn't stop, just drove out and back to her house, and I came home. I thought about that, not many girls would have driven in a stripped-down T without a top on a possibly rainy night, and I began, I guess, to think about Helen more than I had, which had been not at all. In fact, Dad and I were showering one night after that, and he said, "Julian, you could do worse than marry Helen, she'd be as affectionate as a kitten!" I said, "Goddamn it, Dad, why the hell do you keep shoving her in my face? Forget her!" He just laughed.

I talked to her later and asked, "Would you like to eat a steak broiled on mesquite coals out there on the hill before you go East?" She was going East in a short time to finish up her job.

"Why, yes."

So, I picked her up and we broiled a steak. I have a picture of her standing beside the T, on the slope of Gila Butte that evening, late. I cooked a nice steak, had crushed pineapple with it—and forgot a spoon! Had to make one out of the can lid. Embarrassed me. She backed into a cholla [cactus], which jumped at her, and I knocked it off with a stick. So, we were sitting about the fire, she on one side, me on the other. I figured she was engaged, at least I understood she was.

Knowing she was leaving shortly for Pittsburgh to her job, I asked, "Why, if you like the desert, don't you stick around awhile?"

She looked at me and said, "What do you mean?"

Well, of course, nowadays, why, that would have been taken any way you want to put it. In those days, no sir. I thought—or didn't think—awhile and said, "Well, maybe I mean will you marry me?" and I'll be dogged if she didn't say, "Why, yes!" Well, I'll be teetotally damned, I like to fell off the hill and sat there for what seemed like a long time. Mind you, I'd never sweet-talked her, never held her hand, never kissed her! I finally said, "Is it customary in your neck of the woods for an accepted man to kiss his girl?" She allowed as how it was, and I was sunk.

Now, this isn't especially meaningful, to use the modern expression, unless I tell you that one time, Helen was reading a letter from her Dudley Pendleton, in which he said he could hardly wait for her return, her warm arms, and hoped some cowpasture Romeo wouldn't grab her before she could return to him. That stuck in my mind, and all I had in my mind when I proposed, believe it or not, was to enable her to go to her fiancé and tell him she'd been proposed to by a cowpasture Romeo! That was what I'd thought, without really thinking more about it—I was saving my pay to go to Tahiti with my friend Gray, who had a vanilla plantation there and wanted me to throw in with him!

But, I knew that this girl was the one I wanted. If I didn't get her, all right, I'd go to Tahiti. And we came off the hill and I took her home. Next time I saw her—and we'd *not* told anyone, even Pen, about this—I picked her up en route to Phoenix to get some silver soldering done for Gladwin, and here she came, in a nice house dress, me in Levis, and we trundled to Phoenix in the T. Got the soldering done, driving down

Helen Pendleton at Gila Buttes, apparently on the day she and Julian became engaged, March 16, 1935. (Photograph by Julian Hayden)

Washington Street, she said, "You know, this would be a good day to get married. It's the vernal equinox." And I said, "Hell, I haven't got any money," and she said, "I've got five dollars." I turned into the courthouse lot, and we climbed the stairs to the clerk's office and bought a license—no waiting in those days. Then to Judge Westfall's office at 4:45 and a couple of hangers-on for witnesses, and we were married! We stood in a freight elevator for some time, before a man said, "Son, if you want to go down, you better walk, that's out of service!" Helen never remembered that—must have been dazed?

Well, that's how we met and got spliced. Good splice, too—didn't unravel once.

After we got married, we didn't say anything to anybody about it. Except that when we came in that night, Motz and his wife were waiting up for us, since Helen was living there. Pen looked suspiciously at Helen and said, "Helen, did you two get married?"

Helen said, "Why, yes."

And Motz said, "Now what am I going to do?"

"What do you mean, what are you going to do?"

"Well," he said, "I'm *in loco parentis.* I told your mother, Helen, that I'd take care of you and protect you. What am I going to tell her?"

"It's simple enough," said Helen. "Tell her I got married." That took care of that.

Motz said, "Well, it won't work. I'll give you five years at the most."

And I said, "You come around in five years." So he came around in about six years, and I remembered it and said, "Fisher, do you remember what you once said?"

And he said, "Yes."

I said, "Look into our eyes, my friend." He didn't want to. He had been divorced.

My father's reaction? My father insisted that he's the one who did the courting for me. He bragged on that till he died, that he's the one that courted Helen. He liked her. They'd argue literature and everything else, I guess. Hell, I couldn't do that.

How could it happen so fast? Well, I had dated a few others and knew she was the one when I first saw her. Later she told me that she felt the same; we always figured it was some sort of déjà vu, like we'd known each other in some earlier life. That's one reason I won't be too upset to leave this mortal coil—then I can go look for her again.

I didn't know anything about her parents or family, but it worked anyway. I met her sometime after Christmas and we got married March 21.

Soon after we were married, Helen left for the East. When she returned, I picked her up in the Model T Ford at the station. We went over to my father's first cousin's for the night, and the next day we headed down the Gila River for our honeymoon. In those days the Gila River was a river and had water in it. It was a cottonwood and mesquite forest as far as you could see, some of it almost impenetrable in 1935. Not like it is now.

I never did head for Tahiti. I never got there, hell no, but never regretted it, either. I don't think I was cut out for an island life anyway. And then with the war coming, I might never have gotten out of it. And certainly I would never have met Helen. Of course, there might be a bunch of little half-and-half Polynesians around that I don't know about.

Helen was in the choir at Smith. They traveled a lot. She was also a very good dancer—that was a cross she had to bear, because I can't dance, never could. But she was an excellent singer. Her sister Isabelle was a good folksinger, and she did a lot of that. Her mother lived with us for a while when she was older, but I never did get to meet her father. I always wanted to meet him but never did. He was a big man and superintendent of a steel mill in McKeesport. He had a bass voice that was famous all over Pennsylvania. I remember that now, and he was much in demand. He was a man's man, anyway.

During the war, when I was traveling the highway between Yuma and Gila Bend with the Corps of Engineers working on those airbases, I stopped at a place called The Spot, maybe you know the one. The Spot was a little building, a restaurant, sitting on the highway there on the north side. Spot Road, that must be the intersection, then, where the highway gets through to lava country. I got acquainted with the man who ran it. I'd stop in for a cup of coffee. I found out he had worked for my father-in-law for years on the mill floor at McKeesport. He talked a lot about him; he just worshiped him. And my leader in the CCCs when I had a veteran crew, little Matt McClure, he worked for him for a number of years, too. So I wish I'd known the man, he was a good man. His name was Pendleton, Hugh Pendleton.

Then one of my CCC boys, when I first went to Pueblo Grande, in '36, had worked for one of Helen's uncles who grew apples in West Virginia. It's a small world. And Ann Axtell Morris—you know, Earl Morris's wife, *Digging in the Southwest*, Chichén Itzá and all that—she was Helen's sister's roommate in Smith College. It all comes together, doesn't it? It's what Jean Shinoda Bolen would call the tao of synchronicity. (She was a friend of my daughter Mary's at Pomona College.)

*Letter from Helen Pendleton to her friend Laura
MacKenzie in Bridgeport, Connecticut. Julian
and Helen were married two months later.*

Box 335, Chandler, Arizona
Jan 23, 1935

My darling Laura:

Did I mention before the two Haydens, father Irwin and son Julian? Father was originally from Massachusetts, and therefore feels very drawn to us. He's an old duck, and we love him dearly. Julian is the most beautiful specimen of man I've ever seen in my life—six feet three, blond and whiskered, and just as nice as they come. He is, however, something of a hermit, and we've been having our job cut out for us to get any of his very valuable time at all. He's begun to thaw out since we've been out here, and we've seen a good deal of him. Pen [Helen's cousin, Pen Motz] and Emma (our very miraculous biddy) have very determinedly set their caps for him in my behalf, and it's a lot of fun keeping up the good work. You needn't worry, though, lamb . . . I'm only having fun, and so is he. He'd make a hell of a good husband for whomever was woman enough to catch him. . . .

Anyhow, we're pretty proud because we managed to get him at least as far as the bar the night we went to the dance, and in a real pair of pants too. He wears dungarees and what not all the time, and I can't imagine what he'd look like in real clothes.

Much love, Hellie

*Hugh Nelson Pendleton
with his daughters
Helen (left) and Isabelle,
ca. 1912.*

I haven't any idea what Helen's family thought. I once wrote her father a letter, a short one. I don't think he answered me, but then he didn't write letters. Her mother came out to stay with us for half a year when we were working Pueblo Grande. She was a nice lady and very, very much a lady: very soft-voiced, wrote poetry, and all that sort of thing.

She and her husband must have been a contrast, because he was a big burly steelworker, who had been a farmer as a young fellow, and came from the working, laboring side of the family. I don't think he went to college. But they educated four fine children: Serena, Hugh, Helen, and Isabelle. The girls went to Smith. Hugh went to Penn State, became a master mechanic, and worked on Guam, building some big hospitals, at the end of the war. I first met him about 1947 when he was coming back from the Golden Gate Bridge, and he stopped at Tucson with his wife and son. He became an underwater specialist, working in deep water. He became a yachtsman, a sailor. When he was stationed in Toronto, for his company, they were building dry docks and doing underwater work. He and his wife won so many regattas that the Canadians barred him from further competition. Good man. I liked him. And then one of his sons became a professor of theoretical mathematics at Brandeis University.

Pulling George Webb's cattle truck across the Gila River at Gila Crossing, Arizona, 1935. Julian is standing in his car at right.

Probably our honeymoon sounds a lot better than it was, but it was sure good. We went down the Gila River to Gila Crossing. It took us several days to get that far. Went to Sicate and all those places. At Gila Crossing we went down and there was a Pima with his cattle truck stuck in the middle of the river. So, since my Model T pickup that I'd put together had three transmissions in it and big tires, I tied on to him and pulled him out. His name was George Webb. He later, with Ned Spicer, wrote the book called *A Pima Remembers*, which the university published. So nothing would do but to have dinner with him, and we stayed there for several days . . . with the full-moon light, delightful, and the river full of water.

And George took us over to Maricopa Wells, the stage station, which was almost inaccessible in those days. We got some pictures of it. George could play "Poet and Peasant Overture" on the harmonica. It was the *only* thing he could play, but he was good. And we'd sit out there in the evening with our backs against his adobe wall and he'd play "Poet and Peasant" over and over. I tell you it was nice, horses stomping around.

And he told stories. His father had had a flour mill on the south side of the river between Maricopa and a well on this side of Maricopa. His father belonged to the Hia C'ed O'odham, which seems to be a sand hill people, but also a group of Pimas that lived in that sandy area there, just west of the Maricopa–Phoenix road. He took us to a place that had thirty or forty Papago skeletons in it, people who had died of the flu in 1918 or thereabouts. Some Anglos had gotten in and looted it just recently. Skulls lying around, which was a shame. That was in the Estrellas. So anyway, we kept in touch with George from then on out. When George was writing *A Pima Remembers* with Ned, I'd

*Erik Reed at Snaketown, Arizona,
March 1935. (Photograph by
Julian Hayden)*

meet George and his wife at the bus station and they'd stay here for the weekend. Then
I'd take them back to the bus station.

Then we took the old Maricopa Road down the foothills of the Estrella and came
across a beautiful, big late-Hohokam Site. It had a D-shaped reservoir in a natural draw.
A cremation area was washing out, and pots standing there. Of course, I left them. All
gone now, I suppose, but very few people got into that country. And we went over to
Vekol and on to Gila Bend.

When Snaketown had closed, I stayed on to close the camp and dismantle everything. I took Erik Reed to the bus station in Chandler. Erik later became a famous
archaeologist. He was one of the crew, one of the archaeologists there. He was only
about seventeen years old, I think, and a graduate of George Washington University.
Harvard wouldn't take him yet because he was too young, so he was killing time until
they would take him. He was a very brilliant young man. And he and I were buddies,
and he and Helen were great friends. So I took him in to the bus station in Phoenix
and we stopped at the ABC Bar and had a couple beers, and we felt real dashing, you
know. He had his pay-out money. We were walking by the popular store, and here was
a white Stetson. A Stetson and two beers become expensive. So I looked at that hat,
and the more I looked at it, the more I wanted a Stetson. My father, by the way, was a
distant cousin of John B. Stetson, who manufactured it, but they knew each other. So,
I was predisposed.

Julian in his white Stetson with the "go-to-hell" Amarillo twist, Chandler, Arizona, April 1935.

So I went in, and when I looked at the lining, man, that was it. I paid over twenty-five dollars for that Stetson hat, a quarter of a month's wages in 1935, working for a hundred bucks a month and found. And me, with a bride back east, saving money. She'd gone east to finish up a job she was on.

I put Erik on the bus and drove into camp, and nobody recognized me at all. Cook didn't know who I was, nobody knew. It was a hat coming in, not me. So I loved that hat. And Helen didn't know any better, so she accepted it, too.

But that picture of me in the *Journal of the Southwest* [1989], thankfully out of focus, has that Stetson, a beautiful Stetson on top of my head, the only hat I ever owned. And that's a go-to-hell Amarillo twist in it, too. You know what an Amarillo twist is? I worked for days getting that twist in just right.

Josh Allen, our cowboy cook up at Keet Seel excavation, explained to me that the roll in the brim, on the righthand forward side, off the starboard bow, is an Amarillo twist. It was peculiar to people who ran cows in the Amarillo district until it became popular and was always known as an Amarillo twist. By God, when I saw that Stetson and bought it, the first thing I did was put a twist in it. What the hell. It was a beautiful white Stetson with a scarlet lining.

So when Helen and I got down to Gila Bend on our honeymoon, something went wrong with the car, so I pulled into the garage on the main highway, which was sixteen feet wide and only a couple miles of it were paved. Gila Bend was a little tiny town on the transcontinental highway, you understand, on the road to the plank road and the dunes? The garage man said, "Sure," so I pulled in out of the heat, and Helen went to sleep in the seat. I laid my Stetson up on the backseat and went to work under the car.

When I came out from underneath the car, the Stetson was gone. So I woke her up and said, "Did you see anybody monkeying around with my hat?"

And she said, "No, I've been asleep."

So I said, "Well, drat it." Or "shuckins," or something. I went out in the street and looked around. Pretty soon I saw a guy walking down the street with my hat on.

So I went up to him. I said, "Pardon me, mister, but that's a beautiful hat you have."

"Yeah," he said, "it's a good one."

And I said, "Where did you buy it?"

And he said, "See that sedan going down the street? I bought it from the fellow driving it."

I said, "You did?"

"Yeah," he said, "I paid twenty-five cents for it," or seventy-five cents or something.

And I said, "Well, you got a bargain." And I said, "I want to ask you a favor."

"What?"

"Let's go into this jewelry store here, and we'll get the manager. I want to do a little talking."

"Okay."

So we go in, and I called the manager, and I explained to the manager, "This gentleman is wearing a hat which was, I believe, taken from my car in the garage up here." I said, "I want you to look inside the sweatband and tell me what you see."

And, of course, it was my name and everything. So I thanked him, and the man said, "Well, I guess I'm out two bits," or whatever.

"Well," I said, "the least I can do is buy you a beer, mister." So we went up to the bar.

Ultimately I reckon I wore a hole in that Stetson, and then I don't know what happened to it. I should have kept it as a souvenir. It still had the Amarillo twist in it when last I saw it.

So we went to Ajo. Looked in the pit and all that. We went down and looked at Organ Pipe, which was not even in existence then. Took an old dirt road there. The land then was ranched by Old Man Gray [Robert L. Gray] and his sons. So we pulled off on that border road north of Lukeville. Now the name of it is Avenida de las Dos Republicas or some goddamned thing.

And there was a beautiful arroyo a mile or so away from the so-called highway, with broad gravel floors and big mesquites, so we camped there that night. One of the Gray boys came by in the morning, and he looked at us as we were packing up. He said, "That ain't a very good place to camp."

And I said, "No?"

He said, "You know it rains in this country." It was in May, you know.

I said, "Yeah, we took a chance."

"A lot of snakes down here!"

"Yeah. I reckon so."

"Well," he said, "howdy doody," and went on his way. He said who he was. I guess I asked him, because I knew about Gray from Frank Pinkley. That's the only contact I had with the boys until two or three years later.

Helen and I were working in Phoenix. We met Tom Harter and his wife. Now, Tom was an artist, who taught at ASU in the art department. His wife Helen was a sweetheart; I don't know what she did. We've got one of the watercolors downstairs that they gave us. And they invited us to go with them down through Lukeville to Sonoyta. We went down and spent one hot summer day. We met in a bar, which wasn't what I had expected, but that's what we did. We spent the day drinking beer and eating chicharrones, you know, cracklings . . . and visiting with a man named Juan Peralta, who was the chief of customs for Sonoyta.

Peralta was a delightful fellow. We went down on over and looked at the big house there, which is now a garage or something, on the east of the road, just after you cross the line and up on the hill. It was Charlie Wren's hunting lodge. Charlie Wren was a little fellow, a little Englishman in his sixties. That lodge was the hunting and fishing headquarters when he used to take parties down into Mexico.

He had the first natural and sensible air-conditioning system I'd seen. Set up on a hill, there was a cut bank facing the southwest. On the southwest of the house, a tunnel with a door went underneath the house from that cut bank. The tunnel went all around the interior perimeter of the house, and registers rose from the tunnel, rising up the floor from the house. These registers were under the big, very narrow windows in heavy, three-foot adobe walls. And when it got hot, somebody would go down and open the doors, and the southwest breeze—which always blew—would blow in, be cooled by the soil, and blow up through the registers enough to stir the drapes. The wind then went out through the ceiling. It was a marvelous thing!

And Charlie ran the hospitality. He showed us all through, took us into his library; he had one of the most famous and most complete libraries of pornography in the Southwest, or so I was told by the Harters. I looked at some of the books, and I had to read them to believe, but perhaps it was correct.

Charlie was a delightful little fellow, as I remember, sort of had sandy hair turned white, blue eyes, and a beak of a nose. Anyway, we went back out to the bar, met Peralta, and drank beer until time to go home. But Old Man Gray came in. He rode up on his horse, got off, and came in. He knew Peralta, so he sat there with us. We all got along fine. Gray drank rotgut mescal from a gallon jug that they had in the bar. He'd fill a water glass half full with sugar and top it off with mescal and stir it up and drink it one after another. Along toward dusk he left.

After a while he came back . . . in an ambulance. His hemorrhoids had burst on him riding home, so he'd thrown himself across the saddle and headed back to Sonoyta, where somebody saw him and called for someone with a car. They came and got him before he bled to death and took him to the hospital. That mescal was powerful stuff, and after all he was an old man. He'd been doing it for a long time. He used to say that Gray was not his name, and that he came out of Texas after having killed somebody and changed his name. People down there believed it. Whether it's true or not, I don't know. I never asked his sons, I'll tell you.

They kept to themselves pretty well. The government wanted to take their land away from them and did eventually. So that takes care of Mr. Gray. That's all I know about him. Had I become superintendent of Organ Pipe, I'd have cut a deal with him, of course, and that would have been interesting, too.

Henry Gray astride his favorite horse in Sonoyta, Mexico, May 20, 1938. (Photograph by Julian Hayden)

After we visited Organ Pipe on our honeymoon, we went down across the line. The immigration office was way down on the far side of town. Town was across the river, and you had to ford it. The immigration officer was a family man, and his office was in the house. He was lonesome, so we spent the afternoon there just talking, playing with the kids, and drinking coffee. It was nice. Helen didn't have any Spanish, and he didn't have much English. Then we told him where we wanted to go. He told us that we'd have to come back up and go to some other entry because he couldn't give us a pass for more than three days, while I wanted a six-month.

But there was an old border road—it hadn't been used for many, many years—that went between Sasabe and Sonoyta. He thought it might be passable. It wasn't very far, he said, *muy cerquita.* We had to go out through the mesquite bosque to go east. That bosque is all gone, of course, now, but then it was so dense that there was no sunlight in it at all. The road was just a tunnel through the mesquites, on the south side of the river. And somebody volunteered to hang on the running board and guide us through it, get through the woodcutters' roads, and put us on the right road. And he wouldn't let me bring him back, which I thought was nice of him. So we drove then by the openings between the greasewoods, to figure out where the road was. We finally got to El Plomo and to the Sasabe Road.

Years later, when I went in to Rosa's restaurant down there at Fort Lowell and Campbell, I looked at the mural painted by Franklin on the wall. In the mural was a sign, five or seven kilometers to El Plomo. I said to the young man running the place, "Somebody here is from El Plomo?"

He said, "You know El Plomo?"

I said, "Yes, I know El Plomo."

"How do you know El Plomo?"

"Well, my bride and I sat under a bank of the arroyo there in 1935 and had crackers and sardines for lunch one day. And then we talked to somebody who'd been a *deportado* from Los Angeles. We had a good visit." I remember El Plomo. It's not on the road anymore, you know. It's way off the road.

And he said, "I'll bet my father would remember you." And he said he did. I don't know whether he did or not. So I always have a friend at Rosa's now.

But there were no tourists in those days at all. Nobody. We didn't see a single one all the time we were down there. And that was before they built the Tubutama Dam, and the valley was just so well watered. Those big hedges of pomegranates on the north side of the river had their feet in the irrigation ditch; they were twenty feet high and loaded with pomegranates.

There at Oquitoa is the water wheel where they used to grind the wheat raised on the field just below it. It belonged to the Cutting family; I think they were English. They'd been there for many, many years. They had a house down on the flat, just below the mill, well watered, and had vines all over it. Their daughter Patricia was buried up in the Oquitoa cemetery; I've got a picture of that grave somewhere. They were famous people. But the dam dried it all up. It's desert now.

That was some honeymoon. We covered a lot of ground in a couple of months, until we ran out of money. I remember we came up through Nogales and camped north of town; big subdivisions or warehouses are in there now. Suddenly we realized we were broke, and it was the day before Armistice, Memorial Day.

So I went down to Western Union. Helen had some money in the bank in Pittsburgh. My money was used up. I'd have had more if I hadn't bought that white Stetson. I didn't have money enough to pay for the telegram, but the Western Union manager was an old Boy Scout. So we hocked our postage stamps and my jackknife, plus my word of honor as a Boy Scout that we'd pay him back, and we sent a wire to Pittsburgh. Pittsburgh misunderstood and said, "Yes, you have so much money in the bank account." So we had to wire again.

And I think for about two days, all we ate was what cornflakes and oatmeal we had in the kitty. I'll never forget that. It was fun, though. Nogales was a nice little town. It didn't take long to know everybody. In those days you could camp anywhere, almost in the heart of town, and nobody would bother you. You could go away and leave your stuff all day, no thieves. Mexico was the same way: nobody would touch you.

I guess we got home in late July, something like that, I don't know what it was, and went back to California. We had lots of adventures. We saw Father Kino's gold mines, or alleged gold mines, and all that sort of thing.

Helen had never been camping in her life. This was all brand new. She couldn't even boil water, but she learned. She'd never learned to cook. I taught her camp cooking, and she got to be good at it. Her mother would never cook, for they always had colored cooks. She came from a very old family. I think half the signers of the Declaration of Independence were in her lineage, you know, including Peale, the man who painted George Washington on the boat. Virginia. Settlers. Oh, she could belong to all the organizations there are that have anything to do with the early days.

That fall we came back over for the reopening of Snaketown I. We lived in a tent there, and she did the cooking. She made pumpkin pies for our first Thanksgiving. She made them in a tin oven on top of a gasoline stove and set them out on the table to cool. We walked off hand in hand happily toward the sunset and when we came back, by God, the Pima dogs had gotten into them and eaten the filling and left the crusts! "And now," she said, "I am insulted. If they had eaten the crusts I wouldn't have minded. But they didn't eat the crusts."

In the mid-'30s some of Helen's kinfolk came to visit us on the reservation. We ate plain fare of beans and yellow cornbread, so we wanted something special. I made a berry cobbler in my Dutch oven. It cooked over the fire and I got a little distracted, and when I came back to it, oh, was that crust a golden brown and so crisp. It was beautiful. We ladled it out on the plates and cut into it. Cut into air. The only thing there was crust. The berries had all boiled out over the sides of the oven. We went to Chandler for hamburgers, as I recall.

6. CCC

How did I get involved with CCC? This goes back to a man named Odd Halseth who was city archaeologist of Phoenix. I'm not going to get into that very far, but I'd met him a few times, so from 1930 on we worked back and forth. He was trying to promote Pueblo Grande as a retirement place for himself and his wife, Edna, who was a very lovely person whom everybody loved. She and Helen liked each other.

In the fall of 1935, I came back with my bride, and we lived at Snaketown until the first of the year and finished that up. About Christmas time, we stopped at Pueblo Grande on our way back to the coast. We were going to visit my people. And Odd Halseth said, "What are you going to do?"

I said, "I don't know. Do silver work, I imagine."

"Well," he said, "I'm going to make an art center out of this Pueblo Grande, in addition to an archaeological center. The Artist's Guild is already meeting here." That's when the big building was new, but it's now gone. So he said, "Come on over. Come on back here." He offered me quarters with a place to work to do some silversmithing, because I was doing a unique kind that nobody else was doing. I was using prehistoric design, adapting it to modern usage. Nobody else was doing it at that time. I was also carving metal rather than hammering it or casting it. "I'll set aside a space for you, and you can design and manufacture and build jewelry. Your quarters will be in the east wing there." So I did.

But then I began to notice that nobody was watching the CCC boys who were excavating a mound and doing odd jobs around the park with no supervisor at all, no photographs being taken, no notes, no nothing. I couldn't stand that, so I started taking pictures at my own expense and, finally, all of a sudden, I was doing everything outside: notes, mapping, and everything else. But maybe Halseth was a smarter man than I thought he was, for suddenly I found myself doing photography. And I found myself doing this and that. And pretty soon I was running that damn job without any authority and neglecting my silver work. I was working for nothing, in other words. So, then I began to concentrate on archaeology. I couldn't do silversmithing and do that, too, but I couldn't eat if I didn't do one or the other.

Soon Halseth promoted me to job foreman of the CCC, but I was a Republican, I voted for Herbert Hoover, and I'm still proud of it. So I had to change my registration, which I didn't mind doing anyway, because I don't hold with party identifications. After all, Senator Carl Hayden was a sixty-fourth cousin once removed to my father, which makes him sixty-fourth cousin twice removed to me, so we were related. Senator Hayden was a very powerful man, and suddenly I found myself what we called a "student technician" and making all of seventy dollars a month. And Helen

Odd and Edna Halseth dressed for a New Year's party, January 1, 1938. (Photograph by Julian Hayden)

and I with a baby coming [their first child, Julian Jr.]. I paid for it with some heavy silver work.

I was attached to State Park 3A. That's State Park CCC Camp, number 3A. It was in South Mountain Park. All the veteran workers were Oklahoma and East Texas enrollees. The program was administered out of Santa Fe. The military ran the camps, per se, but the locations and the programs were operated by the National Park Service out of Santa Fe. So I'm under Santa Fe, you see. Then when a junior foreman opening came up, I was made a junior foreman and from seventy dollars a month I went up to about sixteen hundred dollars a year or something like that. I worked there two years as a junior foreman, and then I was promoted to senior foreman archaeologist. And I'd have gone a lot higher—I'd have gone to Santa Fe if I'd had a college degree, but . . . The director used to chew on me when he came down, "Damn it, get a degree in beekeeping, just get that B.A.! Then we can move you." And I said, "I'm happy." That's how come I always ran crews.

I made adobes [mud bricks] at Pueblo Grande. I could do that part of it and wasn't interfering with anybody's authority there. We made 80,000 of them on that job. I worked archaeology; I worked heavy construction in between jobs; and I continued to do silver work. Well, I was a silversmith. A jack of all trades.

When Halseth and I had our fallings out, as everybody did with him, I went out and built roads, came down here and built buildings, and did this, that, and the other

Helen and Julian with their daughter, Mary, and son, Julian Jr., at Pueblo Grande, 1937.

An unidentified Civilian Conservation Corps worker from Texas at Pueblo Grande, about 1937. (Photograph by Julian Hayden)

Julian Hayden at Pueblo Grande, 1937.

thing in the CCC. I thought I never would come to Tucson again, because when Helen and I first passed through here in '35, I made a left turn off Stone onto Congress, going east in front of the Valley Bank building. A policeman blew me down, old fellow, with a big, white mustache.

He said, "Can't you read signs?"

I said, "I don't see any sign."

"Well," he said, "It was up there," or something to that effect, and he was meaner than hell.

He said, "It wouldn't be so bad, damn it, but I gave you a warning this morning!" Well, I figured that being a stranger without more than eight cents in my pocket and a bride and a Model T Ford, I better keep my damn trap shut, so I did. But I never forgot it. Swore I'd never come to Tucson again.

And I stayed away from Tucson for a long time, except when I had to come to the Arizona State Museum to see Emil Haury. Later I found out from Nancy Pinkley Whiting (Frank Pinkley's daughter, who was sort of a member of our family) that the old cop worked for the bank as a guard when he retired. He had sore feet, and that's why his temper was so bad—he was famous all over Pima County for it. But it damned near cost Pima County my presence.

Then came the University Indian Ruin here in Tucson, and I was hired by the CCC to oversee its excavation. Randolph Park was nothing but mesquite and creosote bush and a baseball field and some barracks for CCC and *ramadas* here and there that my predecessors had built. We had a site camp for juniors under twenty-one or whatever, I forget. So, when I was detached from Phoenix, I came down here for four months to excavate the University Indian Ruin. I had boys from Pennsylvania—Fishtown and "Philly" and Scranton. They were *some* boys: they were numbers runners, Golden and Silver Gloves contestants, night-fighters, real tough kids, yet they were good kids. I had one of the best excavation crews I've ever had, once they decided it wasn't sissy. Sixteen boys out there for several months.

We did a wonderful job. *They* did a wonderful job. We trucked out every day from Randolph Park. The university had a laboratory building there and caretakers on the site. The summer of '39, I guess it was, I had twenty-five men there and we built the first building at Saguaro National Monument. Now it is some sort of a toolshed, I think, but it was a residence at that time. There weren't any buildings out there. We built them. Made the adobes and everything else—my men did, rather. I was just the foreman. I didn't have to pay attention to it. They knew more than I did.

And we did that, and we fought fire out on the Papago Reservation. We did whatever we had to do. There was another side campsite in the Tucson Mountain Park. One of the buildings they built is now the headquarters building at the museum [Arizona-Sonora Desert Museum]. So we worked together. Also, they were working out there anyway at Saguaro, also building roads out there. We did a lot of roadwork with the kids when they came in. That's where I met Joe Wilder's parents, Carleton and Judith. Joe wasn't even hatched at that time, although he was a gleam.

Once the inspector from the IG's [inspector general's] office came out; he looked things over. My superintendent was here and some others. A lot of equipment—shovels, hoes, rakes, and wheelbarrows, and so forth—had been left behind by juniors when they left. So I had to sign for them. Then we had to inspect them and condemn them and throw them away, which was done while I was there and while the major was there. One of them said, "Throw them in that well there. It's a dry well. And cover them up." Soon as he left, we pulled everything out, of course, and hid it.

And it wasn't too long before the superintendent at Wupatki, up by Flagstaff, said someone had stolen his wheelbarrows. And he had to pay for them. Well, by some coincidence, after dark one night, a truck came from Phoenix, some wheelbarrows got on it, and it went to Flagstaff, and the superintendent didn't have to pay for the wheelbarrows. That's the way we worked it.

The same with food. I was given so much a week for dry rations. Dry rations came from Phoenix. Vegetables I bought here at fifty dollars a month. And certain other things I could buy here, so I just took what wholesale grocers would trade me for, and I got stuff my veterans liked. That's the way you had to do it. And as far as politics goes, I want to say this: When FDR [Franklin D. Roosevelt] came up in 1940 for reelection, the captain at the veterans' camp at South Mountain—there were two hundred men there—called them all out on election day. He lined them up and said, "We're going into south Phoenix. We've got a special polling place for you. You know who put you here, and you know who's keeping you here, and, by God, if you don't want to stay here, vote the wrong way." He loaded up two hundred men, and they voted one hundred percent for FDR. That was going on all over the United States at that time.

But we foremen, remarkably enough, we all voted for Wilkie, or whoever the hell it was, Landon. There might have been one holdout. Of course, they couldn't track us. We voted in our own precincts. But I went to Osborn precinct where I was living. I went over to vote, and I announced myself as a Republican, and the marshal said, "Republican. Have we got a Republican booth here?" I looked all around and there it was, under the stairs. It was a Democratic state.

We had nothing to do with the forestry camps. They had their own camps, and so did the Bureau of Reclamation. They tried to take boys from one area and put them in another part of the country entirely. They put Pennsylvanians in Tucson. I'm talking about the National Park Service, CCC. Maybe the others did the same thing, but I don't know. And eastern Oklahomans and east Texans, they came out to Yuma and wherever, see. A lot of them went up in the northwest, anywhere to broaden their experience.

And I tell you, I wish we still had those camps, because I've known more people who went in the Cs when they were eighteen for, what was it, twenty-five dollars a month? I think they got to keep five dollars or six or eight or something like that. The rest went to their families. It was the first time that some of these boys had ever had a square meal. It was hard times, man, we had to work.

A man came through here last year who had been on my crew in Phoenix at the excavation of Pueblo Grande. He was from eastern Oklahoma, about eighteen years old. Of course, I had forgotten all about him. There at Pueblo Grande I had him in the laboratory doing something of some importance, I've forgotten what. Well, he showed up here fifty years later. I'd never heard from him, but he'd come through Phoenix and stopped at Pueblo Grande and told them that he had worked there. They told him where I was, and he came down here to see me. This is what the CCC did for a lot of people. Make no mistake. He went home, chopping cotton for two bits an hour, and he found a girl. She was a little burr-headed Okie girl, and they got married. He knew there was something better.

He saw an ad for training aircraft mechanics in California, so his uncle mortgaged the farm for the two-hundred-fifty-dollar fee. You had to mortgage the farm to get that much money in those days. And he and his burr-head went to Inglewood, California. It was a scam, but he went to Douglas Aircraft and talked them into putting him on the floor, sweeping. "Now," he said, "you know what I retired at recently?"

I said, "No."

He said, "I'm an aeronautical engineer, and I've worked on the satellites, and I've worked on the moon rocket." It all goes back to that experience at Pueblo Grande. It was the first time anyone had ever depended on him, had ever told him he was dependable. They never taught him how to work anything other than chopping cotton. The Cs did that for a lot of men. So, politics or not, it did some good, because they worked; they weren't pampered.

In the mid-1960s, my younger son was doing some archaeological work up in northern Arizona, and he was given a Job Corps crew. He couldn't get some of them to work because they were going to get paid anyway. No discipline, no penalties. So, he was sick about it, but if they had been in the Cs, they'd have worked. The disciplinary system in the Cs was military. We didn't have jails, the brig and all that sort of thing. The worst thing was to be sent home. That was a disgrace. We didn't send many people home. They lived there in the barracks. They had to come to work or else they didn't eat.

Old Jim Clarke was a company clerk in the veteran CCC camp. He was a World War I man, a lean old fellow. And after dinner he'd come down and lie down in the couch in the office and bring out his pair of pet Gila monsters, with a string leash. They'd wander up and down the couch and over his belly. It was all very friendly and very kamiliky [sociable], you know. He'd feed them an egg apiece once every couple of weeks. Now and then he'd take them down to the arroyo, and they'd walk up and down the arroyo with these two Gila monsters leading the way. It was all very nice. And nobody messed with them. Everybody kept their distance, for no reason that I know of. But I never knew of them speaking harshly to anybody. Oh, Jim loved them. Matter of fact, I think old Jim got some real companionship out of them.

You remember the veterans' bonus that was given back about 1939? All the veterans who had served overseas got a bonus, depending on the length of service. Old Jim got a good-sized bonus while I was down here in Tucson with the veteran side camp. So old Jim up and married him a young bride up in Phoenix. He stayed in Phoenix, since she didn't want to come down here. She was a young bride, maybe nineteen or twenty years old. And he was, whatever age you'd be, considering he was in the service in 1918, and this was 1939. He thought the world of her. Jim took his bonus money, and believe it or not, just like the story books, he bought her a little red wagon and a washing machine, so she could take in laundry and add to the family finances that way. Then she could deliver the laundry with the little red wagon!

I heard a lot about that because old Jim and I were pretty good friends. And when I had the camp duty and had to be out there for a week at a time, I'd sit in the office in the evening while he patted his Gila monsters and we'd talk, you know. I got pretty well acquainted with his wife without having ever seen her. And then, by golly, you know what happened? She met a young man, and she ran off with the young man and took the washing machine and the red wagon, too! And Jim was indignant. "By God," he said, "if I have to buy a red wagon and a washing machine for every damn woman," he

Julian's Gila monster sketch and poem from Bunk House Bunk: Denizens of the Dam. *Julian illustrated this and* Bunk House Bunk: The Real Story of Bouldoover Dam, *C. A. "Biz" Bisbee's booklets on construction of Boulder (now Hoover) Dam.*

said, "I hope somebody knocks me in the head. Why, she's ungrateful!" I never heard of him doing such again. But you see what happens when you have two Gila monsters? Or what happens when you lose a young lady with a red wagon, you wind up with two Gila monsters. Everybody has got to have a pet.

I like talking about Gila monsters. My father and I went over to Blackwater, a Pima Indian village, near Sacaton, between Sacaton and Casa Grande, to visit old Tom Blackwater, the son of the man for whom the area was named, I guess, or named after the area. I've got photographs of him. Anyway, we were talking outside the building, outside his house, Pima house, made out of saguaro ribs and mud and whatnot. And two Crow Indians came up. They may well have been missionaries, come to think of it. They were big men, six foot three or four, and probably weighed two-forty. And they had bright, glistening braids down their fronts, one on each side of the head, and chests. I was listening while my father and they talked. Old Tom slipped away into the house with a sort of look in his eye.

He came out with a big Gila monster on a string leash. And the Gila monster was leading the way, waddling along. The Gila monster saw these two Crow missionaries, and just like a flash, you could hardly see how fast he moved, he reared up on his hind legs and charged them, hissing like a steam engine blowing steam. And he headed for those two Indians. Of course, Tom had the other end of the string, but those Indians took one look, and they turned and went one around each side of the end of the building. Tom didn't say anything and he didn't smile, but his eyes twinkled a little bit. He walked the Gila monster back into the house, and after a while the Crows came out front again. Dad and I decided that maybe we better leave, so we left. Gila monsters, you don't want to mess with them.

I never worked for the university itself. In 1964, Haury went back to Snaketown, thirty years later, after the original work. By that time, I was an excavation contractor in Tucson, so I sent one of my rigs up there. Matter of fact, I bought a machine for the job for the university. Picked one up. They paid for it. And I sent one of my operators up to get started and train their man and all that. And I went up once a week to see that everything was all right throughout the job.

So they gave me a title of research associate. I have no degrees, but the research associate title gave me some dignity, which they needed. Pure b.s., you know. I think the only thing we ever got out of it was a mimeographed invitation once a year to my wife to come to the faculty women's coffee-tea. Only three times I lectured on campus. I was a "heretic," so was seldom invited. Project grants and research nowadays? I fund mine *por la bolsa* (out of pocket).

7. At Home

My days of silversmithing certainly helped me get a better handle on a whole lot of things, including psychology. Silversmithing is great. I'd rather do silversmithing than anything I know of a sedentary nature, because it takes so many different skills—most of which I don't have, but the ones I do have, I know something about. I learned the basic skills myself. And when I was working on the tank ships, I learned how to do square-knot work. It's what the la-di-das call macramé when, to my surprise, it became very stylish a few years ago.

Freddie Pleasants, a very nice guy and a very delicate gentleman, lectured on primitive art at the university. He was a great friend of Gwyneth Xavier's. Sometimes he went slumming and took some of us peasants out for dinner. He said, "Did I ever show you my macramé, Julian?"

I said, "No."

So he brought out some, and I said, "What did you call that?"

And he said, "Macramé."

And I said, "Well, hell, that's just our old square knotting."

"Oh," he said, "you know about it, do you?"

"Yeah, I learned something about it when I was working on the ships. I learned some tricks from a Venezuelan political prisoner, Leonard Diaz. And he learned it in a penitentiary in Venezuela."

"Oh." His nose was plumb out of joint for the rest of the evening.

Leonard taught me a lot of tricks, how to do square knotting, what you now call macramé, so I made a beautiful square-knot belt on board the *William Rockefeller*. I've always been able to do things. I wanted to make a silver buckle when I came back from the East, but I couldn't find anything in New York that suited me. I thought I'd make a nice fouled-anchor buckle out of ivory, but I couldn't find any ivory, and what I could find I couldn't afford. When I came home eventually, I kept it in mind and got to thinking that maybe it'd be fun to use some prehistoric designs in silver. So I made a necklace out of four dimes and a quarter.

I put the quarter on a streetcar track, which rolled it out until it was oval, and I made a pendant, a bat figure from Peru. And I got out the dimes, drilled holes, and filed out the openings. I struck up an acquaintance with a manufacturing jeweler who soldered the thing for me, soldered the wings on, and soldered the beak on the bat.

My father said, "You are defacing U.S. currency."

And I said, "It's my property."

He said, "It is not."

I said, "Damn it, it is."

*Julian using an
engraving block to
aid in carving a
silver brooch.*

*Julian "square knotting" a
macramé belt aboard the
SS* Rockefeller *in 1930.*

He said, "I'll teach you to whose property it is." So he called the U.S. marshal, and the U.S. marshal said, "As long as your son doesn't try to pass it, it's his property." So my father had to swallow that one. He was faintly irritated for some time.

So when I came home, I set out to make the big buckle that I wear, the big circular one with the warrior on it, wearing the mask of the rain god, or the sun god, from the Temple of the Warriors in Chichén Itzá. I didn't know how to do it, so I cut a negative in the charcoal block, scrounged up some silver coins and melted them down, and poured it full of silver, and I worked it all down from there. No detail on it or anything, just a big disk. I made my own tools out of rattail files and tempered them. I knew how to do that, or I found out how to do that. First thing I ever made, practically. And, I taught myself because nobody knew how to do what I wanted to do, so I learned how by myself, and all of a sudden I was a handicraft instructor. My stamp for the rings I made was a turtle with my initials inside because I'm so slow. That's how I got started, and one thing led to another.

And then I found out that there was a place, back in the 1890s in the Old World where France bucked up against Switzerland, that was the seat of engraving in the round, or carving in the round, of metal. There were two types of engravers in those days, I've always understood, without researching it further: line engravers, which you're familiar with, initials and so forth, and engravers in the round. The young folks came to the New World, and they didn't want to serve an eight- or nine-year apprenticeship before they joined the guild. So while some of them became line engravers, which is much simpler, the ones who were engraving in the round dropped the whole thing. By 1930-odd, I was told, there were only two of us engraving in the round west of the Mississippi. Anyway, that's what I was doing, was carving, bas-relief in silver with burins, hand-engraving tools. But, that's about as far as I ever got. I never learned how to do repoussé, and I never did any casting, both of which

Julian's trademark turtle stamp, used to identify jewelry he made.

I'd just love to do, but I just never did. So I have very limited skill in my field. I can solder, and I can design, and I can build, and I can carve, and all that sort of thing, but I don't know how to do repoussé. And I don't know how to cast metal the way I'd like to.

I love it because I can sit all day long, perfectly happy, and when I'm through I've got something I can look at. And I can give pleasure to somebody else, too. I usually use prehistoric designs, which I adapt to modern usage. So that's where I built what reputation I had and how come I exhibited. I exhibited every year at Flagstaff at the Museum of Northern Arizona. I had a one-man exhibit with photographs, designs, and some of my carvings. I sold on consignment regularly here in Tucson up until the war started.

We got into the production end of it when René d'Harnoncourt, who was director of the Museum of Modern Art, came to Phoenix in about 1941. He was mounting or had mounted the exhibition of pre-Columbian art, the Museum of Modern Art, very famous show. I was working, doing nothing but silver at the time. The CCC camps had closed. I was finishing a couple of reports, but making a living doing silver. He saw what

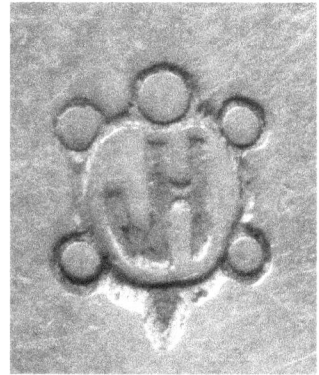

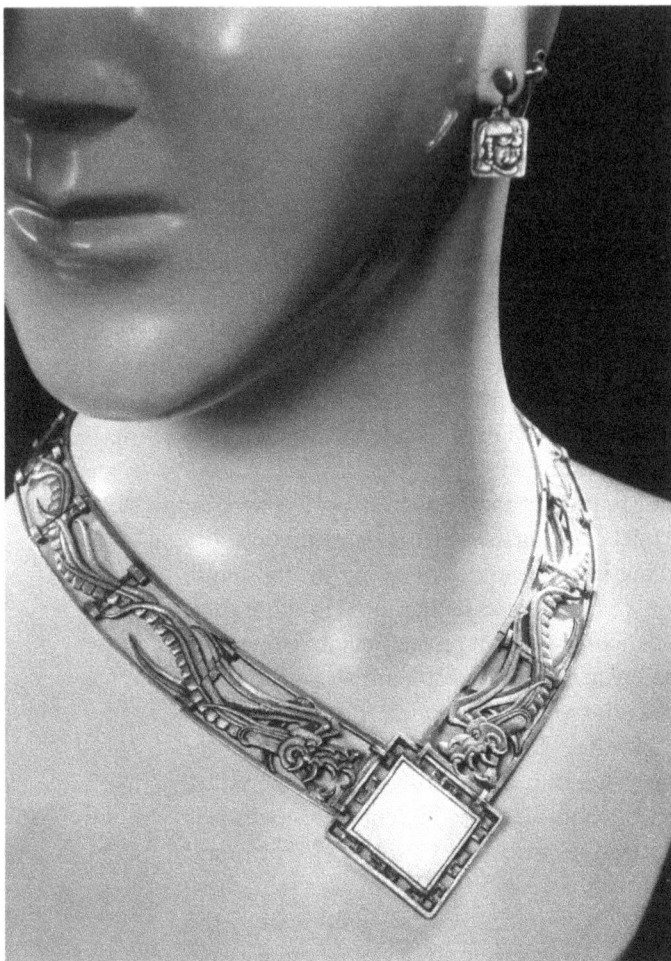

One of Julian's necklace and earring sets with inlaid stone.

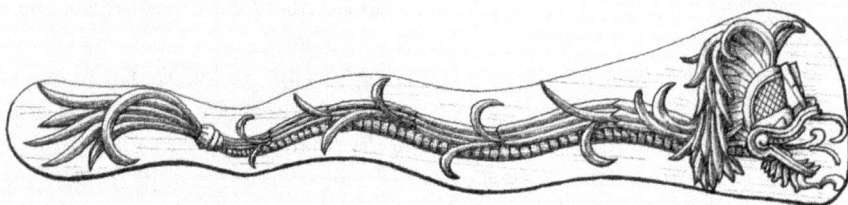

Design for a silver bracelet that Julian made for himself ca. 1933, carved in heavy relief. Julian wore this bracelet regularly until his death in 1998. Julian once noted that in the 1930s, not many men wore bracelets, "but nobody ever gave me any trouble about it."

I had, and so he bought everything in my collection that wasn't spoken for. That startled me, and Helen, too. He went back to New York and showed it to Lord & Taylor. Lord & Taylor said, "Send us all you can get."

I had a friend who was doing lost-wax casting. So we teamed up, and I'd spend a couple of days making an original, a master, and then he'd cast a dozen in an hour and a half. And he'd send them back to me and I'd clean them up and put the catches, pins, bails, and whatnot on them. We'd send them off to New York at wholesale price and let Lord & Taylor sell them at retail. Major Strange had a gallery here in Tucson, and he was handling my silver, selling it for me.

We all made money. We were just doing fine. We got rolling and building a good reputation, becoming really known, it seemed to me. But by that time, the spring of 1942, we were at war. I had an oxygen tank that had to be given up to the war effort; we leased them, just the way we do now. So I figured I better go get me a job, and I quit doing jewelry.

It takes patience. You don't slap it out. This pendant here took, oh, the large part of a full day. You don't make beans making them for five dollars. But that's all right, too, that's the fun of it. It's nice relaxation, get away from contracting or from doing nothing. And also a good way to dodge responsibilities like writing reports.

I cut quite a bit of turquoise. I traded a man a ring for some. He had a vein of turquoise in a big boulder lying out in the field up between Miami and Superior. The boulder, bigger than I am, had a vein of turquoise. He'd chisel that turquoise out. He cut some nice pieces, beautiful blue-green stuff. Down below was a talus of what he called refuse, but they were fully usable pieces. So I made a ring for his wife, with a carved frog on each side of the turquoise, and traded him for all the turquoise I could pick up and a couple cut pieces that he had, including one that was a ninety-eight-carat stone. I thought that was a fair trade, and so did he. I've still got one or two pieces of it left.

But silversmithing nearly cost me my vision until Bob Solosth helped me save it. In 1936 when I met him, Solosth was an orthoptician—in other words he exercised people's eyes to correct their eye problems, at a time when that was not universally accepted. Now they call it vision therapy and it's damn near legitimate, but in the 1930s it wasn't. Anyway, he saved my eyesight. I had "locked" my eyes engraving on a picture frame for a hundred and sixty hours in one month. My eye focus locked at seven inches. The pain was so terrible, to me, that I was suicidal. But when I got the picture frame delivered, it paid for the delivery of our first child.

Solosth broke the focus. Then my eyes were just drifting all the time; I couldn't focus on anything, so Solosth built me a new one, a new focus, but it took a couple years. I went in once or twice a week for a couple hours at a time. No money could have paid for it at all, certainly not what I was making those days. I paid for it by making him jewelry, carving him silver. That's the only way I could pay for it, and that's why he took me on, because he thought I had promise. After all, at the time I was applying for a Guggenheim and all that sort of thing.

Paul Ezell used to tell about going on a field trip with Dean Cummings and the class to Mexico, doing archaeology, of course, and Greta Sarrels was one of the students, as was he. She was from Nogales, where she was raised. Paul was driving his car, but it

The carved sterling silver picture frame Julian made for Harold and Winifred Gladwin in 1936. According to his account book, the frame was made from over 30 ounces of silver, required 36 hours of design work, and took 170 hours to carve. At $2.00 per hour for his labor plus materials, Hayden charged the Gladwins $463.00 for the completed frame.

A page from Julian's jewelry account book. The first entry, dated January 25, 1938, details three sterling silver rings Julian made for Robert E. Solosth, a Phoenix orthoptician, in exchange for "work on my eyes" needed after Julian's eyes had locked at 7-inch focus while making the Gladwins' picture frame.

Major Strange, who operated an art gallery at 281 North Stone Avenue in Tucson, Arizona, is the most likely author of this unsigned letter of recommendation for Julian's 1941 Guggenheim application in support of his silverwork. René d'Harnoncourt (general manager, Indian Arts and Crafts Board, Washington, D.C.), Harold Gladwin (archaeological patron, Santa Barbara, California), Harold S. Colton (director, Museum of Northern Arizona, Flagstaff), Frederic "Eric" Douglas (director, Denver Art Museum), and Charles Amsden (secretary, Southwest Museum, Los Angeles) also provided references.

To: John Simon Guggenheim Memorial Foundation

Gentlemen:

It does not lie within the realm of possibility for me to give you an unbiased report on the work of Julian D. Hayden, nor upon his attitude toward his work. I am too thoroughly of the opinion that the need is urgent, and that the man is thoroughly prepared, both as a student and as a craftsman.

Let me, therefore, have recourse to some of the observations that I have been able to make while his work has been on exhibition in my gallery. About the first person to come in was Clara Lee Tanner, Department of Archaeology, University of Arizona. She was so pleased that his work was getting the recognition that the display involved that I had to sit and listen to a full hour's effusion. The next person was Professor J. R. de la Torre Bueno, F.R.E.S., etc. His comments were no less effusive.

I have shown Mr. Hayden's work to artists, architects, archaeologists, jewelers, craftsman, historians . . . and I have not yet been able to find one who did not thoroughly agree with me that he is doing something very much more important than making jewelry of archaeological design, or supervising a dig. *He is restoring to America, in a very simple and comprehensible form, some of its artistic heritage which has been in serious danger of being lost.*

Because of my peculiar bias I am afraid of overstatement . . . but it does not seem to me to be an overstatement when I say that to the full and complete development of an American art tradition, the work that this man is doing is certainly as necessary and as fundamental as the preservation and perpetuation of the Grecian and Egyptian classic forms. It cannot be until the indigenous American art tradition has been unearthed and recorded and integrated into the existing body of art tradition that we can have a possible fulfillment of the purpose of art.

As for the man himself, I have been much impressed with his simple honesty and integrity of purpose as reflected in his attitude toward some of the things that he has done with a craftsmanship so exquisite that few could refrain from being somewhat boastful.

I believe that the Guggenheim Foundation will be making a real gift to this nation if it finds some means of making it possible for him to continue, and I am sure that the products he creates will more than offset any material or maintenance cost.

---

broke down, so he got under and worked on it. He called out to someone, "Bring me such and size of wrench."

And Greta said, "Okay," and gave him the right wrench.

He cocked his eye at that, and when he needed something else, she handed it to him without any delay or question or anything else. He took it, and when he called for something else, he got it immediately.

He said, "By gol', I'm going to have to take a look at this gal. And began to think, 'this girl's got something.' And you know, right then I made up my mind I was going to marry her." And he did. And they're still together, ever since.

But Paul Ezell was not a mechanic. He was driving an old Hudson, and it needed a lot of work. He was going to grad school and starving his way through, the two of them. So he took a special course in auto mechanics so he could repair his own car. That took the Hudson out of service, and they lived down by Fort Lowell and Alvernon in Tucson, quite a ways.

Greta needed to go shopping, and at the time I had a World War II four-wheel-drive Dodge ambulance, one of those big arks, you know. I bought it for about a hundred dollars from a welder friend of mine, George Audish, to tow a trailer with, if and when I got a trailer that I could put equipment on. So I said, "Well, it's not doing anything, you might as well keep the battery up, and do you want to borrow it?"

"Yes."

So I showed her how to drive it.

She was so terrified of the traffic in Tucson that she never took Speedway or Grant at all. She took side streets, whether to go to town or the university or wherever. But the minute she got in that thing and looked down upon the world, she went right down Speedway, Grant, or Fort Lowell just as big as life. Oh, she was so happy. I guess she had it for six weeks before Paul got that old Hudson back together, and then she gave it back to me, and she took the side streets again. But there wasn't anybody in town that would argue with that big Dodge. It weighed four tons, I think.

In the early 1950s when Paul Ezell was a grad student, we went to Las Vegas to see the first announced nuclear test at Frenchman Flat. Greg Hathaway was head of Highway Patrol, and we flew up in Greg's airplane. We each took five bucks with us that we talked our wives out of to gamble on. We went to the Sands. Finally, we blew our five dollars. It took me only a few minutes; it took Paul about an hour. He'd just come back from Mexico, working in the archives down there. He had a gray suit on, beard, smoked a pipe, and he just looked so damned professorial that it was comical. He took that gambling real seriously, because he didn't have many more five-buckses than I did. So he finally lost his five dollars at the craps table, and he turned away. A contractor friend of Greg's came over to Paul and said, "Hold out your hands." Paul did, and the fellow filled them with chips. "What's that for?" Paul asked. "That's your share of my winnings," the guy said, "I bet against you and the house." Paul took those chips to the window and received about two hundred twenty dollars in silver dollars. He had to carry the sack over his shoulder. He took those home and put them on the mantel of the fireplace; later he used them for a down payment on an old Army jeep. I went to the Pinacate with him in it, and Laguna Prieta, in 1953.

In the morning we left the hotel quite early and drove up Charleston Peak to see the blast. At the hour we turned our backs to the flats and waited until the flash had cast our shadows on the rock behind us. Then we turned to see the results. Awesome. I never wanted to see another one.

On the return trip, I think it was on this trip, Hathaway asked if we wanted to fly over the Pinacate. Paul and I had both spent a lot of ground time there, but had yet to see it from the air. At Phoenix, or was it Tucson, we rented a Tri-Pacer and headed for the mountain. A storm blanketed part of the peak in clouds, but it was beautiful. We flew into Elegante and buzzed the major craters and even nearly spun a wheel on the summit itself. On the way back it was windy, so windy that we bounced and jolted all the way. The headwind nearly stopped us, so that it was necessary to tack back and forth like a ship to reach Tucson. Paul was a little green en route and Greg had his hands full. After landing, Greg mentioned that it was the roughest flight he'd ever taken, and Paul agreed. They asked me, and I said, "It seemed okay to me." They rawhided me about that, but really I was so new to light planes that I had nothing to compare it to; I thought it was always that way.

Paul and Greta had some hard times. He was working on his doctorate, and he was busted. They were hungry. And Helen and I knew that, of course. They lived up on Friday Drive off north Alvernon there. We used to have them over to dinner whenever we could. Anyhow, they got real short, and I said to Paul, "Look. You say you're an old jackhammer man with the CCCs." He was a leader in the CCC camps. "Come on and work for me for a while. Hell, I can put you on, but you better shovel caliche better than anybody else, by God, I'll show you no favors."

He hesitated.

I said, "Damn it, we'd like to have you. You speak Spanish, I've got a Mexican crew, so ..." July, I think it was, up here on Stewart and Third streets or something like that, in one of those caliche fields southwest of Country Club and Speedway. Shoveling caliche is like shoveling staples, if you know what I mean. He jumped right in the foundation trench with the rest of us, behind the hammerman, Johnny Arias. Johnny was a little hundred-and-ten-pounder who was running a hundred-and-ten-pound hammer. Paul went in there with a pick and shovel and a couple of the other boys, and they loosened up that hardpan and then they shoveled it out.

At noon Paul said, "I'm going home but I'll be back." So he took off. Mind you, he was soft. In his youth he was a powerful man, short, broad shoulders, fit. God you should have seen him in his prime; he'd make Mr. Atlas look sick. And my boys said, "Well, he won't be back. That gringo, *muy flojo.*"

I said, "He'll be back." And he came back. With a gallon jug. Of amber water. And I said, "What's that?"

He said, "Tea." And he drank tea all afternoon. Next morning he was back on the job. He worked till he toughened up and put a few bucks in his pocket. He finished up, and then I guess he decided to quit.

Years later I said, "What was in that jug, Paul?"

He said, "It was half water and half scotch whiskey." How in the hell Greta found money enough to buy him any scotch whiskey, I don't know. But he was burning it up as fast as he drank it, you know.

I saw Johnny Arias a couple of years ago, and he said, "Where's Pablo?"

"Mmm, retired now."

"You know," he said, "I never thought he'd make that day out." They still talk about him. You know damn well he earned his money that first day. But, of course, the Mexicans, they poured it on him. You bet he earned his money. He was tuckered.

Paul was born and raised in Wyoming, so we had something in common. His family homesteaded in the eastern plains of Wyoming, and the other folks in the country, they wanted Mr. Ezell to become a schoolteacher. They wanted a school, and they set one up, but he wasn't going to teach—that was sissy stuff. So he left the country again and disappeared, after siring Paul and a couple sisters.

Mrs. Ezell, left alone for the rest of her life, cooked for boardinghouses and miners and all that sort of thing, but she raised them all. The kids worked their own way through college, if they went at all, and I think they all did. I know Paul did. But she was bound and determined that Paul would become a doctor or a lawyer. Paul rode the rods to come to school at the University of Arizona, where he got a doctorate in anthropology. She was finally satisfied with that. She finally decided that since he'd become a professor, he was okay. Paul was bucking the image of his father and trying to accomplish what his mother wanted while still going his own way at the same time.

Yes, Paul and Greta went through some rougher times than you know. Before the war, Paul had gotten his master's here and couldn't find work, so he went into the Border Patrol, immigration. He was stationed at Wardsworth and working undercover. I saw the pistol that he carried undercover. He'd cut the hammer off it and put a little ball bearing on the cocking part of the hammer so that he could fan it. It was deadly but very small.

He worked on the other side of the line because he spoke German, I think, and he certainly spoke Spanish. He apparently worked a large part of the border from the Colorado River to the Gulf of Mexico. I remember reading in Barbara Tuchman, *The Zimmerman Telegram*, about a woman living in Mexico who had headed or helped a large spy ring of Germans in World War II. Paul knew her.

He traveled a lot, getting much of his information from red-light houses, because that's where the madams and girls knew everybody and everything that went on. But it was a risky job. Finally Greta said to him, "Look, Paul, I never know if you're going to come home alive or dead. As long as you insist on staying with it, all right. I'm going to make my own life, so that if you come home dead, I can continue. And if you come home alive, that's great. I'm going my own way." And she did from then on out doing research work. And by God, it held, it worked. I think that was remarkable of her . . . and of him.

One time Paul went hunting with Alan Olson and Madelon, Paul's youngest daughter, and Paul accidentally shot Madelon in the arm out here at Three Points. We were shocked, of course. That's trite. But Alan came over and told us about it as soon as he could. Alan had taken them to the hospital, and then he went immediately to their house, got all the weapons—he'd already taken Paul's—and took them to his house for hiding. Paul was suicidal for quite a while. And we were all very careful not to talk about firearms, or allow them to be seen by anybody. Madelon took it a lot better than he did.

Madelon took it in her stride. I'll never forget when they fitted her for a prosthesis. She wore it for a while and then threw it off. In effect, she said, "By God, if they don't like me without it, they can go to hell." She never wore it again to my knowledge. I don't know anybody more independent than she is or more competent. Or smarter. She handled it the only way she could, and it was the right way. And the other way would have killed Paul, I think. Oh, she was a wonderful girl. Still is.

Paul and I argued many times, bickered and cursed each other. I'd call a couple of times and he wouldn't call back, so I'd tell Helen that I never want to hear from that SOB ever again. Next month he'd call, and we'd be best of friends. When he'd call and be in a foul mood, or toward the end when he was ill, I'd just hang up and then call back with bagpipe music playing into the phone; that'd calm him down. He loved bagpipes.

My brother, Perry, had five ready-mix plants. No, construction was not in the family, and we had nothing to do with each other's business. When he was in high school, he went to work running a power shovel for old man Braman, in Riverside, who had an old, broken-down rock and sand plant. He thought he had cancer, and he knew he was having union trouble, so he made a proposal to Perry, who'd been working for him thorough his latter years of high school, running a shovel. Perry eventually married his daughter, Marjorie.

So he said to the other son-in-law, who was an accountant, an office man, "You two boys buy me out. You give me a fair price, I'm not going to give you a damn thing. You buy it out and pay it out of earnings, and let's go." So the two boys bought it out. They were making beans, but when the war came they had the only sand which was acceptable to the Corps of Engineers for March Field. The only suitable sand in the whole of Southern California. Their plant was in High Grove, on the way to Colton. So they were off to the races. And they didn't miss any opportunities, either. They took them all.

Perry paid cash for everything. He never had any credit anywhere, which was almost their downfall eventually. But by the time they got to the point where they had to have some money to really expand, they had five ready-mix plants all the way from the Mojave through Southern California. They were hauling their own bulk cement from Colton.

Julian and his younger brother, Perez "Perry" Hayden, in Riverside, California, 1953.

You know these big cement hopper trucks you see on the highway? They've changed the design a little now, but in California they had a tare—the wasted weight of the machinery—and the net, which is the payload. The trucks and trailers were very heavy steel rigs, but my brother was hauling his own cement, and it griped him to haul all that iron around and not make any money on it. So, he went over to Broadeck's in Pasadena, a big aluminum processing company, gave them a design, and said, "Break me these aluminum hoppers out of sheet aluminum to haul cement." They said, "We can't do it. It won't work." He said, "Never mind, you'll get paid. Make 'em." And they did.

And he made enough money off the saving in weight and the gain in payload to pay for everything. Oh hell, he didn't sell them to anybody, but he saved himself a helluva lot of money. Broadeck's called him after a while and said, "We're interested. Do you mind if we make a few?" He said, "No, be my guest." They sold six hundred that first year. It's the only time I ever knew him to miss a buck. They're used all over the world.

He's the same brother who designed the transmission cooler [Hayden Trans Coolers]. That's the way his mind worked. He had a hundred fifty or so Dodge trucks hauling ready-mix, big ones. He drove a Chrysler Imperial, got a new one every year. He used to come over here and brag about it. He'd show us all the positions the seat would take just by pressing little buttons, you know, just like a kid with a toy—that's why we liked him. He wasn't bragging, he was just showing it. Anyway, this big beautiful Chrysler Imperial developed a high-water-temperature leak in the block. And the Chrysler factory said they'd send him a new engine and he could just throw the old engine away. But he was still puzzled; there was a problem there.

So he went out for a drive, and when he came back, he was feeling around the transmission and got a third-degree burn on the ball of his finger from a line leading from the factory cooler back to the transmission. All automobiles in those days had a tube in the bottom of the radiator, and if the water or transmission got too hot, the water temperature rose, and that heated the oil and water, so you had a circular situation. He thought about it for a minute, and he went down to Dunham-Bush's agency in Riverside or San Bernardino—they handled heat sinks for the electronics industry. The salesman had been trying to sell him a little section of a radiator for some reason. So Perry said, "The demonstration block—do you want to sell it?" "Hell, I'll give it to you." So he brought it home, plumbed it up, and put it on his Chrysler. Then he drove it up to Mount Shasta pulling a trailer, and that temperature never got over a hundred and ninety.

Dunham-Bush made the coolers for him, then, and eventually he started making his own. I went over with Helen one August in my pickup, and he gave me a block, used, 'cause my car was running hot. Coming home, I thought I was going to have to put Helen on a plane in Gila Bend to get her home because it was so terribly hot. So when I got home, I put that block on. I went back over in two weeks and left my camera on the floor of the cab, and at any time I could lay my hand on that block and on the lines—the temperature was well under 190 and probably under 170. Then the imitators got in on it, and at one time he had over forty imitators. I asked him about it, and he said if people want to buy crooked coolers, let 'em buy 'em; if they want the best, they can buy mine.

And when Perry built them for racecars, Carroll Shelby, a famous racecar man, used them for differentials, among other things. The chief engineer of Ford Motor Company was down at Daytona one time when my brother was there with Shelby, and he got real excited about this. You know, engines were getting more powerful and smaller crankcase capacities and were having trouble. So he took my brother to Dearborn [Michigan]. And he said, "Before we go in I want to tell you something. Everybody you're going to meet here is a PhD. Don't tell anybody that you've never been to college or they'll throw us both out." So he didn't.

Oh, he invented lots of things. My brother didn't have the education. And probably a good thing, too, because as my illiterate mechanic friend who worked for Hunziker said, "It would have just messed his mind up." He just barely finished high school. Just barely. I don't think he ever read a book. He was a man of action. Always working. He worked in archaeology with my father a couple of summers. But he was one of those men who could see right to the heart of the problem.

An outfit built a big earth-filled dam up at Abiquiu, New Mexico. Mittry Brothers had the contract—I used to work for them when I was a kid. You know the dam, maybe. They built one of the longest conveyors in the country at that time, several miles long,

Julian working on building his adobe home in Tucson, while his children, Julian Jr. and Mary, along with Chapo the dog, look on, ca. 1947.

hauling material for the dam. They put the head pulley-way at the delivery end where the dirt spilled out. That drove the conveyor. But the bearings kept pulling out of the end plates. So the conveyor company flew my brother over there and had a big conference with Mittry Brothers' engineers and everybody else. My brother said, "I think if you do this . . ." "Oh," they said, "our engineers say that that won't work." "Well, then, what do you have me over here for? Put me on the plane." So he came home. But they did what he said, and they never lost another head bearing. He just had that ability to see right to the heart of a problem. He's a rare one.

Sometimes people will come here to visit and be impressed with this house. They scan the walls and admire the architecture; it looks like an antique. Later they'll get up the nerve to ask, "How did you come to find such a lovely old adobe home?"

I squint at them and then say, "I built it." And I did. We lived in tents here while I put up the walls after work and on weekends.

They ask the same sort of thing with my car, that '52 Chevy two-door out there, which has become popular with the customizing set, the hot-rodders and low-riders, I think they're called. They'll see me in a parking lot at the store and ooh and ahh over my car. Sometimes they'll ask me a question I don't quite know *how* to answer: "What are you going to do with it after you die?" I'll be right interested to see how much "doing" I do after that happens.

Lew Walker and I had traveled some together, to the Kofa for one place. Later he retired to the town of Julian in the San Diego Mountains. He was a good man, but I remember one time he didn't help me at all.

After we moved into this house, I didn't have sheetrock up yet, just the insulation, but I kept finding bits of insulation on the table. And after a while we began to get a wild-animal smell in the house. Helen, I guess she was the one that caught it, said, "We're going to have to get rid of that old cat of ours, old Blackie. He's becoming incontinent and using the basement for a bathroom." So I went down and there was scat down there containing mesquite pods.

I said, "Damn it. Cats don't eat mesquite pods; this is something else." We still didn't see anything until I was sitting in my easy chair there, and I happened to look toward the kitchen. Here came a ring-tail out from where the cat food was, headed across the doorway and went under the stove. So I got up quietly and got my camera, and I had a flash attachment at the time, and I set it up. When he came out, I got a beautiful picture of him.

Then I went to look for him. He was in behind the stove hanging up on the gas line, and he looks up at me and says, "Son, that's far enough," and I said, "Yes sir." So we just cleaned up after him. We could hear him in the nighttime going around tops of doors and climbing on the shelves.

So I called Bill Woodin. Bill said, "Don't talk to me; a great horned owl just came down my chimney and I'm trying to cope with that!"

So got on the phone again and called Lew, said, "Lew, I've got a damned ring-tail cat in my house."

He said, "So what, I've got five families of them in my rafters. You want me to do something about it? To hell with you." Okay, okay. Thanks a lot.

We finally got tired of it. So I took some Flit and Flitted the places that he might hide, left the door open, and he went away. There'd been a terrible drought that year, and a lot of animals were down.

I got to thinking, as I have many times over the years since my father died, and I realized that Dad was just like me to have along. Almost always. Once in a while he'd butt in on me, sometimes with almost disastrous results, but on the whole he let me go my way. And Helen and I certainly let our children go their way. We occasionally would gently make a comment, but that's all we ever did.

My son Steve can walk into a group of fishermen, Mexican fishermen, American cowboys, or bankers, and in five minutes they're turning to him. That's a talent. He doesn't say much. I'm very proud of that guy and proud of his mother, for making him what he is. He got a lot from her. So anyhow, for what it's worth, he's going a long way, and he's finding his niche at last. Just as maybe I did, in my advanced age. We're slow bloomers, us Haydens. From Helen he got a gentleness and a literacy and an appreciation for literature that I couldn't have given him. Particularly the appreciation for literature, because I never had much to do with it.

Our daughter Serena was a pretty good shot with a rifle. You bet she is. Serena was in Korea with the Red Cross after she got out of college. They sent her up to the demarcation line at Panmunjom. One day she and another girl had the day off, so they borrowed a jeep, and they went for a ride. They came across the First Cavalry out there in the boondocks having a shooting match with forty-five-caliber automatic pistols. So Serena and her friend stopped to watch. The officers and the noncoms thought it would be nice to impress these two pretty girls with their skill with the automatic, and they even let them fire a few rounds.

Serena had never fired a pistol before, but she whipped them all. She beat them all. Skunked them. She'd never fired one before. So they made her an honorary member of the First Cavalry, gave her a battle jacket and a helmet, and gave her an engraved loving cup, made out of Korean bell bronze, and some other trinkets. Then they set up an All-Korea match, in which she would be the only woman invited. She got the invitation two days after it took place, so she never had to prove up. And she's still an honorary member of First Cav. I'm very proud of her, and rightly so.

She was a damned good shot, but that's where I got in trouble. She was on the high school rifle team and one night at dinner she was telling us about how well she'd done that day at school. So I said, "What were you firing?"

And she said, "A Mark Anschutz," a famous target rifle.

I was interested, and I said, "Well, when I was on the rifle team in high school we used Springfields," a certain model, I've forgotten now.

And that little scoundrel Steve, he got up from the table, walked down the hall there, and stopped in the doorway. He turned and looked back and said, "A muzzle-loader, no doubt." So I put my face in the plate and finished my dinner without a word. You have to raise your young sprouts to have proper reverence for the old, which he still has.

When Steve came back after he'd been to Mexico for a year or so fooling around, he worked for me down near the Mexican border in some opal claims that I was involved in for a couple of years doing assessment work. When he came out, I said, "What are you going to do now?"

He said, "I think I'll go up to Alaska and go fishing."

"Well," I said, "Steve, why don't you stay here, stay around, and learn how to run a backhoe." I had a fleet of them here, several of them. "We'll teach you how to run it, and I can get you in the operators union," which I could. "You'll have a high-paying trade wherever you go." Good operators are scarce.

And he looked at me for a while and he said, "Pa, I know what you're thinking. I'll learn how to run one backhoe, then I'll be running two of them, then I'll be running three of them. And you'll be in the Pinacate. The hell with you, Pa!" And he took off. He had done just what I would have done, so we get along fine. I like that guy. Good guy. He has about as much respect for me as my wife had. And I liked her, too. That keeps a man in his place.

I may come back as a lizard. Sit out there in somebody's patio and talk C-14 to myself . . . and eat cheese. English cheddar. I think that'd be fun. Maybe I can persuade Helen to come over and nibble on the cheese with me the way that one [a large male spiny lizard] did last summer. He brought his sweetheart over and persuaded her to eat side by side with him.

That lizard seemed to be happily mated there, eating cheese from my fingers. He always thanked me when he left, by pumping. Very polite lizard. Some naturalist told a friend of mine, "Nobody ever trains lizards, it's impossible. Fairy tale."

And she said, "It isn't a fairy tale." She'd seen it.

Julian gives his son Steve a lesson in operating a dozer, ca. 1950.

"Where did all this take place?"

"Julian Hayden's patio."

"Oh my God," he said, "Anything can happen in that patio."

My father forced me to copy longhand whole sections of *Fun with Stars*. I never cared for stars since, except for my old friend Orion.

Oh, my father adored my brother. When my brother was working nights and trying school by day, my father hassled him a little. One day father short-sheeted my bruder's bed (always "bruder" and "muder"). He came home, dead tired, and collapsed onto the bed. Then he found the situation and chased my father out of the house and around the block. My father ran to me and glowingly bragged, "He woulda killed me if he'd caught me!" My brother became a multimillionaire, and I didn't.

Father died at age eighty-seven in my brother's arms. I'm sorry my father and I became friends so late in life. He came to visit. I had the tents on my two acres while

I built the house. I was feeding four kids and had lots more folks eating because I was employing twenty-five fathers. My father groused around the house at this and at that. In particular, I had ordered a new hi-fi for the family. He complained about it, too. I was fit to be tied, and I called him on it. I told him, "You once said that a man has the right to enjoy his own dunghill regardless of how it looks to others. Well, this is my dunghill." We started to be friends after that. I wish we'd started sooner.

I don't know how Lunch Bunch got started. Oh, hell no, I wasn't a charter member. I was invited occasionally, but I never went because I felt out of place there—that was the Historical Society. I didn't know anybody. I thought it was more or less a closed corporation. Bunny Fontana and George Eckhart were two of the originals. They used to just eat here and there.

I started after Helen died, because it was a nice thing to do. Before then I always ate lunch with her—never missed, except once a month. That was one of the nice rewards of being married to her, you know. You know how that is.

Helen and I were married forty-two years. Started every morning with a smile, except a couple when I was brooding about business or something. She always fixed that, too.

8. Seri

It is a temptation to reminisce in far too much detail when the names Tiburón and Gwyneth Harrington Wulsin come to mind. Tiburón in 1941 was remote, unknown, romantic, while Gwyneth, as it developed, was so very colorful in her understated way, so varied in her experiences, so rich in knowledge learned and earned, that memories of both are permanent.

I recall vividly my first sight of Gwyneth, in 1935, spring, when a team of Soil Conservation Service [SCS] ethnologists descended upon the Pima Indian Reservation to study the Pima. Our group of archaeologists, working at Snaketown, drove over to Santan Community Center to witness the introduction of the SCS folks to the Pima Indians, who turned out in force. Dr. Lewis Korn, University of Pennsylvania, headed the group, which was largely composed of female ethnologists from Columbia University, and who themselves were predominantly members of the intelligentsia of the time. Dr. Korn introduced the team. He called Gwyneth to the fore and said, "And this is Gwyneth Harrington, who has worked with the Wind River Sioux and understands them, so she will understand you, and you will all get along very well." There was a general hissing sound in the auditorium as the Pima ladies drew their breath through closed teeth, a gentle sound of startled amusement. Gwyneth was much embarrassed by this introduction and dug her toe into the floor like any shy child, tall and rawboned as she was. Our crew members enjoyed this all, for we considered ourselves dirt archaeologists and not high-falutin' ethnologists from Columbia! As it turned out, Gwyneth was not one of them either—a good Scotswoman, she was herself a dirt archaeologist, although she had worked with Korn in Venezuela as an ethnologist.

In what seemed to us good Columbia style, one of the female ethnologists visited the home of the Presbyterian deacon and leader of the Bapchule village. She got out her sheaf of forms and proceeded to question him. He submitted for a while, but when she asked what position he assumed when enjoying (my term) relations with his wife, he arose with dignity, took the shotgun from the corner of the room and said, "You will now leave with your entire party, and you will not return." Gwyneth was much upset by all this sort of thing and did not participate, eventually moving to the Indian Arts and Crafts Board staff, where she worked with the Papago and met Juan Xavier, who was assigned to her as driver and interpreter. He was college educated, a former member of the Papago tribal council, and descendant of medicine men, an excellent choice for her task.

In May of 1941 I encountered Gwyneth again at the Arizona State Museum in Tucson. She was working as ethnologist for the Arts and Crafts Board in Papaguería, and she had several times been to the Seri shores, traveling alone in her old car in her summer vacation times, despite the heat and the risk of being stranded in case of break-down. She liked the Seri, and the Seri liked her, for she had instant empathy with them. After all, she had had broad experience with Indians in many areas, had lived with the Guajiros in Venezuela, the Wind River Sioux in Wyoming, had studied voodoo on La Gonâve when Sergeant Wirkus was jefe there, and so on. I myself had just returned from a fishing and archaeological surveying trip along the coast south of Seriland, and Gwyneth and I compared notes on the coastal sites we had seen. A very pleasant visit, and I returned to Phoenix, thinking no more about it.

Late in June, to my surprise, she called, inviting me to join her and Juan Xavier on a trip to Tiburón Island, where I had long dreamed of going. That was impossible to refuse, even though I had to admit I couldn't help pay my proper share of the expenses, being essentially broke at the time. So I left my family in Phoenix, and my Helen drove me to Tucson to deliver me to the party and to meet Gwyneth, a case of mutual liking on the instant. We left for Mexico the next day.

I did not know the relationship between Gwyneth and Juan, so I happily pitched in to help pack and unpack, set up camp, doing more and more of the work to help pay my way, as I thought. Then I began to notice that Juan was withdrawing and becoming more and more silent. Thinking about this, I realized that perhaps waiting on Gwyneth was Juan's prerogative, so I backed off and took care of my own affairs, which solved the coolness and we got along fine. Gwyneth, of course, said nothing. And I figured correctly that the reason for my presence was chaperon *pro forma*, as well as for the chance to see the island and the archaeology with the Seri. After all, this was 1941, and the university society as well as the Papago society was less permissive than nowadays.

The drive to Kino Bay with Gwyneth and Juan was not without incident, as was always the case when traveling with her. She attracted incidents. We crossed into Mexico late at night, and the customs officer told Gwyneth that we could not enter with all those canned goods until the health officer had examined them the next day. So she remarked casually that coming down she had noted a certain constellation she could not identify, and she asked if he could name it for her. So the two went outside, returned shortly, and we went happily on. I don't know how many pesos it cost her, but the "bite" was neatly and tidily handled. I had not experienced it before, but she was an old hand.

Passing through the small town of Santa Ana en route to Hermosillo, Gwyneth was reminded of an incident on an earlier journey to the Seri. Returning from Desemboque in her old Chevrolet, the car broke down right in front of the military headquarters. This was a prohibited zone, and the sentry came immediately to order her to move. She couldn't, of course, and a major came out to reason with her. Gwyneth looked perfectly helpless and appealed to him for mercy. He realized her quality, ordered a mechanic to repair the car, offered her coffee, and introduced her to the other officers. As it happened, this was late in the afternoon of the Fifth of May, a national holiday, and Gwyneth not only was the dinner guest at the officers' mess, but danced half the night away, to the pleasure of all concerned. Next day she drove happily homeward, car running beauti-fully and she well-danced.

Hermosillo was a small town in those days, and we had no problems passing through and asking a traffic officer for the turnoff to Kino Bay. Just turn west along the fish truck road, it's three miles wide and can't be missed! It had rained hard in the past few days, marking the start of the summer rainy season; the San Miguelito vine was already climbing the saguaros, and the milkweed vine was beginning its thick cover over the trees. Road ruts were deep and filled with water, and one had to choose between them, sometimes wrongly. We took the wrong pair once, sank, and hung up on the shock absorber brackets. So Juan and I stripped down and slid under as best we could, digging the earth away with our bare hands. And then it was dark, so we camped.

I noted next morning, while walking about waiting for Gwyneth to awake—she was a night person—that here and there was a single hole with an arcuate bank of granular soil on the upstream (east) side, and then I saw the giant solitary black ant responsible for the hole and the protective berm, which would divert a shallow sheet flood on the very gently sloping Gulf Plain. *"Muy sabio, las hormigas!"* I remarked to Juan while we waited that morning, that the day was marching on, and how did he put up with this late sleeping? Juan stared at me and said solemnly, "Julian, I just give myself up!" So I did likewise. The road actually was three miles wide in places, as the fish trucks had dodged ruts and mudholes over the years.

We came to the massive adobe walls of the ruined Costa Rica ranch, which had been destroyed during the revolution, as so many other haciendas had been. Nothing remained, as I recall, but the roofless hulk of the main building with walls three feet thick and with a *jacal* and ramada sheltering against a corner of it. The Coronado family lived there, and we visited with Piedad Coronado, Luz, her daughter, and the grandchild. Luz had been sweeping the dirt floors and had the skin of a kit fox wrapped around her brush broom. I asked why, and she said the chickens were afraid of foxes and stayed out of her way while she worked. That made sense, and I took a picture of it and her. We didn't ask, but Angelito Coronado, who was of help to Dane Coolidge, in 1932, may have been the husband. The family was certainly Mayo Indian, with light hair and hazel-green eyes and light skin. According to Coolidge, the Mayo trace descent from Norwegian sailors of long ago. Gwyneth posed with the ladies for a photograph, and we moved on.

So we got through the still-virgin and uncleared Gulf Plain and near sunset camped on the soft and spongy salt flats east of Old Kino, a collection of jacales and adobe huts. We did stop to photograph a group of old ladies in black who were attending the cemetery east of town, sky overcast and dismal in the late afternoon light. In the night I awoke, awakened by the wind, which had changed from a land breeze to a very strong wind from the west, from the sea. I got up and looked, and the wind was blowing right into the heart of a storm riding fast from the east, where the low hills seemed just afire with lightning. So I awoke the others with some difficulty, argued them into the car, and we drove for Kino. Got there just in time and stopped on a dirt street corner outside a little store with a wooden awning. Here came the storm, a *chubasco* of the first grade, and it rained with great violence, lightning horizontal below the low and solid black cover of cloud. Roads and plaza, such as they were, filled immediately with water to a depth of inches, and now and then, as the storm continued, we heard adobe huts collapsing. We were comparatively dry beneath the awning, and Gwyneth visited with the store owner, a pleasant lady who stood inside and watched with us. Gwyneth said she'd not thought to be spending the night on *"una espina"* and got a big laugh. She meant *"esquina"* which means corner, not spine, of course. She was, not so incidentally, a mistress of the art of winning friends and sympathetic interest by making a fool of herself, an art I also have made use of in my time, sometimes unintentionally.

Luz Coronado and her son with Piedad Coronado and Gwyneth Harrington at Rancho Costa Rica, Mexico, 1941.

Next morning we rounded up Carlos Suarez, a man with a dapper mustache, and Federico Enriquez, tall, dark, lean, and sardonic with a shock of hair, who owned a twenty-six-foot fishing boat with a mast and a Model A motor. They were fine men but not mechanics. We left Kino Bay happily enough, and halfway to Tiburón the motor died. We drifted enjoyably while they worked on the motor, and I thought we might be there long enough to memorize the outlines of Isla Tassne, the pelican island [Alca-

Luz Coronado with a broom to which she had attached a fox pelt to keep the chickens away while she swept. Rancho Costa Rica, Mexico, 1941. (Photograph by Julian Hayden)

traz Island] outside Kino Bay. I kept my mouth shut and hands off as long as possible before asking if I could be of help. By that time no face would be lost if my offer was accepted, so I repaired the engine, and we motored on. A simple problem, luckily: an insulating block in the Model A distributor had shorted out, so I made another out of a book of Bull Durham cigarette papers, which worked very well indeed. Our faces were all in good shape.

We went on, up through the Infiernillo Strait and around the northeast corner of Tiburón, arriving at Tecomate in the midst of a fleet of *pangas* [skiffs], folks coming in to camp with their dogs, children, and all their camp gear. The water had failed at the Agua Dulce water hole earlier, but now it was back to normal and the Seri had returned.

Gwyneth was greeted by all as the old friend she was. She pointed out a young man who was the apprentice medicine man, Santo Blanco having recently died (I had photographed his grave atop Punta Antigualla, north of Kino, the day before). We went ashore, and I realized that Juan was suddenly not with us. I asked Gwyneth, she said he was singing to the Little People. I listened and could hear the rattles and the soft singing in the arrowweed thicket. When I asked her how Juan and the young man knew each other and could communicate without a common language, she replied that people of power always recognized and understood each other. In time, I learned the truth of this.

Juan Xavier and a
Mexican fisherman
aboard a panga *near*
Kino Bay, 1941.

It was getting dark after all the visiting, so we made camp. Juan and Gwyneth walked inland some distance with their cots and suitcases, while I slept in the boat, on the forward deck, wedged in between the bitts and the bulwark. In the night a chubasco hit, the low ceiling again, a solid sheet of lightning, heavy rain, wind most violent. The boat pitched until I thought it might go end over end, and the anchor dragged but ultimately held. Next day we spent time hunting for suitcase contents and cots, and Gwyneth continued her interviewing.

A party of Mexican fishermen arrived in a small, flat-bottomed dory with outboard motor, six men, as I recall, mostly young fellows, after shark liver, which was a premium in those unsynthesized days. They lived aboard the dory and slept ashore, having with them a heavy cast-iron frying pan, a sack of green Guadalajara coffee (*"no hay mejor, amigo!"*), some wild rice, some chiles, and some fresh limes, and an appetite. Cooking was done in the stern of the dory, on a five-gallon Standard oilcan filled with sand. We went to the cobble shore of Tecomate Bay, dug fifteen gallons of *almejas*, those delicious tender bivalves, steamed them in the shells, and ate them, squirting lime juice into the opened shell with one thumb and flicking the meat out with the other. The cook roasted the coffee in the pan with sugar, *carbonizado*, and that was a wonderful meal. Later I realized that the heap of shell would, barring storms, stand perhaps for years to come. Thus are shell middens formed. Gwyneth photographed us, a happy group of young men.

At Tecomate, Isla Tiburón, 1941. Juan Xavier is at the far left in the front row; Julian is second from left in the back. (Photograph by Gwyneth Harrington)

And that reminds me that "Seri Bill," William Neil Smith II, who years later lived on the island with the Seri, made a fine color film of Seri life, and in one scene posed with a Seri man holding a pelican outspread between them. He had said that had been a famine year and all he and the Seri had to eat was pelican. I noted that he and the Seri were standing on the very cobble shore from which we had taken those fat and sweet almejas, which had amply fed us. But then perhaps I was the only person viewing the film who would have known that.

Speaking of color photography, there was one magnificent woman whose name I've forgotten, who was tall, slender, had a regal stance and walk, and who wore a bright red garment which reached the ground, like an housecoat. She posed for me standing at the prow of a blue panga, with the west headland of Tecomate Bay forming a backdrop in the blue sea. I almost got the perfect picture, but her face, shadowed, was underexposed, so that her fine features and festive face painting do not show well. Heartbreaking.

We left Tecomate that day or the next and sailed down the strait to the dune camp of Palo Fierro on the west side of the strait. Here were many more people anxious to visit again with Gwyneth, old friends, and they all came running down to greet her, the men standing back a bit, with dignity. Here I photographed the women showing Gwyneth how to carry a basket on her head—without her knowledge, for she did not like being photographed. We spent several hours there, while she asked about dreams and stories and the well-being of her friends. I was interested to see a group of young men approaching me, one carrying a .22 rifle, an old hex-barrel, single-shot Winchester.

While Julian's color photograph of this Seri woman was poorly exposed, his black-and-white exposure was more acceptable. Teco-mate, Isla Tiburón, 1941.

Guns, I had heard, were illegal among the Seri. So when the leader handed me the rifle and indicated I was to fire it and gave me a cartridge, I knew I had to put up or shut up—and this was certainly preferable to a wrestling match or a knife fight. I looked the piece over, aimed at a seashell about fifty feet away, and fired, hitting low and to the right. The men looked at each other and smirked. I handed the gun to the leader, and he hit the same spot I hit. So I took the piece back, selected a splinter of shell from the sands, slid it under the rear sight, elevating it, and smashed the target. So I was in like Flynn, and we all had a very pleasant visit indeed, without a single mutually intelligible word.

One of the men gave me a miniature panga complete with a lateen sail and mast, named *Sierra Kunkaak* (the sacred mountain of the Seri on Tiburón). Cut of elephant tree wood (*torote*), painted with native blue paint, the separate gunwales pinned with ocotillo thorns, it is now in the possession of Richard Felger, along with a later model boat made of planking with outboard motor whittled from a block and attached, given my son Steve twenty-five years later when he was surveying on the Seri coast.

Girls flocked around Juan, a very handsome man, and painted his face with glee. I took photos whenever possible, with no problems at all and no questions of payment,

Seri women showing Gwyneth Harrington how to carry a basket upon her head, Palo Fierro, Isla Tiburón, 1941. (Photograph by Julian Hayden)

since we were friends. Unfortunately, I was short of color film, having been on short commons for some time, and couldn't afford more. So I missed some good pictures. I did get one of Francisco Barnett, the five-year-old son of Miguel Barnett, who stopped dashing about in his floursack chemise to smile enchantingly at me. Now I see the portrait of Miguel Barnett, a man of sixty or so, in the books, as well as that of the mother, Victoria Astorga.

Fishermen came in while we were at Palo Fierro, towing three turtles, which were promptly butchered by the old women. The party had been out an hour, and turtles were plentiful. I have described this elsewhere, in *Arizona Highways* [1942].

We left Palo Fierro after a most enjoyable and profitable stay, Gwyneth's notebooks filled, my archaeological notes made, and sherds collected, and we crossed the strait below Punta Chueca without stopping at the camp. We spent the night around a point in privacy. During the night we heard great splashings and roaring in the strait, which the Seri told us later were the sea animals fighting. That was certainly true, for the next morning, as we waded out to swim in the shallow waters, we encountered an elbow joint which had been bitten cleanly about six inches from the joint proper, and that bone was a good eight inches in diameter. Big jaws. We innocently waded out, not knowing of the stingrays which infest the shallow waters, and later we realized how fortunate we had been not to have been struck by one.

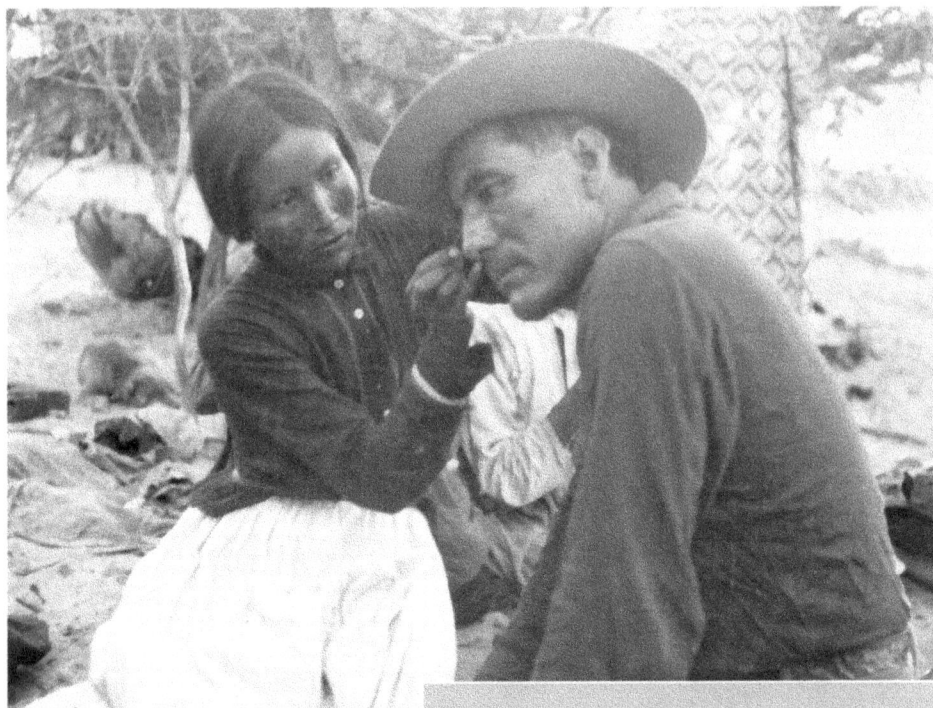

Unidentified Seri woman painting Juan Xavier's face at Palo Fierro, Isla Tiburón, 1941. (Photograph by Julian Hayden)

Francisco Barnett in his floursack clothing, Palo Fierro, Isla Tiburón, 1941. (Photograph by Julian Hayden)

Unidentified Seri fisherman, Palo Fierro, Isla Tiburón, 1941. (Photograph by Julian Hayden)

An incident occurred there which might be related now but surely could not have been told nearly fifty years ago. Gwyneth had been in the water, I was going out some distance to swim, and as we passed we looked at each other with that always new electric jolt of recognition about which one usually does nothing. She rose from the sea like Venus on the half-shell, tall, broad-shouldered, lean with no excess weight, breasts like round shields set high, she was someone to remember, clad as she was in a clinging, transparent blue shift! I myself was in my prime and a powerful man then and was equally bare. We hesitated slightly, took each other in with an all-encompassing look, smiled slightly, and went our ways. I never forgot that, nor, I suspect, did she! Gwyneth was always aware of *la différence*, one of her charms, and since she never went beyond the awareness, she was beloved by her women friends, too.

We sailed back to Kino Bay, where Gwyneth paid off Carlos and Federico, and Maria, Carlos's Seri wife, handed his money to me to keep lest he drink it up that night. We boiled turtle that night at Carlos's house, the ventron with its layer of meat propped up in front of coals till done, then served in the shell with fresh green chiles and canned string beans and tortillas. A veritable feast. And we left the next day, without incident.

Some other memories occur to me. Pete Ferguson, campmate, fishing partner of mine before World War II on frequent trips to the Gulf coast, used to tell of Seri visiting the fishing camp of La Quinta Olga, operated by him and his partner Don LeMastre, in 1933–1934 or thereabouts. La Quinta Olga, by the way, had been built earlier by the son of then governor Calles of Sonora, as a getaway resort for his mistress, a Russian girl named Olga. When and why young Calles abandoned the place I don't recall, but Pete and Don had leased it and were thirty years ahead of their time, so went broke. Meanwhile they had worked hard to establish the camp and knew all the ranchers, Seri Indians and others for miles around. Including Sr. Aguirre at El Dátil, inland, who used to round up Seri men every year with his armed cowboys and herd them to his ranch, where they worked as slave labor until the season was ended. Aguirre (El Pinto, or Pinatado, from his varicolored skin) always appeared at the door of his ranchhouse when visitors drove up, holding a loaded rifle at the port, prepared for any eventuality.

The winter of 1933–1934 was especially cold, and fishing was bad, so a band of about forty Seri came north to Libertad and camped near La Quinta Olga. There was only one panga in the group, and it was manned by fishermen who caught turtle when they could, to feed the band. Others, women, children, and some men, came afoot along the coast. All depended on the uncertain catch of the fishermen for their food and were half-starved at all times. When a turtle was brought ashore, all gathered frantically about it, emerging from the scramble blood-stained and dripping, the turtle shell left clean-stripped on the sand. Ferguson once handed a Seri a nearly empty flour sack. The Seri crammed a mouthful of flour into his mouth and, as Ferguson put it, "Smoke flew out his ears." Another drank a bucket of whitewash, thinking it flour water, without a change of expression.

The Seri men were clad in tattered denims and torn shirts, but each wore a brightly colored handkerchief about his hips, a survival from the days when a pelican skin was the only clothing worn. Each wore a felt hat, stiffened with red, white, or blue clay, perched atop his long hair, while at his belt was a long knife, a prized possession. The old men also wore, often, a "corona," a curiously made "oil-derrick-like" headgear of split wooden strips or of straw, brightly painted. Women wore heavy canvas skirts and jackets, buttonless, ragged, hanging open, relics of some long-past missionary visit.

At night the Seri people gathered in a circle about a fire on the sand, toppling one by one in sleep. They were often drunk on bootleg mescal, obtained from Mexicans, or on marijuana, and fought bloodily during these bouts. The Mexicans at Libertad would have nothing to do with the Seri women, although Mexican ranchers often drafted the men at rifle-point to work in their fields. Both people detested and feared each other.

Mr. Newcomer of Phoenix corroborated Ferguson's description of Seri life in telling of his short visit to them in 1932, and his photographs do not contradict him. He found the Seri in one of their temporary camps on the mainland, ragged and hungry, living in brush shelters, and he was impressed by their destitution. Except for clothing and a few utensils and substitution of pangas for balsa rafts, Seri life appeared little different in 1932 than it was when W J McGee saw them in the 1890s. McGee's photographs show them to have been a starving folk, struggling for bare existence against the Mexican ranchers and soldiers, naked except for the pelican skin about the loins, without utensils other than occasional pots and pans, using frail craft (balsas) made of reeds for fishing, and hunting small game with bow and arrow.

As the party of hungry Seri walked north toward Libertad, the men spied a wild bee's nest in a cliff, and their leader, Ramón Blanco, brother of Santo Blanco, the famous medicine man, climbed up after the honey. He fell and was killed. So his mates took his liver, divided it among themselves, and ate it, in order to partake of his power. This is a worldwide belief and seems perfectly natural to me, but it is undoubtedly the genesis of the tales of cannibalism.

One old man had a lovely daughter of fifteen or so and offered to trade her to Pete for a dory. Pete was tempted, thinking it might be interesting indeed to take this girl, clean her up, send her to Los Angeles to his kinfolk, educate her, and see what might develop. But he didn't. He may have been diverted by the financial straits of the camp and by Don's developing kidney stones. Pete drove him to Phoenix, lying in the back of the pickup, squalling the whole way. Stones had perforated by the time they reached the hospital. The roads were not good in those days, all washboard, no pavement.

9. The War Years

My father was a Marine Corps sergeant. Joined up for World War I. He was too old and had bad eyes, but he signed up anyway. I think he was just bored with being the father of three and of living in Montana. His outfit was poised to fight at Belleau Wood, but his squad was taken to the rear to guard a munitions dump. My father never got over that. He wanted the glory and excitement of the front, and he never heard a shot fired in anger. And always wished he had. Then he wished I had.

I tried to sign up for the Seabees. Went to Phoenix for the physical but wasn't called with the group. They went to Bougainville and were wiped out by our own artillery. They were sent ashore to build a landing strip amid the palm trees. Our own artillery was using proximity fuses, and somehow or another those shells exploded just above the palm groves. Almost everyone died.

I was silversmithing when the war came along. I had three children, so I had a family deferment. I was a big, healthy, raw kid who looked ready for the military, but no one ever chided me about not being in the uniform—except my brother and father.

I'd finished up at Ventana Cave in '42, and I wrote my part of the report. I had closed the CCC camp, then did some more work at home, in Phoenix, and finished up the University Ruin report, so I went back to silversmithing to make a living. After a while it got obvious that I had to do something else, because the government confiscated my oxygen tanks since, obviously, silversmithing wasn't going to help the war effort or anything else.

So I went over to Goodyear, Litchfield Aircraft Plant, and I thought maybe my experience in delicate work and so forth would qualify me, but they offered me a job sweeping floors at fifty cents an hour. I said, "No, sorry." So I came back to Phoenix, walking down Central, and I ran into Red somebody who'd been a truck driver in my crew when I was with the CCC Veterans' Camp out at South Mountain Park. We were talking, and he said, "Why don't you go with the U.S. Engineers?"

I said, "Who are they?"

He said, "Their office is right around the corner, they might be hiring."

So I went in. Some major looked up, and he said, "Can I do something for you?"

I said, "I don't know, are you hiring?"

He said, "Are you a safety man?"

"Why," I said, "of course I am."

He said, "Where did you work?"

"Three and a half, four years in the CCC," I said. "I made lots of safety lectures."

He said, "Can you be in Yuma tomorrow morning?"

I said, "Yes sir." By God, I was in Yuma tomorrow morning. That's how that happened. Gwyneth Xavier was living with us at the time. I came home and told Helen, "Well, you and Gwyneth have got to pack the house when I get a place to stay. Meanwhile, I've got to be in Yuma in the morning. I've got to get a bus out of here tonight." I felt sorry for her, but nothing I could do.

So I was in Yuma that night and stayed at San Carlos Hotel. I began to get acquainted, and the next morning I went out to the base. There were only six of us on the job. So I went down to Judge Westfall, I think his name was, and I rented a house on Fourth Avenue right across from the library—a big market's there now. The rate was twenty-five dollars a month as is, or thirty dollars if he painted the inside.

I said, "Twenty-five is fine." So I rented it right there. Before he realized what was happening, OPA [Office of Price Administration] froze the prices. God, that house is worth a thousand dollars a month today. Now, all of a sudden, we had thousands of men working out on that air base. We lived two years and a half there. I spent the war at Yuma on construction of the air base. I was a civilian safety officer of fifteen hundred men and countless equipment. I helped start the job at Yuma, being the fifth or sixth man down there. Yuma didn't know what was coming. Back then the airport was just a little puddle-jumper field. You know what it is now.

I went into the office, and Captain Floyd—Mr. Floyd he was at that time, since he hadn't been commissioned—was an old Bureau of Reclamation engineer. He was a rough, tough old fellow. He was a man who put the railroad into Butte, Montana, down at Silver Creek, which some said couldn't be done. But he did. And he also electrified the street railways in San Diego for the Spreckels people. He designed and did all that work. He'd been quite a man in his day. Still was. So I introduced myself.

"You're the safety man, are you?"

And I said, "Yes, sir."

He said, "Do you know your business?"

"Yes, sir."

"Well," he said, "maybe you'd better get with it."

Yuma Army Air Field decal.

"Yes, sir." And I turned around and walked out. Didn't see him again until I had business with him. That's the kind of guy he was. He looked like a bullfrog, he talked like a bullfrog, he swore unconsciously, and he was marvelous. And he built an air base. He'd talk to the generals just the way he'd talk to me. And they respected him for it. They finally commissioned him—he worked up to be a major by the time the war ended—which made him madder than hell because it subjected him to military regulations.

So I went out looking around. I went over to Winterhaven, California, just across the river. There was a rock crusher and cement plant over there, and I'd heard a rumor already that the plant was about to fall down, so I figured I'd take my little book and go look at it. It was true, the operator didn't dare grease some of the fittings up at the top of it because the timber was so rotten. So I went all over it with the operator, wrote it all up, came back, and went in to see Mr. Floyd. Floyd read my paper and said, "This means he's got to tear it down; you're condemning the plant?"

I said, "Yes."

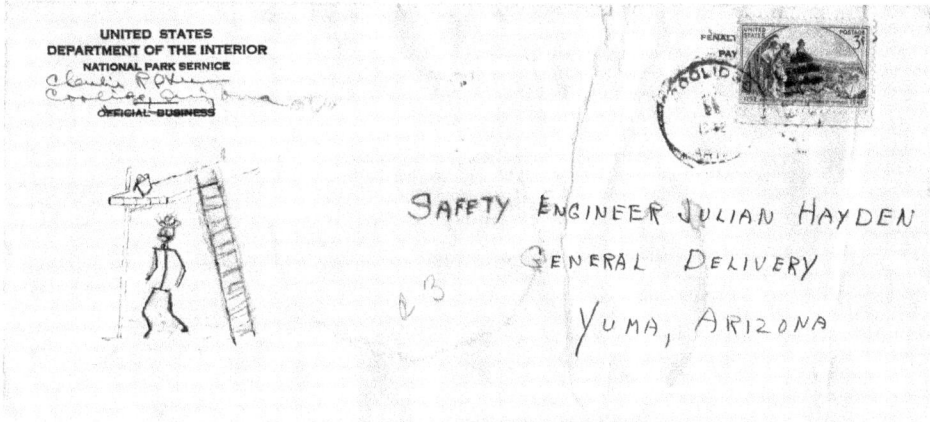

A 1942 envelope from Charlie Steen, addressed to "Safety Engineer Julian Hayden" with Julian in caricature at left.

He said, "You can't do that."

"Why?"

He said, "We don't have jurisdiction over material suppliers."

I said, "He doesn't know that."

"Well, condemn the son of a bitch then!"

I said, "I did, sir."

The operator's name was [C. H.] "Ralph" Trigg. I only met him once or twice. I don't know if he ever knew what I did for him or not, but he found the money and built a good plant. Eventually, he provided all the material for all the military work around Yuma, made a fortune, and retired. If it hadn't been for me he wouldn't have done it, and I never even hit him up for a cup of coffee. So I paid my way through the whole damned war just by that one operation.

From then on, I had a good time. I had supervision of a hundred dump trucks on the road. It was just wide enough for two dump trucks and had deep sand on each side. Two shifts a day out of Yuma, running out to Telegraph Pass in the Gila Range.

I supervised the safety of the entire building of the runways and the buildings at Yuma, the whole thing. I was in on everything. I didn't have any help, either, not until the last few months when they gave me a helper. I put him out someplace and kept him busy there while I went about my business. I had the mess halls and everything else.

I had two bosses: I had a civilian boss, George Arndt, who came in from Los Angeles, an oldtimer, a wise old boy, and we understood each other perfectly. He came out about once every six months to see how I was doing. He didn't want to see the work, he just came out to visit. But the commissioned officers, they'd come out wearing the brass, though most of them were ex–shoe clerks. Reserve officers. They'd start telling me how to run my business. So I'd take them out on the job, and by the time I went up and down that highway once, they'd be asking me where was a good place to hunt ducks. And they never came back again.

I was supervising the running of these dump trucks. I was tough, too. The thirty-five-mile-an-hour speed limit, it was enforced. Thirty-five miles an hour. I used to go out at night . . . You know dump truck drivers, construction drivers, like any other drivers, they have a telegraph system. I could leave the base and within four minutes out at the crusher in the Gila Range, they'd know I was on the road. Once in a while my brother would come over to visit from Riverside driving a Lincoln Coupe and bring his wife, and so I'd borrow his wife and little girl and the Lincoln, put a red lens in my flashlight, and go touring along. Here'd come a truck passing me. So I'd just pull up alongside of him and give him a red light. "You're not playing fair!"

I'd say, "Yeah. And you're driving too fast." I carried a book of tickets. I worked through the highway patrol, Merle Chafey; we worked side-by-side. So I'd give a ticket half the time. As a matter of fact, Merle stayed off my roads. He took care of the west end of the county, where the tourists were. He didn't want any part of construction. He was a good man and we got along fine. I enjoyed him.

This Yuma air base, a single-engine flying school, was training fighter pilots. It was feared that we might be fighting the Japanese within the limits of the continental United States, so it was a rush job. We had high, high priority. As I say we had one hundred trucks, more or less, of which I think only one operator had a certificate. The rest were all wildcats. They came in from all over to work.

In another fiasco, the Yuma County ration board promptly took all of the rubber away from the Yuma Army Air Base—all the tires, wheelbarrow tires and everything else—because planting season for the farmers was coming up, and the farmers wanted new tires. I learned this one morning, and I promptly ran into Captain Floyd and told him. He said, "Well, what are we going to do?"

I said, "Look. I can have every truck off the road within twenty minutes."

"But," he said, "we can't do that, we've got to build this base! We're fighting a war!"

I said, "We are, but Yuma isn't. It's the only way to go. If these men haul in violation and wear their tires out, we got all kinds of trouble. How are they going to get out of town if they've got no rubber?"

So he said, "Shut them down, then." And so I went out, and in about twenty minutes there wasn't a truck rolling anywhere, and at that moment in came General Vandercook from San Francisco, head of the entire Western Training Command.

He said, "Where are the trucks?" And Captain Floyd told him about it. He called Long Beach, and that night there were two boxcar loads full of brand-new truck tires on the road. And I had to sign for them. I had to issue them and take care of them and account for every damned one of them. I got paid two thousand dollars a year. I guess it served me right, but we had the trucks rolling anyhow next morning.

These truckers got paid by the ton. I even bought two trucks. I had sold a fleet of trucks for an old cowman, John Boyer from Aguila, who made some money with them on that job. He got tired of it and wanted to go back to rassling cows. He was a great old boy. He said, "I think I'm going to sell them trucks. I'm tired of this." Big ten-wheel Internationals, they were good trucks and pretty scarce. He had about fifteen of them.

And I said, "John, I've got an idea. You going to sell them yourself?"

And he said, "Why, yes, I guess so."

I said, "I'll tell you. You know what you want for them?"

And he said, "Yeah, I know what I want for them. Damn it, they're my trucks, aren't they?"

"Well," I said, "I'll make you a proposition. Let me sell them for you. That way you won't have to mess with it. And you give me anything over your price."

"Oh," he said, "if that's what you want to do, go do it." So I advertised in Spokane and Seattle and San Francisco and Los Angeles and Denver, and I could have sold ten thousand damn trucks the next day. A big Dane came over from Los Angeles and paid cash for the whole outfit. And John slipped me my override. First time I ever saw more than eight dollars in my life. It was a nice piece of hundred dollarses. So I bought two dump trucks and I put them on the road to ride with the others. That would be illegal nowadays, but nobody cared in those days, for we were trying to build a base. I hired a couple drivers that I knew, and I was rougher on my men than I was on anybody else. If somebody was complaining, I said, "Ask my drivers." So I didn't get much of that.

I really had control from then on, and I had no accidents. Oh, it was just some of the fun that I had. Six in the morning till midnight for two years and a half. If I caught a man with his clearance light out or something, he went in and fixed it. Oh, he'd get so mad, he'd miss two trips, you know. Cost him money. But it worked.

I'll never forget the time Morrison Knudsen contracted moving-target ranges on the base. He brought in a hundred and sixty long-haired Navajos from Black Mesa. They got in late at night in big stake-bodied trucks. And you know Navajos are jokers. Very few of these men spoke English, just the leader of the Yellow Hair clan. Coming down, one of them, an old man, had whittled a pistol out of cedar wood, and he'd put shoe black on it. And he stuck it in the MP's ribs. The MP was a young fellow from Georgia and he damn near died of fright. And by God, that old man damn near got shot, too. That caused a commotion; they had to go over and straighten it out. Keep in mind that these Indians were civilians.

The next morning they all came in to be fingerprinted and mugged and what not. That was my job, too. I did all of that. The leader came in, in front of all these Navajos, hair done up and all, and the office help, and anybody else available came to look. The man looked at me and he lets out a squall, "Dághá Niłchxon! Yá'át'ééh dine'é!" And we hugged each other, you know. Henry Yellow Hair! I knew him at Keet Seel. Helen knew him, too. When we went up on our honeymoon, we had stopped and visited him in his hogan.

The office people tiptoed around me for about a week. Oh, those are things that make jobs worthwhile, you know. The Navajo had their own barracks, but when they were free, the young men would go down to the railroad station, which had a beautiful lawn. They'd strip down to their breechcloth and wrestle. Once in a while they'd break a bone, too—they wrestled hard. So the police got into the act, and I had to go down and straighten that out. "Damn it, let them alone. They're Navajos. This is their custom. It's not hurting the town any." After that I got along fine with the police. We had more fun.

When did Barry Goldwater show up? I think the cantonments and barracks were being built at that time. The runways were in, and they were flying. Wing Commander Donaldson came in in a P-46, I think it was, one of these single-engine fighters with an Allison engine, that they used to paint shark's jaws on, remember? He was a little fellow, just as sharp as he could be with a go-to-hell cap with the wire taken out, you know, and enormous red mustachios. I don't know how the hell he sat in the cabin without rubbing them on the sides of the canopy. But he fought all the way through the Battle of Britain.

I think the army had just graduated a class, and Donaldson came in and put on a lecture and demonstration for the cadets. He barrel-rolled down the runway and rolled out of one end of it, almost striking sparks with the wing tip. And he upped and looped and landed and taxied right up to our office. Donaldson did what he had to do and demonstrated combat tactics with somebody else. He was a hell of an interesting soul and impressed those kids and all of us. Then he said goodbye and taxied down the far end of the runway. He turned around and picked it up just like that and barrel-rolled all the way north and right over that hill which has the water tank on it now. And he disappeared the other side, and a tremendous cloud of dust went up.

A cry went up, "He's down!" And Colonel Barry Goldwater was search and rescue, so he promptly jumped in his plane and took off to see where the wreckage was. He couldn't find it. Next thing you know over the radio came, "Tally ho, boys! Cheerio!" or whatever you holler in England. He'd just squirted some exhaust at the sand dune the other side of the hill, and he kicked up the dust and went up the road. So we all laughed at Barry Goldwater with great relief. We had to laugh at somebody; we were pretty scared.

From the Gila Range they were mainly hauling rock to use as a bed for the runways. We had a couple of crushers out there, on the north side of the road. Turn off just before you get to the foot of the mountain and then go up that wash there. I suspect you could still see it. They crushed gravel for concrete aggregate.

That's where I learned about vitamin C. When I went there, we couldn't keep anybody working out on that crusher. It was in a basin and there was no air at all; it was just a hell of a place, just impossibly hot. The men just couldn't take it. And when I went down in June, I fell right into the middle of that. I was thinking about it, and I remembered having read before in *Time* magazine [probably June 29, 1942] that some British doctors had solved the problem of heat exhaustion in the Kimberley diamond mines, which had been a problem for a long, long time. These doctors took sweat scrapings from the black miners, and found not only the salt they expected to find but also quantities of ascorbic acid. So they started giving the men quantities of ascorbic acid, and it solved it. So I went downtown to the drugstore, and I guess I was the only civilian that ever bought any ascorbic acid there. The man behind the counter hardly knew what I was talking about. I took it out and gave it to the crusher operator, who turned out to be a good friend of mine—most of the time. He passed it out to his workmen and that was the end of it. After that the contractors kept ascorbic acid, vitamin C, on hand, at my instructions. And I've always had it here. I take it every day and my men took it every day. All my employees took it. I used to fight with the army surgeons over it. They said, "Oh, no, that's superstition, there's nothing to it." The Army isn't always up to date, either.

My favorite was Doc Eaton. I met him right away, because I had to have somebody to take care of the workmen who got hurt. He was a man of about forty, round and chunky. He loved that small town, because he knew everybody. I went down to see his office. He kept up with the latest developments in medicine. All of the journals, and they were all filed, and he could flip to the latest. He even knew about vitamin C, which most doctors didn't. I respected his medical knowledge. But I wasn't above blackmailing the son of a gun. We got to be good friends. And we lowered our severity rate, which means the length of time a man's off. We cut it way down real quick. I think we respected each other. And I had the deadwood on him, man, it always helps to have a deadwood on him.

We had a case in which a Mexican dump truck driver got drunk on vodka. He caught a wheel in the sand off the road, and flipped, and landed on his side. So he stood up in the cab, which was on its side, and climbed out through the open window. Gasoline was pouring down around his feet And he lit a match for his cigarette. One of our inspectors, Red somebody, I've forgotten, a wonderful Oklahoman, pulled up right behind him and said, "Hey, you want some help?"

"No, I don't want any help," and he threw his cigarette down and up he went. So Red pulled him out, and he called me somehow. I called the doctor, and the doctor said, "Wonderful case. Sixty percent skin graft and all that."

I said, "Fine. Where is he, down at Yuma Hospital?"

"Yeah."

"Well," I said, "I'm going to tell you something, Doc Eaton. That man's not eligible for treatment."

"He's not! Why?" Industrial commission rules, you know.

I said, "Because he was drunk and refused help."

"Well, then, he'll be out at six o'clock tonight. Burns or no burns."

And I said, "No, Doc, he won't."

"What do you mean?"

I said, "You're going to take care of him, and you're going to treat him right. And you are going to do something for me. I won't have any more malingerers. If I send a man in with a busted thumb, you put a splint on it and send the son of a bitch back to work; that's what you're going to do. Every time."

He thought quite a while. Long silence. He said, "Okay."

There weren't many people in Yuma, six thousand maybe. The town ended at the Y, as you come east. There used to be a service station, right in the fork in the Y; it caught fire one morning. Yuma hardly had a fire truck, but whatever they had, they went up there and, with the construction trucks in from the air base and the military trucks we pulled in, we put it out. It was all right. All had to hang together, because if it had burned much more it would have been in Yuma.

I didn't have much to do with the city police, because I was working in the county. But the sheriff, Pete Newman, was a legendary character. I carried a card under him so it would give me some jurisdiction over civilians who weren't working on the base. I used that card now and then, with Judge Lutes's assistance.

Everybody slept outside in the summertime, of course. Down the road, just at the dropoff into Roll Valley, an old Mexican and his wife were sleeping in their brass bedstead under a mesquite tree. In the heat of the night, a car came careening into their field there and ran right into their bedstead and dumped them out. The old man jumped up, screaming for the *policia*. And the man said, "By god, I'm the policia! I'm Pete Newman, what the hell's wrong with you?" He was on his weekly toot.

And everybody just smiled and said, "Oh, that Pete. He's a pistol."

He was a good man. One time I was just leaving the house after dinner, going out to patrol on the highway. I saw a couple of fellows walking along, hitchhiking. One of them had just stopped and opened his ditty bag and pulled out a pistol. I looked at that as I drove by and turned around and came back. And I said, "Son, you got a pistol in that?"

He said, "Yeah."

"You mind if I look at it?"

He was hitchhiking, and he said, "No," and he showed it to me. Loaded.

I said, "What do you carry it for?"

"Oh," he said, "I don't want to get held up."

I said, "You in the service?"

He said, "I was. They gave me a dishonorable discharge over there for something or other."

"Well," I said, "packing a gun and getting a DD, going together, you might have a problem. Why don't you come along with me. We're just going to talk about this." So I picked him up, and we talked it over with Pete Newman.

Pete said, "Let me see that gun." He looked at it and said, "Son, will you take fifteen dollars for it?"

He said, "Why, sure."

Pete said, "Here. Here's fifteen bucks. Now get out of town. Just keep going, and for God's sake, don't put another gun in that bag." Now, that was a good man, you know? He could have rapped him. I didn't think he would, or I wouldn't have taken the boy in. But he saved that boy some serious trouble. And if the man had been hungry, Pete would have fed him. But that's what you've got to do in a small town.

Also I had a little trouble in Yuma. Or would have had if I'd stayed. I got word that the operator of the landfill outside the base was unhappy, so I went out to see what was the matter. He showed me. All of the scrap from the air base was being buried out there in the sand: lumber, brand-new uniforms, shoes, copper, rubber, everything. They had no salvage whatsoever. Although my Helen was saving rubberbands—everybody was saving everything they could, but the desert training command was in full swing, and at least a dozen trucks, the big trucks, a day were bringing in scrap, much of it recyclable, and were dumping it. The operator of the tractor was getting real unhappy.

So I took a Brownie camera out. If I'd been caught with it, I would have been in trouble. I photographed it, and I sat there for a half-day and tallied the contents of every truck. I got the photographs developed, and I filed a report with a box number I had somewhere in the coast and got no answer, which made me unhappy. Then the inspector general sent a Major Longman in for what they call squawk week. In the army those days, every so often a man from the inspector general's office would come, and anybody had access to him, from the lowest private to the generals. Everything was confidential; you could complain about anything and everything, and they wouldn't do anything to you. So I waited until this pressure was off, and then I went in and introduced myself, and I told my story. "Well," he said, "Mr. Hayden, you just go on about your business and we'll take care of this." I gave him everything I had.

By the second day that fill was fenced and under armed guard, and the colonel later on got a commendation for having the most efficient salvage yard in Western Command.

Julian's ration book from 1942.

But he was looking for whoever blew the whistle. So I got transferred to Muroc (now Edwards) Air Base. My captain was already up there, and a couple of people from the office, because we at Yuma were closing down and finishing up construction.

So I went up to Muroc, whereupon I got in trouble again. There was a big garbage dump between the civilian barracks and some other buildings, I forget what they were. Just a big open garbage dump with no cover on it. Some of our contractor's employees were in a trailer camp nearby, and there were a lot of flies, and the babies were getting dysentery. So, I complained to the chief surgeon on the base, and he told me to tend to my own business, so I said, "Yes, sir." So I came home. I got home every other week for a couple of days.

I talked to my father about it, and of course that got him up. So, he got hold of a friend in Redlands who was a buddy of Senator Phillips. All of a sudden that dump was cleaned up. And they were looking for whoever started that one. I don't know what his title was, but the top dog in the California state health department almost lost his job. This thing went all the way to the top when Phillips got at it. But we didn't have any more flies.

I was a safety officer at Muroc for the engineers. We used to go up to the jetport at Palmdale where the top-secret jet planes were. They were still experimenting with them. I don't know who built them, Northrup maybe, I've forgotten. One of them used to come over at five o'clock every afternoon, come down low right over the trailer camp. It came so fast you couldn't see what it looked like. The trailers rocked and the babies would cry and the dishes would fall off the shelves, and it would disappear. Every so often it would flame out and that was it. Send a truck out for the wreckage, and pick it up and put a prop on it, always. And a canvas. You drove up past their hangar and you looked the other way; if you didn't, the guns came up.

Yeah, I'm going to make one brag here. I guess I've been bragging all evening, damn it, but nevertheless. In my cabinet in there I've still got my safety records, files, some of them anyway. Two million, two hundred thousand man-hours I supervised. Only one man was killed, and I think two men were permanently injured. And I'm pretty proud of that. But the best thing of all were the friends I made.

As range safety officer, I patrolled to check for violations, and I had the brass to make things stick. I pulled up to watch men unload steel from the rail yard. The guy running the crane had a laborer steadying the load. The problem was they were right close to a power line. I went to the operator and said, "If you get that boom near that line, it'll arc six feet and power right through your laborer. If I ever see you that close again, I'll fire you on the spot." And I would have. Fifteen years later I was here in Tucson at El Rancho market, and a guy came up and asked, "Remember me?"

"No, should I?"

"Aren't you Julian Hayden?"

"Yes."

"Well," he said, "I was a crane operator at Yuma Air Field and the day after you warned me about the arc, I got too close and it did arc. Fortunately, my laborer was away at the time. Since then I've been all over the world operating heavy machinery, and I never forget your face or that incident." I think I almost felt like crying. That's one of the nicest things anybody ever told me. I'm real proud of that; I figure I saved some guy's life somewhere.

We used to have fun. We had a big building, the first of the big B-29 hangars. It was ninety-six feet to the center of the truss. We had a red clearance light up on top of it, part of regulations. It was up on a ten-foot two-by-four with braces. Ground Safety called me one Saturday night, got me out of bed, and said, "Light's out."

I said, "Okay." So I called the electrical superintendent and got him out of bed.

He came over and he said, "I'm not going up there. Think I'm crazy?" It was windy, broken moonlight, clouds. Just a skeleton of the hangar was up, with no sheeting.

"Well," I said, "get one of your electricians."

He said, "I wouldn't send anybody up."

And I said, "All right goddamn it, give me the bulb." I put it in my coat pocket. If I'd stopped to think, I wouldn't have done it, but I had to do it. So I climbed the damned hangar, went up over, and got up there. I shinnied up that pole, replaced the bulb, and came down. When I got back down on the steel I had to pee. So I stood there and I relieved myself. I saw a shadow suddenly move very quickly down below. Well, he didn't say anything and I didn't say anything. Next morning I went into the plumbing contractor's office run by Mrs. So-and-so, a rough-talking old German lady.

She said, "Hayden! I understand you've gone into the soil compaction business!" Office was full of men. She said, "I didn't know your dauber was that long!" I just turned red.

So I made a lot of friends during the war. Some of them I still know, too. I had a helluva good time. Sure we worked ten, twelve hours a day, but that was fun. If I hadn't done that I'd have been a PFC in a mess hall somewhere washing dishes, and that wouldn't have done anybody any good. At least that's the way I looked at it, and besides that's where I was told to be, so I stayed there.

I had a marvelous job. Nobody could have had a better war than I did, since we had to have one. I came across my government file a while ago, hunting for something, and found my justification sheets. In civil service you had to justify your existence once a year, putting everything you do and giving the percentages of time you spent on it. Mine always came out with one hundred percent of my time spent. I don't know how

*Nearly every year, Julian and Helen made a linoleum-block print
Christmas card featuring the Hayden clan rendered as Hohokam
figures. This 1945 card depicts the family (left to right: Mary, Steve,
Serena, Julian Jr, Helen, and Julian) after they had moved to Tucson
and begun constructing their house.*

the devil we ever would have won the war without me. I sometimes think I was quite a
guy, until I think about some of the other jokers who weren't but had a record as good
as mine. I was head of protective security, had to fingerprint everybody who came on
the job—civilians, send the cards into the FBI, keep criminal records on everybody who
had them, had to keep certain people away who belonged to certain organizations, and
make sure that that was so. I had to take care of any spies if we found any spies—we
picked up a couple, you know.

I was up at Muroc much of two winters and one summer, I think. And I came
down here to Tucson in the summer of 1945. I know it doesn't add up, but it was still
there. I had three and a half years altogether. I was happy to get down here, because I
had already bought this two acres [in Tucson] and we'd never seen it. I bought it from
one of the inspectors at Muroc. He'd bought this land in 1927 when the boom was on,
and his wife didn't want to live on it. She wanted to live in San Bernardino. So I bought
it. Paid him eight hundred dollars, for these two acres, which was a strain, but by God,
we paid for it. That's the way it was in those days.

I left the family in Riverside, and I came over. Stayed in BOQ (bachelor officer's
quarters) on the base, Davis-Monthan, that summer. Long days. I'd work till about six
at night, then come over here. I bought a couple of surplus Army pyramid tents, worked
some angles to get some lumber, and put the sides up. I got the tents up, a concrete floor,
and put the power in and water in. We had propane.

One weekend I went over and got the family. The tents weren't quite ready, so I
put the family in federal housing—a dump—over at Sixth and Irvington. Helen cried
herself to sleep, it was so bad; I thought I had done well to find anyplace at all. I had
them there for about two or three weeks. The kids got over here just in time to start
school. It was awful rough on Helen, but she did a good job. We survived. God, she
was a good sport.

Letter from Julian to his parents, Irwin and Mary Hayden.

Rt 2, Box 193
Tucson, Arizona
Sept 25, 1945

Dear Folks,

Well, the kids are all asleep, Helen is painting her nails, Spot is chasing insects around the tent, Willie is asleep with Mary, Torty the Tortoise is holed up in the corner by the icebox, our pair of praying mantises are busy eating mosquitoes and looking sanctimonious, and the moon is just breaking over the Rincons. We're home at last.

And it's turning cold, and Helen is now putting on a pot of coffee. Wish you, Dad and Ma, could be here with us now, the weather is perfect, clear hot days and clear cold nights, with cumulus building up over the Sierritas and the Empires in the afternoons, and breeze all day, flowers still blooming along the roadsides, paper flowers and desert marigolds and a poppy-like flower, and grasses heading out, the staghorn cholla still blooming pale pink and the barrels with their brilliant orange or scarlet or crimson flowers against the brilliant sky and the earth-colored Catalinas. The Catalinas are a constant source of joy to us, changing color all the day long, cliffs bright and canyons dark, with mysterious veils of rain occasionally drifting over or in front of them, like dusty webs. Yes, we like our place.

. . . We're pretty well shaken down, with bottled gas for the range, and running water outside (shortly to be in the kitchen soon as I get the sink installed), a pit toilet complete with ventilator and commercial seat, very comfortable, showerhouse with stall and dressing room (also with running water from hose and bath nozzle), etc. etc. Power turned on, not even a complaint from the inspection dept of the power co, so my wiring job was OK. I still have to put up sheetrock at the corners of the living tent, to cut down on the cool breeze at night and make it easier to install screen if and when it becomes available. Kids have regular GI bunk beds, two high, and like them exceedingly, and have a tent to themselves for playing and sleeping and studying. Helen and I live in the kitchen tent, sleeping on the studio couch.

. . . Love to you, from us

10. "Hayden Says"

My business itself shouldn't be of any interest. I was just a pea-shooting contractor. I don't know how some people get started, but it was fairly simple how I got started in construction in Tucson. During the war I ran into an old fellow in Yuma. I've forgotten his name now—it's all written down somewhere—but he had a gasoline jackhammer. A pavement breaker. It wasn't like the ones you know nowadays but just a vertical cylinder with a spark plug in it. It was essentially a diesel cylinder. You pressed the piston down to suck in the fuel. Then you released the plunger very quickly and it would come up and fire, and then it would go down and start banging. It banged down on the steel, the points that you were cutting pavement or rock with, but it would come up with equal force into your wrists. It weighed one hundred and six pounds. Called a Barco.

He had a carrying board for it. And he'd been doing assessment work for prospectors up in the San Dieguito Mountains of California. Packing it around on his back, along with a battery, a six-volt battery, and so forth and so on. So for some reason I bought it from him, because I figured it might come in handy someday, I guess. I didn't know. Anyway, I bought it and carried it around.

I had intended to take four or five months' annual leave. I hadn't had any all through the war, leave, "comp" time, or anything else. But the Corps of Engineers was mad at me, and with another fellow, too. It wanted us to go over to harbors and docks in San Pedro when they closed this office after the Japanese surrendered. I didn't know anything about harbors and docks, and didn't care anyway, so I stayed. So, we both quit in November of '45. But the Corps evened the rap on us: they wrote us a check for all the back time we had and then took it all back in income tax. So I only had about a month to work around here.

I started digging foundations for the house with that Barco. John Harlow, the landscaper, came by and said, "Do you dig tree holes?" We got to talking, and pretty soon I dug a tree hole for him at so much an hour, three dollars and a half an hour, I think. I furnished the gasoline and a hammer and the strong back. Then somebody else wanted some holes, and then somebody wanted foundation trenches. Tucson is underlain with caliche, and soon everyone found out I was the only man in town who had either the equipment or the interest to do any caliche digging. All of a sudden I was digging caliche.

I figured I'd better get a license, so I went down and saw Oliver Drachman, registrar of contractors. And we got acquainted. It didn't cost me anything, five dollars or so, no examinations, no bonds, no nothing in those days. So I took out a general license and a couple of specialty licenses in excavating and grading, concrete work, and construction.

Julian digging with the Barco jackhammer in Tucson. The two wall tents are those the Hayden family lived in from 1945 to about 1950. The 1930 Model A was named Lillian.

I should have taken out a plumbing license, but I didn't—I thought I was pushing my luck as it was. So that's how come I wound up contracting.

By that time my wrists were so beat out I couldn't even hold a claw hammer. I had to hire somebody to run a hammer. And that's the way we got started. I've been at it for thirty damn years. Just willy-nilly without intending to or anything. I really wanted to build adobe houses, although I'm awful glad I didn't, because I don't want to be that close to people. This house I'm living in is the only one I ever built. I worked on some, but this is the only one I ever built.

I want no part of building for anybody else. I'll dig the foundation and that sort of thing, but I won't build for them. I like to get on a job and get done with it. And I don't want to be called back by somebody saying, "Well, that door is a little bit too long" or "it's too narrow" or "you should have put this tile there." The hell with it. I don't want any part of it. There may be money in it, but not for me. We ate. We figured if we couldn't make enough digging ditches, we couldn't make it at all.

One thing leading to another, we put in septic tanks and drain fields and eventually got into concrete. I figured if we couldn't do that and charge a fair price, and pay our men properly and take care of them and do honest work, why, the hell with it. But it worked out. Generally we were subcontracting to a general contractor. Of course, if I was working for an individual, I'd be contracting then. I bought the first Leroy compressor in southern Arizona. I didn't have any money, but a brand-new outfitter had just formed in Phoenix. It was run by a couple of war veterans just getting started, and they had the Leroy line.

And Harold Ashton, a graduate civil engineer at the University of Arizona, was running a service station down across from Baum and Adamson down on North Stone. I had two gasoline jackhammers and was using a Model A coupe that belonged to Helen. Also, I had bought an old Chevy pickup, 1940s. By golly, Hal had a sharp eye, and he noticed that I was working three or four men. So he went out and bought an air compressor, a good-sized one. He had two air hammers and hired a couple of Mexicans who knew how to run them, and he was digging foundations, too. And he could put out so much more work than I could that it was pathetic. So, I had to have an air compressor.

Anyway, I got enough money to make a down payment on the Leroy, and I paid for it through the Southern Arizona Bank on the installment plan. It was a big portable one on wheels, and we towed it behind the Chevy. We parked it right here in my living room, which was the garage at that time. I washed it down every night and serviced it every night. I patted it all weekend, you know. We hauled it out every morning and hauled it back at night.

Remember Phil Hunziker? I ran into a man out at Southern Arizona School for Boys when we were doing a job for them. This man came out and looked at the big backhoe I had rented, and it had Hunziker's name on it. It was a big cable-rig.

He said, "I knew a man named Hunziker when I was teaching at the university."

We talked and I said, "Well, that's his machine. I'm renting it from him."

He said, "When you see him, you give him my best from professor so-and-so of mathematics."

So, I told Hunziker, and Phil said, "Yeah, that's the only one in the university engineering department who knew what I wanted. What I wanted was to know how

Julian with the Ford dozer in 1953.

to chase a decimal into a corner, but I damn well wasn't going to do it, 'cause I could hire somebody to do it. Look, there's two PhDs sitting at that desk in the next room. They're working for me." You get the point.

I always like to have my hands on things, so I made my own cement forms and designed them and worked on them. One thing and another. And as I told you before, because a man tells me something is true, I look at him and wonder what his qualifications are, and if I'm not sure, I reserve judgment on it. I may have to do what he says, but I don't have to believe what he says.

I've been an archaeologist field man and trowel man—that's where you're down in the dirt. That's where I got interested in soils. I can differentiate soils and tell you the source of about any soil you want to know in an archaeological site. And I can do the same thing in a construction site. I worked hard to learn all I could about caliche, alluviation—hell, I've even forgotten some terminology now—and the movement of water.

The other thing was salt erosion that I learned about when I was working on Pueblo Grande and that I published on [*American Antiquity*, 1945]. That was a great help, of course.

The movement of water in soils has always been a challenge to me. I want to know why it does what it does. What happens when effluent is put in the soil? What about all the bacterias, the greases, and fatty acids, and all the other oddball chemical combinations you get in household sewage? Why not? I don't see anything different from that to doing something esoteric, and this is important.

Then I found myself trenching for septic tanks and drain fields. Naturally, as an outgrowth of my excavation business. So, I go down to the county, and I ask what are the codes, and they show me. I said, "This doesn't make sense. You want six inches of gravel underneath the effluent and eighteen inches above? What's the eighteen inches above for?"

"Oh, that's because the water rises up in the gravels and evaporates." That didn't make sense, but that was the code. So, before long, I started putting eighteen inches under and six inches on top. I uncovered a number of fields that had failed, and hell, they were flooded. There was no place for the water to go. By the time the water got up in that gravel, it was backing up into the house. Any old farm boy knows that but not an inspector and not a code writer.

So I developed techniques which the academics said wouldn't work. Of course, I had my own sewage leaching field out here. I'd dig down in it to see what was happening after a couple of years. There was moisture thirty feet away from it but not below it. Water moves sidewise in a soil; it doesn't go down, because the bottom of a ditch will seal off. I suppose there are other reasons, too.

Now, you stop to think about it. You send water down a ditch, whether it's sewage or anything else, and it'll pick up colloidal clay, the fine suspended clay particles, and then those will settle out, particularly when the water is standing. They will seal the bottom of that ditch, and no water can penetrate. But on the sides of the ditch, the water level will fluctuate, whether in a residential sewage system or in an irrigation ditch. Anything that is deposited on the side of the ditch will dry up and fall off or be eroded away by flowing water, so your sides will always take water.

They used to have to calculate the area. For a house of a certain size and a certain postulated number of occupants with so much water use, you had to have so many square

Hayden Excavation Service installing a septic tank in the Tucson area, April 1959. Manny Hughes, who worked for Julian, is at far left; Julian is steadying the tank. (Photograph by Irwin Hayden)

feet of bottom. Now, we calculate the required number of feet on the trench wall and ignore the bottom. And by God, that's something I developed right here, got it into the Pima County code. It took me a long time, and I put in a lot of systems that were illegal, because it wasn't in the code. Now it's state code; it's even EPA code. Regardless of who developed it, I imagine a great many people thought of the same damn thing, good old farm boys. And I'm enough of a good old farm boy from watching to see that. It works. I made a living here for years installing septic tanks, and designing tanks, and designing, more particularly, the method of disposing the effluent in the field, out in the soil. Soils fascinate me, and the problems of disposal and expressing water within the fields is intriguing.

Otto Fritz was the county sanitarian, and we got pretty well acquainted. I figured out how to handle him. I proposed something very carefully, and every so often, I'd sorta work it around, and later he'd call me up, and say, "You know, Julian, I've been thinking about this, and I think this is the way to do it." That's what I'd planted in his head, you know. It can be done if you're careful, so everything I ever came up with I got into the county code. That was fine. And the incidence of failed fields just disappeared—went to zero as long as they were put in properly.

Finally I got in trouble out at Yale Estates on Wilmot Road. I was supposed to do three hundred houses. Yale Epstein was an honest builder, one of the few honest developers at that time. He wanted me to do the septic tanks and drain fields for all those houses. "But," he said, "damn it, your price is too high and I just can't afford it."

I said, "Okay." The other man's systems have the certificates of inspection, you can get a license on a *charanga*—a jalopy—as well as on a Cadillac. All this substandard stuff would pass inspection, so why should they pay me a hundred dollars more per system, right? And I wouldn't do it any other way than I'd been doing it.

He came over one day, and he said, "I got a low bid on the paving, far lower than I expected, so instead of buying a car, I want you to put the systems in." I never heard of a man doing that before or since, so I did.

I put a lot of them in, and they brought in an FHA [Federal Housing Administration] inspector from Arkansas. He'd never seen a system like mine, and he blew his top. He said, "Every backyard here is going to be flooded." And he shook me down, but I wouldn't put it in his way. I didn't like his way anyhow.

So I called Barry Goldwater and Mo Udall. And who else? Well, I got practically everybody. I don't know whether I got Carl Hayden or not. And I may even have written a "Hayden Says" ad about it—but going up against the FHA was just like coming up against a foam rubber mattress. Finally they wrote me, the big shots in Washington, and said, "Just where did you take your engineering degree, Mr. Hayden?" I threw up my hands, and so did Barry Goldwater and so did Udall. They couldn't break it. And I'd worked for Udall, both Stew and Mo, putting in sewage systems for them, which are still working, as far as I know.

Then after a while, FHA was having so many failures around the United States that they contracted two engineers from UC Berkeley to study the problem of drain fields which were failing and septic tanks which weren't operating properly. They wrote a marvelous report. They were good guys; I'd have liked to have met them. I got a copy right away. They went all over the states and checked all the codes they could find, and they wound up saying that septic tank codification is a matter of codified ritual, not based on anything other than localized superstitions. They said there's always some man in any county who knows his soil conditions, but except for those scattered men, the codes have nothing to do with fact.

So they laid out a system which is exactly like mine, and I was making tanks which nobody else in the state was making. A solid partition with a hole in it midway at liquid depth for increased efficiency, which I got from Victoria, Australia. I had to go to Australia to get a tank design which I could believe in. It's not a state code: it's a federal code now. We had some resistance here in Tucson and Pima County.

So that was fun. Got a lot of satisfaction out of it. We weren't accepted into the best society, but we didn't care about that, either. One time Helen and I were up at a party in the foothills, why, I don't know. I'd put in a septic tank for one of the guests, and I guess he didn't expect to see this old ditchman at a falutin' party. He came over to Helen and growled in a rather derogatory voice, "Do you know your husband digs sewers?" If I'd heard him I might have gotten riled, but Helen just smiled and said, "Yes, and we meet some of the nicest people that way." She could disarm a porcupine. Damn right. We met a lot of nice people.

We first started building septic tanks about 1948. Form building I love, because you're working backward, in reverse. Starting in about 1950 I had the first steel

Helen Hayden in 1954.

Hayden family Christmas gathering in Tucson, 1956. Left to right: Juan Xavier, Fergus Mera, Gwyneth Xavier, Dorothy Morse, Helen Hayden, Phoebe Mera, and Mary, Steve, Serena, and Julian Hayden Jr. (Photograph by Julian Hayden)

septic-tank forms in this end of the state. I'd send one man out with a pickup truck with a set of forms, set it in place, pour it, and come home again. Come back the next day and strip them out and move them to another job, see? Oh we poured hundreds of them. It made us ten dollars or twenty dollars a tank, what the hell, as long as it made a profit.

Old John Mason was precasting septic tanks. He had a little tiny tank that he made, and I used to buy them from him. We'd haul them out and dump them in a hole. I knew John and his wife and their sons, they were nice people. But John died, so I bought the business and set it up down there at Tucson Rock & Sand, where that big hotel is now at Pantano and Speedway. We set it up right beside the cement plant there, so it was very convenient.

One thing leads to another, so I finally built the tanks for the Titan missile sites. Then Phil Hunziker, the contractor, talked me into building precast manholes down at Patagonia. I knew that was the only way to go, but they weren't acceptable in Pima County. The city and county wouldn't take them, because they said concrete manholes would rot out. Finally, I got them accepted. Hunziker convinced the city it better be done. Phil's company had the intersection of West Congress and the freeway torn up. It was a hell of a busy corner, and he had to put a sewer in with a sewer manhole right in the middle of the intersection. He had to block up the whole thing. And he said to the city, "Look, Hayden over there is making those concrete manholes. He's got them made; they're sitting there in his yard in storage; they're cured out. Let me pour a concrete base here," he said, "and he'll bring it out, set it in and we'll have it filled tonight. Otherwise you're going to wait a whole weekend."

Well, they let him do it. So we took it down, hell, it took an hour and a quarter to load up a truck here with what we needed, go down, set it up, and be home. Maybe an hour and a half and the job was done. So the city gave up. That was a break I'd been waiting for, for a long time.

Jackie Stum used to be with Johnson Construction, precasters out on Demoss Petrie Road—now you know how long I've been here: it's Grant Road today. They got into casting beams and slabs, and Tanner bought them out on the Casa Grande Highway at that big yard they were building. T-beams, precast beams, and all. Old Pappy Johnson and Jackie and I were all very good friends. So I remarked one day, "You know, it's expensive building forms, isn't it?"

Jackie grinned, and he said, "Yeah. While you're building forms, you sure eat beans. But once you've got them built and paid for, you can have a little side of meat with those beans once in awhile." And it was the truth. That's when we started to turn to the profit side of the ledger, after twenty-five years or whatever. You see, that's the difference: he lives to contract, he loves it. He also intends to retire when he's fifty-five. And I contracted to live, which is just the opposite.

All I wanted out of it was to be doing something that interested me, and to feed the family and educate the kids and get me some money to do what I wanted to do, go to Pinacate or whatever, see? And take care of Helen, of course. There's a difference. Different approach. So I was perfectly content to stay right in the middle. I was too big for the little boys and too small for the big boys. So I was chocked in that notch. The big boys would call me when they didn't want to be bothered. And the little guys couldn't get up there, so it worked out fine.

Pouring precast septic tanks in 1962 at the Hayden Excavation Service yard, possibly for use at the Titan Missile Silo Site. (Photograph by Julian Hayden)

Hayden Excavation Service employee Pete Muñiz, ca. 1963. (Photograph by Julian Hayden)

Years ago Web Brown started up in business, and he started following me around. Finally, I caught on to what he was doing, because I was losing work to him. So whenever a man would call me, he'd want a bid on a sewage job or whatever, and I'd say, "Fine." So I'd size them up, and the man quite often would say, "Now is that your best price?" And I'd conceal my rage because that always made me mad.

And I'd say, "Yes, that's my best price, but I'll tell you. I know how it is, dollars are short. Why don't you call a man named Brown? And you might let it be known to him what I've quoted, because he might be able to give you a lower price." He did, he always gave a lower price, and I was giving the man my estimated cost, and sometimes a few dollars under it. So after several months of that, Brown called me up. He said, "Hayden! How do you stay in business?"

I said, "What are you talking about?"

He said, "You know, I've taken a number of jobs away from you and I've lost my hind end on every damn one of them. How do you do it?"

And I said, "I don't know, Web, maybe I'm just a better businessman than you are." Bang! Down went the receiver, and all of a sudden he quit following me around.

The subdividers came in in '46 and '47. Until then it was mostly individual contractors building individual houses. Carter Henrisey built a lot of brick houses, particularly on the north side of Speedway between Tucson Boulevard and Campbell. They were rather small, fine houses, but they're still standing. Brick was cool, particularly if you double-walled it. And it was all made right here, we had three or four brickyards. We have three different brickyards represented in my patio brick out here. That's why the marks are upward. Tucson Pressed Brick, Louis DeVry, Bill Grabe, all friends of mine. The yards were on the Santa Cruz in the Saint Mary's area.

American Homes had the first subdivisions, down around Fifth and Swan, in 1946. The city building code and the FHA code, too, called for the waterlines to go overhead. You weren't allowed to put them under the floor. And in the winter of '46–'47, we had cold weather. My thermometer outside the tents here read six one night and seven the next night. I had a brass faucet plumbed out of the wall, just right up against the adobe, and that burst in the night, it was so cold. Oh, it killed palm trees and orange trees all over Tucson. All the ceilings fell in those American Homes houses, so they changed the code and put the waterlines under the floor after that.

Pueblo Gardens was built in the 1950s sometime. That was a Del Webb project. I remember Pueblo Gardens, and Western Hills, too. Jake Jacobson, vice president of Del Webb, called me. I was doing an awful lot of trenching at the time, with my machine. He said, "I've got a contract job for you." So I went over. Three hundred houses, hell of a lot of them. Big job. So we got together and made a price, and he brought out the contract, about a dozen legal pages. And you had to take a reading glass to read them. And I started through them, and I handed them back to him, and he said, "What's the matter?"

I said, "Jake, damn it, I can work the rest of my life and not earn enough money to pay a lawyer smart enough to read all of that and understand it. I don't want the job. Thank you anyway." He looked at me and he grinned, and that was the end of it. A friend of mine took it. He called me and said, "I got a wonderful job!"

"The hell you have, what is it?"

He said, "I got the trenching on Pueblo Gardens," or Western Hills, I don't know which.

"Oh," I said, "by the foot?"

And he said yep.

"What'd you get?"

He said, "I gave it to them at seven cents a foot."

"But," I said, "Freddie, that's less than cost. It was going to cost me ten cents, or more, if I took it, and there's caliche there. I know where the caliche is, and so do you. What'd you give them seven cents for?"

"Well," he said, "if it was a single house, I'd have said ten cents, but here's three hundred houses!"

I said, "Do you mean if you had a thousand, you'd pay them? What's the matter, are you crazy?" Well, of course, it busted him.

I had a foreman, a very nice young foreman, lived up on the corner. We were pouring custom septic tanks for people. A crew would dig the hole, and he'd throw the forms up in the truck and take them over and set them. Then he'd call for the concrete and pour them, and the next day he'd strip them and go set another one. We were getting down to a routine. But about the fourth time he did it, he forgot something.

He didn't come back. So I finally went down hunting him, and he was down in South Tucson, and standing looking sadly at the tank. He'd left the center braces out and poured the concrete, so the forms had buckled, and there were so many yards of concrete down there with the bent steel. The mix was still plastic, fortunately. And I said, "Uh-oh, better lift the braces out."

And he said, "Yep. Shall I go home now?"

I said, "Why, hell, no! You got a shovel. Get it dug out before it hardens. I'm going to let you do it, too, because you spilled it." So I stood around and watched him, we didn't talk, he dug it all out.

I helped him pull the forms out, and he said, "Now do I go home?"

I said, "No, you take it down to the welders and get them straightened."

He said, "Shall I show up in the morning?"

I said "Damn it, Dean, you're not going to do it again, are you?"

He said, "No."

"Why," I said, "you're just beginning to make a good hand! You do it a second time, you can go talk to yourself down the road. But not the first time." He made me a hell of a good man.

I knew Steve Gollob. I met him in '39 when we were working out at Saguaro National Monument. Coming back from work one night, he slid off the high-crown dirt road in the mud. East Broadway was a high-crown dirt road. Wssht! and you're off in the ditch. So, I pulled him back up on the road with my CCC truck. He was from Central Europe. He'd been gassed during World War I, and then he came out here and homesteaded at the northwest corner of Broadway and Pantano. He took up all that land where all those shopping centers are now. Gollob Road is named after him. He had all that homesteaded, too. Prudence Road was named for one of his daughters, I think. He had that whole area over to Camino Seco.

He had a big concrete barn that he raised mushrooms in. He was also a plant pathologist at the university. He had a tremendous deposit of alluvial soil there on the terrace, on the Pantano. Somebody was hauling soil out of it, and then I did. Gollob charged so much a load. I needed a dump truck, and I needed a loader for my other work, so this filled in. I hauled out of there for years. I mixed gray soil and silts and Red Mesa topsoil and gypsum, and I screened it. I built my own plant, when I was still working with Audish. It was good advertising, anyway. It kept equipment available, and men available. I had as many as thirty men working at a time, but usually only six or eight. Usually we had three or four crews here and there. I didn't make any money at the soil business, but it kept the trucks and loaders working and available when I wanted them on my contract jobs.

I did work for the Desert Museum. The Arizona-Sonora Desert Museum began in my backyard. Bill Carr drew up the papers, and we signed them in the patio.

I dug more damn holes out there and poured more damn concrete. Then it was small, when we all knew each other, then it was possible. My men liked to go out there—my operators, my drivers—we'd go out on Saturday. I'd pay their wages, of course, but I'd contribute the equipment. We'd take septic tanks out and dig holes and set 'em. We did a lot of work—furnished topsoil and garden mix. Around the otter pond, that's all planted in the special garden mix that I made out here in a big drum. I gave 'em most of it. Once in a while I'd send 'em a bill. Then they got big and had no more use for little guys like me, so, by God, I got mad and just quit doing anything out there.

At the first meeting of that board of advisors for the *Journal of the Southwest*, some joker wanted everybody introduced. You know, people say various things when they're called upon, some of them want to talk for twenty minutes and some don't say much. When it came to me, I said, "My name's Hayden, I hang around the fringes of things, and that's that." That startled them, I think, didn't it? At the next meeting I didn't want us to all be strangers, so I amplified it, and I said, "I'm the only person here probably who is an honorary life member of the American Society of Sanitary Engineering." That startled them, too, didn't it? Probably the only one in the state as far as that goes. That sounds big, but you've got to notice the "-ing" on "engineering." Didn't say "engineers"; it says "engineering." That's for us plumbers, you know.

Pete Mejia, who worked for the city of Tucson, was famous. I was digging a cesspool down on Anita Street or someplace like that next to the Santa Cruz, one time. We were just finishing it off, and Pete came by. He said, "Hayden, what the hell you doing?"

"Putting in a cesspool for this place because there is no room for anything else."

"What are you doing that for, there's a sewer right behind the house and there's a sewer right here in the street."

I said, "There's nothing in City Hall on it."

He said, "That figures. Come with me." And I walked back, and here was a sewer main and collecting line right behind their property line. He showed me the manhole up there some distance, out in the street, and he said, "Look, come down here. Have one of your men bring a shovel, dig down right here." And there was a manhole.

"Well," I said, "now what in the hell are we going to do?" He said, "We're not going to do anything, finish that damn cesspool." He knew the location of every manhole in the city of Tucson because he'd been there. And when he died, why, hell, the city's never been the same, the utilities department. He knew the waterlines and the sewers one end to the other. He was a great old boy. One time Pete and a bunch of other city employees were fired over some little tiff, but Pete knew he'd get his job back because he was the only one who knew where anything was.

Reminds me a little bit of Omar Turney of Phoenix, who used to be a city engineer in Maricopa County. He was the man who mapped all the prehistoric canals and wrote *The Land of the Stone Hoe* and so forth. He laid out north Phoenix, Central Avenue past a certain point, laid out everything. The city finally let him go, retired him. The new engineers went out, and you know they couldn't tie anything together. They came to Turney and said, "What's the matter here?"

"Well," he said, "simple enough. Some situations are mighty easy to cure."

"How do we cure it?"

He said, "You see this little black book? It's my retirement money." And, by God, they anted up.

At Snaketown II, in 1964 or '65, Agnese Lockwood and her husband Chip came from New York as volunteer workers. Agnese worked in the laboratory washing potsherds and sorting and all that, and Chip worked out in the field, in the excavation of Snaketown II, where Haury had returned after thirty years to where we had dug in the 1930s. Lockwood had attended Point of Pines in 1946, when Haury opened that field school. A number of famous men attended that first one or two years at Point of Pines, a famous field school.

I went out one day a week for the duration to check the equipment and kibitz and so forth. And I was with Chip out in the field down toward the river one day, in a deep ditch, and one of his Pimas was digging down there and knocked out some potsherds way down in the bottom, about six or eight feet deep. We looked at it, and by golly, he'd cut right into the oldest canal, the earliest canal that we ever found out there. It goes back to before the time of Christ. Chip was a modest man, and he never claimed discovery rights on it, but he and the Indian found it and I watched them find it, so I vouched for them. So when the job was over, Chip and Aggie wanted to move to Tucson, and they found a place up on north Campbell.

Chip and Agnese met on the Irrawaddy River in Burma, on the road to Mandalay, when they were working for the United Nations. Talk about a romantic place to meet! "On the road to Mandalay / Where the flying fishes play ..." Alger Hiss was secretary or undersecretary or something of the sort of the UN. That's where they all went together. And Chip and Aggie were always in touch with Alger Hiss, and I corresponded with him, too.

I still remember most of the words to "On the Road to Mandalay." My father had an Edison Diamond Disk phonograph in Montana. One of my earliest remembrances is waking up to the music on that old Diamond Disk with those old half-inch-thick records. And "On the Road to Mandalay" was one of the songs. And, oh my God, I remember that so well, I can sing it all the way through if I wanted to, but I don't think your tape recorder could take it.

Why did I do a newspaper column? About 1950 or thereabouts, the Small Business Administration was lending money, and I found myself in a position in which I had

The Hayden Excavation Service soil-screening plant, November 1962. (Photograph by Julian Hayden)

to have some money. I needed ten thousand dollars to buy equipment and to build my business up in order to stay in business, otherwise I would never get beyond a jackhammer and a compressor.

So I went down to Southern Arizona Bank, and talked to Harry Tennison, a good old Texas boy who liked to gamble. And I said, "Mr. Tennison, I need some money, and I think I need about ten thousand dollars. I know damn well you folks can't loan it to me, because I haven't got the assets to back it up. But, maybe we can find something."

"Well," he said, "I think we can. The Small Business Administration might do it." And he said, "The only way it can be done is for them to take possession of everything you've got, everything you own and ever will own. And guarantee the return of our money. And we can loan it to you with their guarantee."

"Well," I said, "let's see what happens." So I did.

We paid it back. I bought the equipment and built the big topsoil screening plant on Steve Gollob's property on the Pantano River. I went into it properly, and I built conveyors and everything else with a platform and lots of equipment. And then I had to advertise the topsoil, because nobody else had ever screened topsoil in Tucson. We had a big supply of it pretty well locked up.

So in 1956 I went down to an advertising agency, not knowing any better, and they cooked up the damndest mess of type fonts and idiocies I ever saw in my life and they charged me for it. I thought, "Why, shucks I can do better than this," so I started writing my own damned ads. And I did it for damned near twenty years. I spent lots of money on it, but it was my vanity press. I could say what I liked pretty well, and I paid for it, too, in more ways than one. But I never regretted any of it.

And I paid Harry Tennison back, too. With interest. From then on, I could borrow anything I wanted. I had a good association with the Southern Arizona Bank.

Before I went into business for myself, before I needed any money, I was working by myself with a gasoline jackhammer all alone. Helen and I were driving an old Model A Ford sport coupe that needed fixing. Helen needed it, and I was using it for a work truck, for which it wasn't quite suited. I needed a pickup. So I go down to Mundey Johnston, the vice president who ran the local Valley Bank. I gave him a letter from Walter Binson, the president of Valley National Bank in Phoenix, who was a good friend of mine. The letter told Mundey Johnston to do what he could for me if I ever came in. Probably not the most tactful thing to have done, taking Mundey Johnston the letter. But anyway, I did.

I told him what I wanted, twelve hundred dollars to buy a pickup, a Chevrolet pickup. I had picked one that could take my jackhammer. I was beginning to hire people. Johnston looked at it. "Well," he said, "I'll tell you, Julian. You work hard and you save your money, and when you get enough money saved, then you buy something." And meanwhile I was watching him. His secretary was handing him stacks of bounced checks, and he was flipping through them. "Well, this one is okay, my wife has tea with her; this one, I play golf with this one; this, throw out." And that was the way credit was handled at the Valley National Bank.

So I said, "Well, thank you anyway, Mr. Johnston."

When he turned me down, I went upstairs to the small loan department and asked if I could call Phoenix, and he said, "Yes," and I called Luther Brumbaugh, the head of the installment loan department in Phoenix, and I said, "Mr. Brumbaugh, I need three hundred bucks."

"Well," he said, "tell the man to get on the phone," and I did, and I got three hundred bucks which I didn't need and didn't want. I wanted twelve hundred. So I sort of grinned to myself and walked out with three hundred dollars anyway.

And then I went down the street to Southern Arizona Bank. I talked to Hubert d'Autremont, president of the bank, and I walked out with my money on my face. Mrs. d'Autremont was a great friend of Gwyneth Xavier's. Gwyneth's husband, Juan Xavier, had gotten drunk one rainy night and disappeared, so I went over to help find him. Hubert d'Autremont, the banker, and I hunted for Juan Xavier in the rain and the cold until we found him. It's the only time I had ever met Mr. D., but that's the way business was done in those days.

Red Greth used to come pick the ads up every two weeks. Often it was the first draft, pulled at the last second out of the typewriter and handed to him. I'd read them later, when they came out in the paper. I pretty well perfected, in my own opinion, the technique of saying what I wanted to say in five inches of type, and it's two and a half high, which is five square inches. Red remarked a while ago, to a friend of mine, that the newspaper spent more on legal fees checking my copy to see nobody was going to get sued than they ever got out of me. But a lot of people read them. I still run across somebody who read them and remembers me.

Some people wanted to punch me in the nose. A man at a party up in the foothills overheard me talking with someone in proper English, which I can do if I have to. And he came over to me and he said, "Hayden, do you write those ads?"

And I said, "Yeah."

He said, "I thought you were illiterate."

"Hayden Says" advertisement from May 18, 1975, featuring Helen's recipe for Potroast Picante Hayden.

And I said, "Well, you know that A on A Mountain?" and I was perfectly deadpan.

He said, "Well, yes."

And I said, "Well, you know, by God, I've got it whupped, and when they put B up there, I'll whup it, too." And he stared at me for a while and he turned around and walked off, and I never saw him again. I used that damn Tex-Mex, Texas–New Mexico lingo that I enjoy so much, because I've spent so much time with cowhands and construction workers.

Some of the columns were very practical. They talked about how to make chili and other things. One time I quoted Helen's recipe for pot roast. She liked to cook pot roast once in a while, and she cooked up a nice roast, and she put some chile and what not in it and named it Pot Roast Picante Hayden. So I printed it. And a few weeks later a woman called me, and she said, "Mr. Hayden?" And I said, "Yes."

"Remember that pot roast recipe you printed?"

I said, "Well yes, of course I do."

She said, "I cut it out, and I just want you to know my daughter is just taking it to Okinawa now."

When a man is coming in twenty minutes to pick up the ad, you decide what to write. At least I do. I talked a lot about climate and water conservation and climatic change. Archaeology. My father looked at me one time, and his eyes bugged, and he

Helen Hayden at home in Tucson, 1959.

said, "That's almost poetic." I talked a lot about archaeology. That's something I thought I knew a little bit about.

Hell, that's the way I like to write reports, too, sometimes. I don't get very far with it. Like those animal stories I had [*Journal of the Southwest,* 1987]. That was the genesis of them, I would just come in here and sit down and write what I had been talking about out in the patio. Nothing to that—anybody can do that, just maybe sometimes they don't.

I discontinued the column because Helen died. There wasn't any point in it any longer. So I said so, and then I quit. I sold out. That ended that. And I told you one time that when I come up against a roadblock, and it doesn't make sense to try to break the block, I go around it. That's what I did here. I went around it. I took another course in my life, another tack. I found myself on the lee shore, if you want to get nautical about it.

11. Studies in Desert Archaeology

I happened to come across Malcolm Rogers's photo book just the other night when a stack of books in the front room fell over. Luckily I wasn't under it, otherwise I wouldn't be sitting here now. This album fell out of it. I'd forgotten about it. It's a remarkable collection of photographs. Few of them are identified, but I can identify them. Some of these go back to the 1920s, Baja California, the Southern California deserts, and White Tanks.

Here are two beautiful pictures of White Tanks themselves. They are potholes in white tufa in a very deep canyon in the Little Sheep Mountains near the Kofas. They hold water. Malcolm found this place in the late 1920s, early 1930s, and in 1945, when he married his second wife, part of their honeymoon was at White Tanks. In those days it was hard to get to. The mountain sheep habitat in the Arizona-Sonora Desert Museum is patterned after White Tanks.

He and his bride, Fran, built a little camp right at White Tanks. I never thought I'd see the place where they had honeymooned, but when I went over two summers ago with Westec, Inc., in the army helicopters from the proving grounds [Yuma Proving Grounds], we just went over there and sat down right beside this camp. Right beside the tanks. It was so nice!

Malcolm and his bride took the first half of their honeymoon there, and then they came over here to Tucson with Helen and me. They took the second half in a contractor's portable office that I had bought when we closed down the air base work and put out here where the trees are now. We were living in tents. Malcolm and his bride got their exercise by moving adobes around from one stack to another and getting them out of the way. It was great fun. I don't remember how long they stayed.

She was a cute little button, a little dancer, and stacked. She wore the minimum, of course, because she knew she was stacked. She was a nice girl, and we had a lot of fun. So, it was wonderful to see their White Tanks camp: the hearths, the windbreak, and the table formed by putting an old plank from some mine in an ironwood tree. I was fooling around, and I found Malcolm and Fran's initials on the hearthstone. Nobody had ever noticed them before because nobody knew the story of the place, except me. So I pointed it out and took some pictures of it.

We had an Army video cameraman taking down all Paul Ezell's and my words of wisdom on this trip. I sat down on the hearth beside this tree, and he did whatever you do with a video camera for posterity. That was nice. Then Paul wandered in and so I slid over. I assled over into a packrat nest without thinking, so the next scene on that damn camera recorder was me leaning over while the ladies in the party pulled cholla out of my tight Levis. I took that with great dignity and aplomb, I assure you. What

White Tanks, Little Sheep Mountains, Arizona.

else could I do? They never sent me any prints, but there are photographs in this album of that first camp, which took me back.

How did Malcolm Rogers get where he got? Malcolm taught himself. He was interested in archaeology from the time he was a child. He grew up around Syracuse; it's in his biography and his obituary, which I wrote. The information is in Dave Hanna's biography of Malcolm, which he wrote as a master's thesis some years ago at San Diego State University. I have a copy of it if you want to read it. I put a lot of it in there for him.

Malcolm's grandfather, Thomas Rogers [probably his great-grandfather, 1792–1856] built the second steam locomotive in the United States, and founded the Rogers Machine Works [Rogers Locomotive Works, originally called Rogers, Ketchum & Grosvenor] in Paterson, New Jersey. His father was an electrical inventor, Fred Rogers. He invented the variable speed electrical control [the Rogers Variable Speed Changer] used on all streetcars and many electric boats. He licensed the patents to General Electric. Rogers Engineering Works is in Trenton, New Jersey, where my friend Jonathan Gell is doing historic archaeological work now on the ruins of the old farm. And he also invented the electric light meter, which is used everywhere, all over the world. He invented it, but the day he was to file his patent applications, he picked up a British journal, and a Britisher had filed just two or three weeks before, so that was that. Anyway, that's the kind of background Malcolm grew up in.

Fred Rogers, Malcolm's father, was on the *Least Petrel*, the Bancroft vessel that circumnavigated Baja California. Fred Rogers accompanied the ship, examining shell middens, caves, and so forth for Early Man archaeology. This cruise was written up in a book called *The Flight of the Least Petrel* by Griffing Bancroft. They were a family of very smart people.

And you were talking about Raphael Pumpelly. Pumpelly lived not very far away from Malcolm's family. Of course Raphael was the age of Malcolm's father, but Malcolm as a little boy would go over there and spend whole afternoons with Pumpelly in Pumpelly's library while Raphael told stories to him and the other kids about all his travels around the world, including the Camino del Diablo. He got Malcolm very much interested in archaeology, anthropology, and travel, of course. Isn't that wonderful? It's one of the reasons Malcolm had the interests that he had, I guess. He grew up in that.

Malcolm told me that when he was eleven or twelve years old, on the bank of some stream, possibly the Hudson River, he determined that there was a stratigraphy. Now, that was new in those days. Nels Nelson founded the business of stratigraphic studies in 1905 or thereabouts. And my father and M. R. Harrington had studied that and worked on Long Island, prior to 1909, which was pioneering work.

But Malcolm was about twelve years old and possibly a little younger when he found this site of camps on the Hudson River where he determined that Algonquin culture lay below Iroquoian culture. Malcolm's great interest was archaeology. But his father said, "No way, it's a sissy occupation." So Malcolm went to Syracuse University, I think, to become a geological chemist. He never got his degree, but he worked as a mining chemist at Washington and Idaho, and here and there before World War I. Then he was in the Marines, although he never got overseas. When he mustered out, he went to Escondido, his father retired, and they bought an avocado grove, which was great in those days of 1919. From there he started looking for archaeology immediately. That's what got him started.

Rogers went over to Santa Fe sometime in the 1920s [1926] and worked for Dr. Edgar Hewett. He worked at Puye [New Mexico], excavating a structure which lies just outside the cliff. I don't know how long he worked for Hewett, but Hewett used to be director of the San Diego Museum, and that's where they met. And when Hewett went to Santa Fe, Malcolm eventually went over on a visit and worked for a while.

In 1930, we finished up at Mesa House, as I told you, and afterward I finished illustrating the report. I was on the loose, so I packed up my motorcycle, my old Indian. I put a bedroll on the handlebars, and off I went to San Diego. I went to the San Diego Museum, out of curiosity to see what it was like, and I met Malcolm. Didn't mean anything to him and not much to me, either. He was a short man. I looked at my journal a few months ago, and it reminded me of him. He had a penetrating gaze, and a stern face, and I noted it at the time: this guy's a tough hombre, in effect. He was a hard man. And a smart man.

So, I went on and I stopped at somebody's wells on the old Jacumba Highway, and a girl named Ila Horr took me down into the arroyo and showed me some pictographs, which were interesting. Then I went on, and I went down to Coyote Wells. I wanted to go to Mount Signal; I'd never been there.

This was June, more or less, getting hot. So I headed for Mount Signal: I could see it. But I blew a tire halfway down. That's when I learned about thirst. Blew a rear tire, so I took the tire off. I didn't have any patches, and I only had an army quart canteen of water. Not very smart of me. I started walking north. And I walked and I walked. Then I saw a sign: "Bad Water, four miles." I sat there for quite a while thinking about that, whether to go thataway or straight ahead because by that time I thought that Coyote Wells was on the other side of the mountain range ahead of me. Fortunately it wasn't.

When I got in, I was more than a little dry. I had a can of soup, and a young fellow from the service station drove me back down, which was real nice of him. I've always carried extra water since. I was lucky, because if I had headed for that Bad Water, it would have been another story, wouldn't it? So anyway, that's how I first met Malcolm.

And then in 1932 I went down to stay on the *Star of India*. It was in San Diego Harbor. She'd just been tied up after coming off the Alaska run. She was a salmon packer. I came down with the intention of going over to the San Diego Museum and collecting some Mayan designs. There I met Malcolm again, and we got better acquainted.

I don't think I saw him again until '36 or thereabouts, when I was working at Pueblo Grande. He knew Odd Halseth and Mrs. Halseth, and he came over to visit, or was passing through. I met him again, and in '38 he called me and offered me a job for the summer running the excavation at the so-called San Dieguito Site on the San Dieguito River, now called the Harris Site.

So I took three of my CCC men with me, who were getting ready to pay out anyway. We did that job, and from then on Malcolm and I were good friends. He was very fond of Helen and Helen was fond of him. He had a lovely wife, whom we both loved dearly. He later divorced her in a fit of middle-aged madness, which he later on regretted, but that's all right, too. So, we were sort of a family from then on.

I remember Malcolm's 1940 Dodge. We didn't have four-wheel-drives in those days that were available for us ordinary folks. I don't think they really had many trucks that were suitable for this. And I don't think he could have afforded two cars anyway. He and his father financed all their own survey for field work for the San Diego Museum, so he ain't got no money.

They were working without salary. Malcolm was finally a curator and eventually director when the war broke out, but pay was secondary. When I went over in '38 to be job foreman at the San Dieguito Harris Site, Malcolm and Fred, his father, put a good deal of money into that in addition to the Carnegie grant that paid for me and my crew to come over from Tucson. They housed us, Helen and me and two kids. Malcolm contributed to that, too, and then later on when I took a big mosaic photograph of the cross section of the trench, Malcolm found money somewhere to pay for that and pay me a little bit, too.

Another photo in that album shows Malcolm as a very much younger man, holding a metate, up in the Jacumba region of the San Dieguito mountains. He's probably forty years old at that time. It is a picture that we used in *American Anthropologist* with his obituary. I see he's wearing shorts, and you can see how sleek and well-muscled his legs are. When I went over to San Diego to straighten out his affairs after his death, the county coroner asked me how old Malcolm was. His birth certificate said seventy, and he couldn't believe it. I said, "Well, that's what it is."

The man said, "At seventy, he had the muscle tone and the skin tone of a man of fifty or younger. He must have taken awfully good care of himself."

I said, "No, on the contrary, he drank lots of tequila and applejack and smoked a couple of packs of cigarettes a day all his life. He was just one of those men." He had good genes. His father was in his late eighties when he died, and he was still stumping around the country being mean and cussing and snorting.

Another scene looks out of a cave, shows an elderly gentleman looking into the distance; it's Fred Rogers. One shot has him with his famous staff that he carried around, looking off into the desert. He always had one, and it was well polished. People were well-advised to stay away from its reach when he got mad. I thought he was going to use it on me that night we talked about the Hualapai tiger. We were sitting around the Coleman lantern on a job one night, and got to talking about Hualapai tigers, kissing bugs, and Fred said, "We don't have them this side of the Coast Range."

I said, "Well, Fred, what's that?" And there was one walking toward the light. And Fred poked it and it rammed him right in the end of his finger; his finger was unusable for weeks. And he blamed me for it. He was furious at me. He thought I'd done it on purpose. But at his age, he was entitled to it. He was in his eighties. After all, I'm only three or four years away from being as unreasonable as he was.

Later Malcolm bought a small ranch at High Pass, up in the mountains between the border and the highway from San Diego to El Centro. He had divorced his first wife and married a young woman named Frances Grace. Malcolm took his four-wheel-drive jeep and camped at White Tanks in '45. He used a tent, and he and Frances built a hearth and windbreak on their honeymoon. And they also honeymooned right here, by God, in my house. So, you know, it all ties together, somehow. It's fascinating to me: all the little chances that occur in a man's life, and each one slants him in another direction. Eventually he had four children with Fran, to his dismay and surprise. He thought

Malcolm Rogers with metate, in the Jacumba region of the San Dieguito Mountains, California.

he was too old to have children. The ranch went broke. The investments went to hell. When he fixed the place up, I used to go over and visit him. This particular winter they had snow. The roof blew off the office in a blizzard, and I have a picture of the office with snow all over the shelves and chairs and everything else. The outhouse door blew off, and it was a little chilly sitting with icicles hanging from the seat.

I invited Malcolm over to the Ventana Cave excavation in '41, and he stayed with us for several days and looked it over and saw the resemblance between the Ventana Cave lower material and the desert material of Southern California, and California. I don't think he was welcome, because the emphasis in those days was on Folsom and Cochise over in the East, but since then it's been all ironed out, and we're all happy with it. The evidence is that it's Californian, pure and simple, with one or two intrusive points from travelers from the East, obviously, who settled there.

Malcolm and my father had known each other only through me. I took my father and Malcolm to Ventana Cave in 1959. We went down to get some C-14 samples. On the way, between Quijotoa and Santa Rosa, is a little upthrust of basalt. Malcolm looked over, and he said, "If you were to go over there, you would see a trail going from north to south and vice-versa over that hump, and there would be a shrine in the middle of it. And it would be San Dieguito and Amargosan." He was using those terms in those days.

My father said, "How do you know that?"

Malcolm shrugged and he said, "Well, I've never been here before, but I know the country, terrain, somehow."

So I said, "Let's go up." We went over, and there it was, just as Malcolm had said. My father thought about that and didn't say anything.

We got to Ventana, and Malcolm was trying to chop out some C-14 samples out of that study block that we'd left there in 1942. He mashed his thumb, so he went away to talk about it to himself, and my father turned to me and said, "What's with all this San Dieguito talk? What is it?" So I explained it to him.

Fred Rogers at cave.

Malcolm Rogers and Julian Hayden at Ventana Cave, Arizona, April 1959. (Photograph by Irwin Hayden)

"Well," he said, "has it been adjudicated by his peers? Has a committee of his peers investigated these sites and agreed with him?"

I said, "No. Quite the contrary."

And he said, "Why?"

I said, "Well, for one reason, the evidence is so scanty that once a site has been collected there is nothing left, nothing to show anybody. And secondly, conventional thinking is that there is no archaeology in the desert, so nobody would look if he asked them."

"Well," my father said, "in that case, it's completely invalid, isn't it?"

I replied, "Why do you say that?"

He said, "When a jury of his peers come out and pass on it, and approve it, then it's likely to be true. Until then, there's nothing to it at all. Just speculation."

"Well," I said, "you went to Harvard, and I didn't. But I have my own ideas and I'm sold on them." He eventually came around after a number of years and several publications. But that was the old 1905 approach of the anthropologists. For F. W. Putnam and all the rest of them, if you've read your history of archaeology, everything had to be approved. Haury was trained in the same mold.

We were just ahead of our time, is all.

And this isn't quite off the subject, but Tita Braniff from the Instituto Nacional in Mexico held a reunion in Hermosillo in 1974, a gathering of people interested in the archaeology, anthropology of northwest Mexico. I was invited, and I went down and put on a slide show on the Pinacate, which I hadn't expected to do, but four hundred people showed up. She advertised it all over Hermosillo. My Spanish was not good, and I had too many slides, but what do you do?

So I put it on, and I showed some slides of the Yuha Man excavation going in Imperial Valley, which Morlin Childers had conducted. I watched the cairn taken down, and I saw the bones removed from within it, and to my mind, it could be equated with the early material in Pinacate, Malpais, preglacial, which of course was heresy. So I said so: 20,000 to 22,000 with the C-14 dates for the caliche on the bones, and on the bones themselves, which was very gratifying to me.

As I left the lecture hall, Haury said to me, "You had no business making statements like that in public."

I said, "Why not?"

He said, "Your peers have not inspected it, and have not agreed with you. It hasn't been approved."

By that time, I was tired and hot and a little disgusted with myself because I'd had too many slides, and I said, "Well, I'll tell you, Doc, I don't have any peers. Does that answer that?"

And his eyes popped and he said, "What do you mean?"

"Well," I said, "in my opinion, a peer of mine is a man who is competent in his field, has been in my area, has inspected my evidence, and has either agreed or disagreed on the basis of my evidence, not his or his preconceived notions. You say that my statements are improper, which is equivalent to saying that if I went to Snaketown, where I had never been before, and I were to make statements about your archaeology there, then I would be doing what people you say are my peers would be doing in my area."

"But," I continued, "Dr. Haury, I worked two years at Snaketown. I know damn near as much about it as you do. I come a damn sight closer to being a peer than anybody you can send to my region."

So we went off and had a drink. And I think I had a good point. And I still maintain it. Now, that's going to get me in trouble. I don't think it will make Emil mad. I hope not. Not after all these years.

Malcolm was working on Early Man in the desert. He didn't know what he had, and it took him years to find out, but when he did, then nobody would believe him except Leslie Spier, who talked him into writing it up for *American Anthropologist*. He called it the "scraper-maker culture," up in the high ground of the San Diego mountains. It turned out eventually to be San Dieguito II, the second stage of San Dieguito culture.

But when he got into the desert, he came across earlier and earlier stuff, so he finally worked out a sequence which is still perfectly valid and which I still *insist* is valid. Whether Malcolm's dating is wrong has nothing to do with it. He was very conservative. He was in a conservative world. He said San Dieguito I, whether it's in the middle Pluvial, is on this side of 5,000. There was a wet period and then a short dry period, and he thought it was in the wet period. Actually it was in the wet period long before that, like 11,000 or 17,000. But he didn't know that, and he didn't have the tools to do anything with it. It wasn't until Ventana Cave, when we got our C-14 dates, that we began to see what was possible, and he died before he could really put it into print.

But at any rate I was trained by him in the San Dieguito River, north of San Diego, in 1938. He invited me over there, and he obtained this job for me. I was working at Pueblo Grande on Hohokam stuff, so this was all new to me. I went over there, and we were looking for San Dieguito III, which turned out later to be about 8000 BP [before the present]. It's overlain by a sterile zone and then by La Jollan, then by a sterile zone and then by Yuman, Diegueño, in other words. It's all perfectly clear. Anyhow, that's where I learned about it. Not many people knew about it, but Malcolm did.

The Harris Site was a factory or camp site. The San Dieguito River north of San Diego, up near Escondido, in Pleistocene times cut down through valley fill and left terraces. Malcolm noticed, in one of these terraces it cut on the riverside, that there were artifacts coming out of his San Dieguito complex, San Dieguito III, the third stage of his San Dieguito complex.

So he managed to get a Carnegie grant to finance the job, and we went over for him and we all worked together, of course. We ran trenches into that terrace that went right out to the floor of the canyon walls and petered out. We got stratigraphy. It was not a type site; it wasn't even a factory site. It was a camp site, and the tools, the stone, had been brought in, partially roughed out, and they were just finished there. Also, points and knives were trimmed there after they had been broken, repointed, you know. We had all of that.

We didn't have any dates at that time, of course, in 1938. But it was overlaid by a sterile layer, and then there was La Jollan, which is a controversial occupation, controversial origin all down that coast. On top of that were Yuman and Diegueño. Diegueño were still living in the country. So, it was a stratified site. The only thing that's ever been written about it was a very brief report in the Carnegie yearbook.

I made a big photo mosaic, half the size of that kitchen wall, of the wall of a trench. That was quite a stunt in those days. It was the first time I'd ever heard of it, but it seemed to be possible. Later on I saw it written up in *American Antiquity* by some Japanese as a new technique, which he's welcome to.

I laid out this trench wall, which was six or eight feet high or more, so all the stratigraphy was exposed. It was about four feet wide, I guess, and I don't know how many feet long. And I laid it off with string, in a grid. I used Fred Rogers's Leica, which made him madder than hell, because he wanted to do it, but he was too old and crippled up to climb around. I could use only the central section of each frame. I had the negatives of the film machine printed with machine enlargements. And after we shot a section, they each had to be moved, so I had to figure that out, and lay out a grid accordingly and then photograph allowing for the overlaps.

Then, when I got all the things printed over in Phoenix, where we were living, I cut the centers out of each frame, which were in sharp focus, and laid them on this big piece of Masonite, so we had a beautiful picture of the stratigraphy. It took a lot of film and a lot of paper to do it, but it worked out very well. Then during the war it was taken down into the basement when the Navy took over the place for a hospital. Somebody forgot about it, and it eventually went to hell. I don't know if there is even a photograph of it now.

Malcolm wrote it up in greater detail in his manuscript on the San Dieguito complex, which was not completed at the time he was killed. After he died it was published, most of it, in *Ancient Hunters of the Far West*, the Copley book from San Diego. That's

San Dieguito Harris Site (California) profile, 1938.

the one I sputter about because of the format and of some omissions and commissions in there which confuse everybody.

The Harris Site has been misinterpreted by a lot of people since then, including Paul Ezell, Claude Warren, and God, I don't know who-all. But Tony Andretta over in Alpine and I depend on it as being a camp site for the last phase of the San Dieguito culture in that region, on the coastal side of the mountains. A late one, in other words.

In '58, when Paul Ezell and I were at Papago Tanks, Malcolm had fallen on hard times. He'd retired. He made some bad investments at the end of the Second World War and was broke. He had a wife and four children. One thing and another. Malcolm was working as a laborer for a landscaper to make a living, to eat. He and Frances were separated. So Helen and I had an idea. We talked it over, and we said, "Paul, would you call Malcolm, and tell him that friends of his have gotten together, set up a fund, to pay what little can be paid, enough to eke out his veteran's pension from World War I, and make it possible for him to come back into the field, to write his memoirs and write up his reports." Paul called. And Malcolm fell for it. Whether he did or not, I don't know; maybe he wanted to believe it. But really, we put him on our payroll as a clerk. We carried him on our payroll, took over title to his jeep, and paid all his expenses from then on out till he died. And we figured that was fair enough.

Malcolm Rogers lived archaeology. He was staying with us, living in the basement. His last word at night was archaeology, and first thing the next morning picked right up where he left off. I had to work. Had four kids to feed. I'd usually get up at 5:00 a.m. and read a paperback while I mapped the day. One day Rogers chided me for not being more serious about archaeology. I didn't get mad, but I did point out that not only did I have my own family to feed but those of twenty-five workers, too. I could have mentioned houseguests, too, but I didn't.

While living in Tucson, Rogers worked on his manuscript. First his notes were down here in Tucson, and that wasn't so bad. But then it was mail from then on after Rogers returned to San Diego. My God, the money we spent shipping manuscripts back and forth: whole, big envelopes full of Rogers's notes where he'd change his mind, and cut and paste and tear, and throw in scraps as it occurred to him. Helen went through that. I tried to go through some of it just recently when I was working on this report, but I couldn't make head or tail of it without devoting my whole time to it and starting from scratch. But she did. She knew more about it than I did or ever will. She probably knew as much as Rogers ever did. She was a hell of a good editor, as well as an archaeologist, and anthropologist, all of which she picked up because she was smart. Always marry a woman who's smarter than you are, my friend. Always. Every time.

Eventually Rogers had to go back to San Diego to work on his collections, and they wouldn't help. He continued it. And when he died, well, I went over and took care of things—I was his executor, of course. The Museum of Man would not help. They said, "Thanks, you're doing a wonderful service." "Thank you, too." But that's the way the world is, so what the hell.

He hadn't finished his report when he got killed. Helen and I were supposed to edit it. The first draft he had completed, and Helen had typed everything he had ever written. The San Diego folks came over and asked us about it, and we told them, "We'll edit it, when we're ready. Don't push us." Next thing we knew *The Ancient Hunters* was on the

Malcolm Rogers and Julian at the Hayden home, Tucson, 1958.

stands. I had to go buy a copy. And it's a mess. They probably made a nice tax deduction on that, sons of bitches. But what the hell, there's no use fussing about it now.

Malcolm Rogers taught us how to see desert archaeology. All other southwestern archaeologists thought in terms of the Four Corners country, like Pueblo I, II, and III. Paul Ezell, for example, came here under Byron Cummings, and that was his direction.

Byron Cummings, and I don't do him any disrespect, was like many of the oldtimers, a collector first, then an archaeologist. But he was a classicist, a Greek and Latin scholar, who was fascinated by digging up the old stuff. He worked out a sequence that suited him, though it became antiquated in the late 1920s. Cummings wouldn't go along with the changes, which is why eventually he went out. But parts of that have been changed, particularly the early parts, since C-14, or since Landers, or since Blackwater Draw, since the discovery of the association of man and bison, man and mammoth, Folsom, and so forth. That's what broke the pattern, the accepted pattern. It took years and years before the oldtimers would go along with the fact that Clovis points were found with mammoth, or Folsom points were found with bison. They just wouldn't buy it. Hrdlička was conservative. And few academics went along with the new finds. It was a very strictly controlled business at that time.

But that was Paul Ezell's background. He didn't know any more about desert archaeology than the Man in the Moon; how could he? So when he saw the stuff at Papago Tanks, his eyes were opened, and it takes an eye-opener. You train your eyes to see one thing, and that's all you can see.

Originally, Malcolm didn't know anything about Pimería Alta. He worked in Southern California and the southwestern part of Arizona. And he didn't get below the border. He wasn't involved in that. But he set up the archaeological criteria by which we were able to judge what we found in Pinacate and in Papaguería. By extension, he taught us to see all the way over to Trans-Pecos, Texas, and in the long run throughout the Southwest.

Malcolm laid the basis for the whole thing. And it was his encouragement that carried us. After Paul and I took him up what we found at Laguna Prieta in the way of pottery and what we found at Papago Tanks in the way of stone tools, Malcolm identified it and placed it in the historic sequence. That's what encouraged me to go ahead and get involved in the whole thing, because Papaguería was clearly the only place left where there was all of this material lying untouched and unstudied by anybody.

Our side of the borderline had been all messed up: tourists, travelers, other archaeologists, pot hunters, developments, and so forth. There was no place up here we could go. Down there in Pinacate it was untouched, as you know. Nobody got in there until the highway was built and the woodcutters blazed trails. And I followed the woodcutters; I was the next one in after them.

In 1951 Paul and Alan Olson and Tad Nichols reached Emilia Tanks, and hell, they didn't bother anything. They didn't pick up anything; they didn't know what the hell they were looking at, but they took some beautiful photographs. It was just like you and me going to the moon: what the hell do we look for? And when Paul and I went to Papago Tanks, he was looking for pottery. I was looking for Early Man. But I didn't know it was Early Man per se, in our sense now. I was looking for crude stone tools and cracked rock. For Paul, fortunately, all of a sudden his eye clicked, and then he saw what I saw.

Tony Andretta called me this morning, so excited he could hardly talk. We agreed that Malcolm had all the phases of San Dieguito over there in the deserts and on the coast, but they're separated, one area from another. And mine, too, down in Pinacate, we had Malpais I and Malpais II, but they're intermingled. And we have San Dieguito I, which hung on here in the Pinacate until the Altithermal, until 9000 [BP] more or less, but by that time on the coast San Dieguito III was full blown. This was just a bunch of hillbillies down in this country of the Pinacate and the lower deserts.

Archaeologist John Charles Kelley, Paul Ezell, biologist Barton H. Warnock, Tony Andretta, and Julian in 1979.

The Clovis people went down there hunting big game, passed through, and left some of their remains, points and scrapers and so forth. But they didn't stay. They went down there just the way the English went to Africa on safari: they came and they went, but they had no effect on local cultures.

Andretta in the Rio Grande has Malpais I, Malpais II, San Dieguito I, San Dieguito II, San Dieguito III, Clovis-Paleo, right there, sometimes superimposed but all in close enough relationship that you can sit there and see all of the changes in the technology as you come all the way through. Then all of the Texas Archaic comes right down to Spanish times. It's an incredible area. And nobody knows anything about it except Tony and his botanist friend Barton Warnock (who's a hell of a field man), and me. I'm just an onlooker and consultant and prodder, which is sometimes valuable. And it all goes back to Rogers with his pioneer work and the great good fortune I had in knowing him and working with him for so many years.

Malcolm taught himself how to see those patterns and those tools. There wasn't anything on the deserts in those days. There weren't any cliff dwellings, there weren't any pueblos, there weren't any pots, there weren't anything of anything, just cracked rock. But he recognized artifacts. He was a genius in his own way. He was a very conservative man, which befit his time. He talks about 4,000 years old for San Dieguito I, when San Dieguito I is, in Pinacate, older than 9,000. It goes back to the beginning of the Pluvial, probably, back in the glacial zones. He discarded Malpais finally in 1958 or '57 and included it with SD I.

He had no dates on varnish, so he had no way to date it, and he'd never been to Pinacate. Here in the Pinacate we have the whole thing through San Dieguito I on those pavements. It's a "laggard area"—that's a good term. Somebody called a similar thing "a tarriant variant," which is laying it on too much, I think. But it's a retarded area, held back for whatever reason.

But just as we have three stages of development that can be defined in Pinacate by just walking around Celaya Crater Site, Tony has all of them over there in a comparatively short stretch of the Rio Grande, where it flows from the north. It's a big volcanic region in a beautiful, dandy siting. Wonderful. Some day, some day.... We're beginning to wean them. They're coming around.

Tony recognized that he had artifacts, but he didn't know what they were. He'd been working in the Archaic, Texas Archaic, with which he was very familiar. So Jerry Epstein, who is an old friend of Helen's and mine, a professor at the University of Texas–Austin, archaeologist who worked at northeastern Mexico and so forth, was coming over one day, and he stopped to see Tony. He had heard of him, or knew him slightly, and Tony showed him these vast areas of hearths, masses of stone. They were all black, with artifacts, also, crude, what Tony called choppers, which nobody in Texas would accept as tools at all. They were "cores" to Texans and to many other people, but these things really were coarsely flaked choppers.

So Jerry said, "Tony, what's that black coating on those rocks?" Tony said, "I don't know. Fire-burned, I don't know what it is." And Jerry, who had been making fun of me for a long time about my desert varnish and my sequence in varnishes in Pinacate, which is all right since it was a friendly tease, said, "Tony, I think that coating on there can tell you something."

One day, after Helen was gone, Jerry came over with specimens. He had a chopper and a cobble of basalt lying on the table here. After we pushed each other about and said howdy, I said, "What's that stuff?"

And he said, "Well, you tell me."

I said, "Where's it from?"

And he said, "You tell me about it."

So I looked at it. "Oh," I said, "it's a good Malpais chopper. And the cobble is basalt. Both have got heavy varnish on them. Neither one is from Pinacate, that's all I can tell you."

And that damned little clown started capering around the table saying, "Now I believe, now I believe!" He went back over, and he stopped to tell Tony, "You go over there and see Hayden." So one day I came in the house, and someone hammered on the door, and here was Tony and two of his friends who had been working with him, one of them Don Williams from Tumacacori or Tubac.

They were summered at Alpine, Texas, and they used to go up and dig Archaic sites. Tony brought some of this stuff with him. I was able to identify them, no problem. And then he knew he had some backing. We had a little personal go-round, which determined a number of things. I put the Indian sign on him—he's damned quarter Osage war chief, and quarter Irish frontier marshal and half Italian minor nobility—so he sort of believed it. And we've been close friends ever since.

God, that's a big man, taller than I am, and he weighs 230 pounds. Big beak of a nose and piercing gray eyes. Hard. They called him Mr. Ice Man when they were walking back from the reservoir in the Korean retreat, because he never showed any emotion. He told me one time, rare time, when he was feeling a little talkative. Very hard man.

But I booed him. I don't do it very often, I'm pretty peaceful, but. . . . He hadn't heard of me; never heard of Rogers; he knew nothing about this. His orientation was from Texas, and all Texans are oriented within Texas. They're incestuous, self-centered, fornicating so-and-sos. Even the Texans are beginning to wake up. We're getting a few labels on a few people whom we respect. Meanwhile, we're going our own way. I'm real happy about it. Besides which, I won't have to write about Pinacate if I'm helping him over there.

I still get my mule aroused now and then. I can get pretty stubborn. And that will all work out in time, one way or another. At least I did better than Tony—I've got my notes up so that someone else can operate on them. I keep them up, too, which is more than Rogers did.

While at Yuma during the war, I did some archaeology. We had a Lieutenant Kernberger. I think he was post engineer. He had read Malcolm Rogers, and he used to go out in the desert and hunt for desert varnish and Malpais sleeping circles and things like that. We'd talk about it, and once or twice I was able to go out with him. Once we went up to Camp Laguna, where the proving grounds are now, and looked at those Malpais sleeping circles. Yeah, we saw some. I didn't see nearly as much as I wanted.

I did go up to the Kofas one weekend. Malcolm Rogers and Lew Walker had passed through, and they were headed for them, and said, "Why don't you come up Saturday? You can get back Sunday. Don't bring any water; don't bring any food; we'll take care of all of that." So I drove up Saturday morning and went right through a whole convoy of Desert Training Command people coming back from their maneuvers—they were the tiredest, saddest-looking, beat-up bunch of men you ever saw in your life. And those damn tanks and tank destroyers and all the rest of it. I felt a little silly driving up in good health, right up between them, and they were on their way to Africa.

So I met Malcolm and Lew, and we looked at the mountain sheep, and we looked at the trails. On the way back I took one of the photographs I published in my "Fragile-Pattern" paper. I learned a lot. But I damned near starved to death, too, because of those two old desert rats. Malcolm Rogers never had more than a glass of water in the morning, even in August. He had trained himself. As he has told me, he'd get a little dizzy in the afternoon and he'd puzzle why. Then he'd remember, "Ah!" He hadn't had his water that morning, so he'd take his glass of water and there wouldn't be any more until the next morning. Lew Walker was the same way. I think all I had was the hind end of one jackrabbit and possibly a piece of bread in two days. Another day of that and I'd have been hungry.

Lew Walker was an ornithologist. He and Malcolm were buddies. He was about six foot five, and split halfway up the middle, he could take a six-foot stride and think nothing of it. Good photographer. He used to take his old boat and a sack full of cameras down to the Gulf, going down to Baja California. He had one boat after another, because he was always wrecking them. They used to say of him that he had lost enough boats and enough cameras to stock three shipyards and four camera shops. Once his car broke down right halfway down Baja, and he walked across in August off toward the Pacific coast. He thought nothing of it. He only had to take half as many strides as the rest of us.

In a little bay on the west coast, Lew encountered a ranch that had been there since the early Spanish times. The families had lived there all that time. There was a band of mountain sheep up the canyon where water was in a *tinaja*. That family had harvested that band of sheep, Lew said, for at least two hundred years and perhaps longer. Culled them, you know. And they never told a soul about it. Then a party of American sportsmen—emphasize the "sportsmen"—came down and got them drunk one time. They learned about the sheep and went up and shot them all. Lew was still mad about it, of course. Later Lew came over here and worked for the Desert Museum in the early days, with Bill Carr.

Malcolm had no patience with people who weren't as quick as he was. Except with me. He put up with me, and I used to puzzle over it. I'd ask him the same question several times in succession to make sure I knew what he was talking about, because he had a teutonic way of speaking, since he'd had a German tutor when he was small. I had problems with it, and I'm not smart, anyhow, in many ways. I had to ask him several times to make sure I knew what he was talking about. He was absolutely patient. He never once lost his patience with me, in my presence, anyway. And I never knew anybody else that he treated that way. With them he'd get mad, flare up, and he'd run them off. Never talk to them again.

So after he died, I asked his widow, Ethel, his first wife, about that. I said, "I never have understood why he was so patient with me."

"Well, Julian," she said, "because you were the son that I couldn't give him." Well, hell. You know what that did to me.

12. El Pinacate

Frank Pinkley, the "Boss" of the National Park Service's Southwestern Monuments, didn't turn a sherd in the story of Pinacate archaeology, but he did nudge a couple of archaeologists in that direction: Paul Ezell and me.

He offered me the first superintendency of what became Organ Pipe Cactus National Monument, but I didn't take it. Frank Pinkley was in a way sort of a second father to me. We liked each other, and I had great respect and high regard for him. I'd worked there at Casa Grande in 1930. He met Helen and he liked her, and he said some nice things about her in his bulletin.

Along about 1936, I don't know just when it was, he said, "Look, we're setting up Organ Pipe National Monument. How'd you like to be superintendent?" I said, "Well, I have to talk to Helen." We thought that would be wonderful. And we talked about it, came up to Casa Grande and talked to "the Boss," as everyone called him.

I don't know how it came up, but it became apparent that I'd be working for the National Park Service, not for Frank Pinkley. I didn't put it this way, but this is what I meant: I said, "Look, it is perfectly simple, really. It boils down to this: I'll go anywhere in the world for you, Boss, but I really don't give a damn about the National Park Service and the U.S. Government."

So, we agreed that probably I wouldn't have been a good employee of the National Park Service. And I continued to do what the hell I was doing: foreman of the CCCs. National Park Service . . . am I glad I didn't.

Bill Supernaugh was brought in on the job. Good man, I only met him once. He stayed there, and he built the monument. He traveled all over it, which no administrator has ever done since. When the war came he was drafted into the Ski Troops and sent to Denver of all places. Of all the damn places to send a desert man.

When Supernaugh came back, he got Paul Ezell involved in doing the archaeology of that monument, so Paul was working officially near the Pinacate. Paul was working there one Labor Day when young Julian, my older son, and I went down to visit him somewhere over northwest of the headquarters toward the Growler Valley. Paul said, "You know, I'm exhausted. It's hot. I don't get any sleep at all. The sun comes up at four in the morning and it doesn't set till midnight, and I can't get any sleep."

So, I noticed how he parked his car. He parked it east and west. He slept there till the morning sun hit him. I said, "Paul if you turn this car around, we'll sleep on the sunset side and we can sleep a little late. Did it ever occur to you that you might do that?"

And his jaw dropped and he stared at me, and he didn't say this because he didn't say those things that I do, but what he intended to say was, "Why, you son of a bitch."

Paul Ezell and Julian in the Pinacate, 1970. (Photograph by Edward Germeshausen)

And he turned the car around and you know it was ten o'clock the next morning before he got up!

And he learned something. I don't know whether he ever forgave me for it or not, now that's something else. You know how a man will resent that sort of thing.

Unfortunately, since he did that work in Organ Pipe, nobody did any more until they made the damned thing a wilderness area, and so it's illegal to go out and travel around in a jeep. I, at least, refuse to go out there. And I guess others have, too. Those who have gone have found that the sites are eroded away since there'd been some tremendously heavy rains since the early 1950s, and many of these sites are no longer to be seen. It is a strong argument for collecting fragile-pattern areas when you see them. Don't leave them, because the rain will get them if the tourists don't.

Later Paul and I went to the Pinacate together. We'd both read Lumholtz's *New Trails in Mexico* and Hornaday's *Camp-Fires on Desert and Lava*. We first went to Papago Tanks. I don't think he knew any more about where it was than I did. But I showed him how to "see" or look at things. He didn't know anything about the percussion of flake tools, if you like. I got out of the truck. He started looking around, but I started picking up stuff. He said, "What are you doing?" and I said, "I'm picking up tools." He said, "What are you talking about?" "Why," I said, "these are choppers and scrapers and cleavers." I showed him, how they were made.

"My God," he said, "I stood right here years ago and never saw them." I said, "Well, Malcolm Rogers showed me. Now I'm showing you." It made an impression on him, and we spent most of two days, I guess. The wind was blowing, and it was a miserable spring equinox, Easter time. In those days there was a heavy growth of annuals. It had been raining for a couple of years, I guess. Giant mallow, giant nightshade, and amaranth, too, growing along an arroyo there, well over head high. Of course, there wasn't any house there, weren't any cattle in there at all then.

We rolled our bedrolls up right into that dense growth, next to the arroyo, on the north side of the arroyo, trying to keep the wind out. Damned near froze to death. I did, anyway. I had an old Keet Seel bedroll, you know, and damn, it was thin. So the next morning we went across the arroyo and went up into higher ground there. Paul began to see things he recognized. Scrapers. Amargosan tools. Amargosans hung out up in that high ground. That he recognized. Then we looked around, we found some Amargosan clearings, stamped clearings, the sort of things Malcolm Rogers had talked about, or told me about, anyway. And we found some cached manos near the clearings. I took pictures of them.

Then we went over across the little arroyo to the south and here, by God, was the atlas bone of a skeleton with the top of a metate showing below, down-body from the atlas bone. The skull had been picked up, obviously; you could still see the indentation. So we looked at that and uncovered it; it was a beautiful burial. Possibly it was a woman, but I think a man. The pelvis was pretty well disintegrated. Head up. Hands crossed under the pelvis. Basalt metate laid over the pelvis. It was a triangular cross-section mano, typical of Amargosan II. Some pottery, some chert flakes, and some red scoria, part of which had been ground to make a red pigment, which the body had been coated with when it was buried. We uncovered it very carefully, made notes, and photographed it.

The wind was blowing colder than all hell, and we were unhappy, so I took my photographs and went off out of the wind while Paul worked there for a couple of hours. One camera broke down, and then the other camera broke down, which was typical of Paul. It was taking him two hours to get his damn pictures, and then they didn't come out so I had the only pictures, which is Paul's self-admitted mechanical life, in a nutshell.

When we headed south into Pinacate, we went on down eventually to Moon Crater. We didn't know there was a crater there up above us on that rim, you know, for we didn't know the terrain. We were down in the arroyo below Moon Crater on the northwest side, you know. We climbed up on the bank and saw a helluva beautiful little site. Here was some pottery and some burned bones and some glass arrow point flakes. And half an arrowhead of glass. Oh boy, we'd thought we'd found Sunset Camp, which was what we wanted to find. Anyhow, that's what we thought we had found. Man, we went over that thing and we photographed it and we collected it, and then we started wandering around.

We went over to the dunes between the arroyo and the foot of the Moon Crater. And I saw something there that caught my eye: a big block of scoria. I looked at it and, hell, it was a beautiful big mortar about two feet in diameter. A greasewood was still

Moon Crater (Volcan de Chichi), Pinacate, February 20, 1965. (Photograph by Julian Hayden)

standing partly above it. Obviously it had been cached under that greasewood, but the whole area had deflated. Here it was lying on its side with the opening facing southeast, I think. I looked at that, and I took some pictures of it, and Paul came over. I said, "Hey Paul, you see anything odd about this area here?"

He looked at me hard and said, "What are you getting at?"

I said, "You see anything unusual here?" There wasn't any other scoria showing.

"Well," he said, "I don't know what you're talking about. What the hell's the matter with you?"

I said, "Look at that mortar there." And he got mad. He sullied up.

Finally I said, "What in the hell's the matter with you? Did I say something wrong?"

"Well," he said, "you damned well did. That's the way my father used to treat me."

I said, "Paul, I'm sorry. I apologize all to hell, and if you're mad enough to go home, we'll go home right now; if you're not, let's continue the trip, and we'll just drop the subject. I didn't mean to do that to you. I was just having fun."

He said, "That's what my father used to do to me. He'd call me stupid when I didn't see what he saw." Did I ever watch it from then on out, all the years since! Perfect innocence, you never know. That gave me a little notion of what he had to live with while he was growing up.

Reminded me of my father's first cousin, Thomas A. Hayden, who was chief assistant engineer at the Salt River Valley Water Users. He came out of Nova Scotia to Santa Fe dying of TB, but he didn't die of TB. So, he trained himself and became an engineer, a hydrologist. Thomas, too, was one of those men who, if you didn't understand what he said instantly, he'd berate you. And Malcolm Rogers was like that, too, not with me but with everybody else.

So that's how come Paul got into it. That's when his eyes opened, and then he got interested. He got to looking at the San Dieguito in Southern California. Actually he had dug at the Harris Site where Malcolm and I had dug in 1938, and he found the same things we did. His paper, "An Archeological Survey of Northwestern Papagueria" in *Kiva* was up till then the only thing that was ever written on Papagueria, as far as archaeology goes. It was a preliminary paper. And since it was all that was ever done, it was damned important.

The succeeding paper was in *American Antiquity* [Ezell 1955] on something about archaeology and linguistic boundaries. Preceding workers in northwestern Sonora had all found Yuman pottery everywhere, so they said, "Well, hell, this was all occupied by Yumans." Paul proved and established through his work with Don Alberto [Celaya] and so forth that Papagos had imported Yuman pottery, and then they made their own. Now, that was a wonderful break, a wonderful advance. So in that sense it was a great feat, a very good pioneering work, really. A seminal thing. I backed him up in my first paper on the Pinacate.

We went over to Laguna Prieta, south of San Luis, Rio Colorado [in 1953]. Don Alberto Celaya sat with Paul on the front seat of the jeep, and I sat on the hood to hold the front end down. And we took off from the highway at the boundary line milepost that Lumholtz took off from. We've got a picture of Don Alberto standing at that milepost, in my files.

And we headed west toward the right (north) side of the highest dune. Don Alberto had not been there since 1910, and he made one slight error that threw us off maybe a few hundred yards. We cut back south, damn near fell into the bloody Laguna Prieta . . . the most beautiful thing you ever saw in your life, a lake right there in the middle of all those sand dunes.

The dunes were standing high all around it. And here was a basin with a lake in the bottom, the most beautiful cobalt-blue lake you ever saw. It had oxblood-red water on the east side from the alkalis. It was astonishing. And on the far side were some mesquite trees. I got all involved collecting pottery, Yuman pottery, from around the camps in the dunes, while Don Alberto and Paul walked around the lake to trace its rim. And Don Alberto pointed to a hole under a tree and said, "I dug that in 1910. Dr. Lumholtz and I drank out of the water from it." And he and Paul both drank from it. Later I felt badly that I hadn't been there for that drink. It was Thanksgiving time and blowing and cold.

Don Alberto told his stories, of course, about Lumholtz. Paul at that time was a young professor, barely two years on the staff at San Diego State University and still a little bit sullen, as young PhDs usually are. I'll never forget this, because I resented it a little bit at the time. Don Alberto and I got along fine; we were talking about rockets, philosophy, and all kinds of things in my very best Spanish, which I'd picked up from

Alberto Celaya at boundary monument 193 on the Arizona-Sonora border, 1953.
(Photograph by Julian Hayden)

my friends in the dirt trenches and construction sites of California. Paul, however, was fluent in Spanish—he spoke Chihuahuense fluently—and he took me aside and he said, "Look, you shouldn't talk to the old man like that in your Spanish. If you want to talk to him, you can translate it through me."

I said, "Why?"

He said, "You know, you don't speak Spanish very well."

I said, "No, I reckon I don't."

And he said, "Every time you use that darned Spanish, you insult that old gentleman. Why don't you talk to me, and I'll tell him what you want to say."

So I got mad and I cursed him, I think, but that was the end of it. And Don Alberto and I got along fine. Paul "knew" darn well that Don Alberto didn't understand a word of English. Later, Paul and Dr. Dobyns spent an interminable amount of time translating back and fourth through Paul. Years later, after Don Alberto died, I found out that he spoke better English than either of us. He used to come home and tell his daughters and laugh and laugh and laugh. The old bastard. He knew everything we said! Hell, yes.

Don Alberto had worked in Los Angeles as a construction foreman when his children were small because he wanted them to go to American schools. He was a boss on a big building in downtown Los Angeles and excavated an elevator shaft. It filled with water in a heavy rain, so he called together his gang and started a bucket brigade. The superintendent came, "What are you doing that for? Put a siphon on it!"

"But how can you siphon from below to an upper level? I thought you were an engineer." And he told that till he died to give you an example of American engineering know-how. He was just an old boy from Sonoyta, but he knew how to get water out of a hole. Oh, hell, yes, he spoke good English, and we never knew it. He was a slicker, and we had a wonderful time.

One story I've never printed because folks might call it legend, but there's a slight basis in fact. Dr. Solosth, my eye doctor, camped down somewhere east of Tinajas Altas, north of Pinacate, with a party after the war. They were getting breakfast one morning when a man came up from the south, a tall, redheaded Irishman. He walked up and he looked them all over. He turned to Bob, as the leader, "Sir, I'm so and so." (I've forgotten his name at the moment although I've got notes on it.) He said, "I work for the U.S. Treasury Department. I'm a treasury agent. I'm hidden out in Pinacate. I have certain information in this envelope. Now, I'm going to turn around and go back again, and if you don't hear from me by a certain time, turn this over to the Treasury Department."

The man gave Dr. Solosth the envelope and turned around and walked off. Disappeared. Bob forgot all about it, but quite a while later, possibly several years, he went over to the Treasury Department office in Phoenix, where they had a big office, and asked about it. They said, "Oh, yes, so and so."

"Yes."

"You know what happened to him?"

And Bob said, "No."

"They found him shot in the back, fallen into his campfire at Emilia Tanks."

He must have been down there looking for smugglers of aliens or drugs. They moved a lot of Chinese and drugs through at that time.

I heard some other campfire stories, too, but couldn't verify them. There were reports of Axis troops and spies in Gran Desierto. Ronald Ives reported finding a shortwave setup and jar of Mauser cartridges at Cerro Colorado. If you read Barbara Tuchman's *Zimmerman Telegram*, you'll get the gist. Also Ives told me that during World War I, Dr. MacDougal was commissioned to guide an elite Army unit below the line to eradicate a Japanese unit. No records kept, of course.

During World War II the Navy ran border security from San Diego to Nogales. I was at Yuma Air Field. In the fall of 1942 a flurry of agents showed up at our security office, and I turned it over to them. Got out and shut the door behind me. Security was very tight for a while. Rumor had it that a squad was sent south of the line to kill and bury a Japanese unit in sand dunes. Then each member of that group was sworn to secrecy and transferred to a far corner of the globe. Two Japanese soldiers were shot and killed as they carried boxes of dynamite across Muroc Dry Lake in California. Not very smart and not knowing much about the countryside, at Yuma I hired a runaway. He had a thick German accent, so I kept an eye on him. Finally I turned his name over to security, and they checked the man's tent out in the desert. In the tent were blueprints and other information. Obviously a spy. When I asked Ives about such activities, he shrugged and said, "Many things are possible."

I was in the field with Norman Tindale in the Pinacate, as you know, and with Paul Ezell. At night, long after Paul and I had gone to sleep, I'd wake up, and Norman would still have his flashlight on in his bedroll writing notes. I asked him about it. And he had learned as a boy, in Australia, never to go to sleep until all of his notes were down, clearly written, all cross-indexed. The day, all of his photographs, a log of his exposures, with possible cross-indexing, and the same with the artifacts. Then, when he got back to the lab or to the office, he'd spend a little time cleaning them up, turn them over to his secretary, and if years later he wanted an article on something, all he had to do was to call his secretary and she'd bring it in. All he had to do was write a foreword, check the references, and put a title on it, in essence. That's the most organized man I've ever seen in my life.

Norman Tindale and Paul Ezell and I came into Suvuk at what must have been nine or ten o'clock at night. We made camp, and Tindale spotted a windbreak, a circle, right off, even before we stopped. He had a sharp eye. So we made camp and were going to cook some dinner. And he said, "I'll build a fire. Aborigine-style." All right. So he tried to build it, and you know, by God, he couldn't build it. That damn fire wouldn't burn. And finally I said, "Norman with all due respect to your Australian bushcraft, by God, maybe the spirits of the mountain don't like Australian ways. And I'm getting hungry."

And Norman said, "Build your own fire, then." So I did. I didn't have any trouble at all, it started right up. Well, that interested him, so I cooked some dinner. We sat around for a while.

Next morning, we got up, of course, and we walked down to the tank, and talked about the stratigraphy there. There is stratigraphy there, not archaeological but climatic. When we went back up and got some breakfast, here came the Romero boys, all five or six or seven of them. Just as we were getting ready to leave. So we stopped, and unpacked again, and made some coffee and got out the cookies, Pinacate cookies, the Oreos I always carry for Pinacate, you know. Galletas Pinacateñas, Galletas Pinacate.

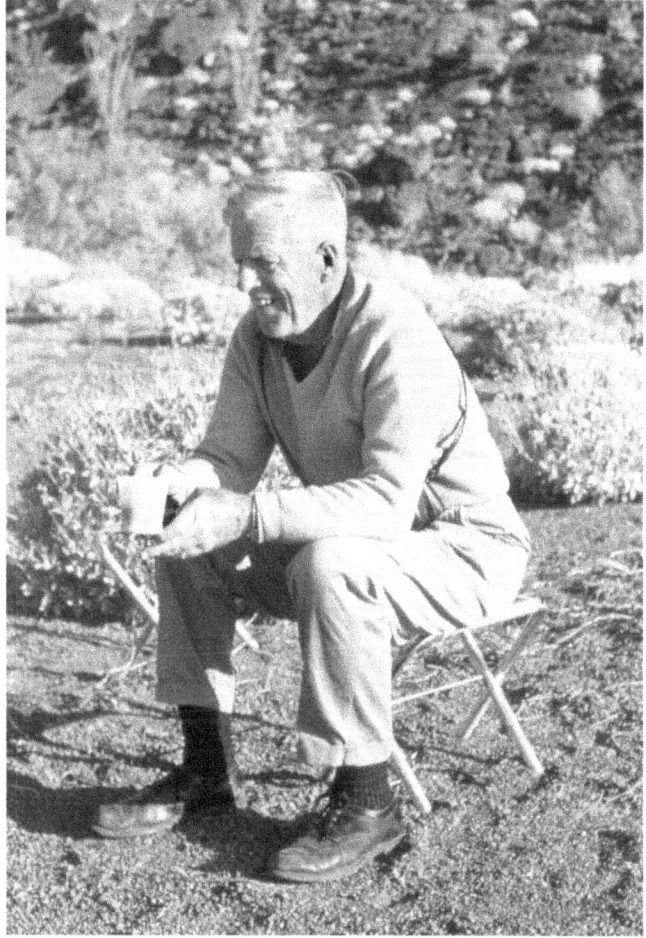

*Norman Tindale at
Cinder Valley, Pinacate,
November 25, 1967.
(Photograph by Julian
Hayden)*

Finally the boys left, and we loaded up and started off, and I looked back and I saw a nice shiny tin can in a creosote bush. I stopped and I said, "Where in the hell did that tin can come from?"

"Oh," he said, "it's me noit cup."

"What do you mean, a night can?"

"Well," he said, "a night can. I don't like to get out of my bedroll."

"Oh," I said, "that's your can?"

He said, "Yes."

"Well," I said, "you know I don't leave cans around camps. I clean up."

He said, "The natives will take care of it."

"No," I said, "before the war, yes, but this is after the war. They've got more tin cans than we have."

"Oh."

So I said, "If you don't mind, Norman, garbage bag's in the back of the truck." And I looked at him and he looked at me, and he got out and went and got it. And I'm probably the only man in the world who ever made Norman Tindale go back and pick up his night can out of the tree!

Ah, he was a good sport. And he was perfectly right, of course. In Australia he'd have left the night can, and some native would or would not have rinsed it out and used it for a billycan for his tea.

After we knew him down there, he wrote that big two-volume work on the Aboriginal tribes of Australia and their territories. Complete. It is the encyclopedia of all the tribes, their dialects, and their territories. I've got it. Stanford published it. He had the draft all done, the whole thing, in his briefcase, and he set it in the back of his car. When he stopped at a supermarket and came out with his groceries, it was gone. He was down here, and he told Helen and me about it. I said, "So what are you going to do now?"

"Oh, I'm going to rewrite it."

I said, "My God, can you?"

"Well," he said, "lots of the photos I can't duplicate." Some of them went back to his beginnings nearly fifty, sixty years before when he was with Aborigines who had never seen white men. But he said, "Maybe I can get something to take their place. As for the writing, I've still got my notes, we can just start all over again." Well, by God, I admired that.

And as he was preparing to go back to Australia, somebody called him and asked, "Your name Mr. Tindale?"

"Yes."

"Well, I think we have something of yours." So he went over, and by God, there was the briefcase. Somebody had taken it, opened it, and found out it was just papers and threw it into another car. The other car's driver hadn't looked into the backseat for a couple months. And here it was. Isn't that an astonishing story, and it's a true story. So I bought a copy, you bet I did. It's one of the great books.

At Bojorquez ranch in Pinacate, I'd go visit. Take a little bottle of mescal or something, and tell a few stories. I'd always take a story from *Playboy*—not the raunchiest, but ones I could translate into my meager Spanish—and they loved it. They soon became fast friends with my son Steve, and one day told him, "We love your father, and he can tell the most wonderful stories." I was always welcomed at that camp. In the old days each cow camp had a storyteller who spun yarns and sometimes did a chore or two. I'm practicing for the job.

In 1935 or so I was just a kid and up on the Gila River, the Pima Reservation. We'd made a few friends up there. One of them, an older man, used to listen to my stories. One day he turned to a friend as we sat there and said—and I tell this not to brag but because it makes me happy now just as it made me happy then—he said, "You know, that Julian has the voice of a bird and he tells the most marvelous stories."

Why did people in the Pinacate and the Cabeza Prieta area never figure out making mud blocks? Almost nobody figured that one out. It's an Old World thing, except for, I think it's in Peru and possibly Bolivia. Paul Ezell worked in Bolivia for years, though, and he talked with an old man who insisted that the art of making adobe blocks came from Phoenicia, and it was introduced by Phoenicians who'd been separated perhaps on the Amazon or somewhere and they'd come up. They used the same name as the

Sr. and Sra. Bojorquez
with Ramón Bojorquez
at their new house at
Papago Tanks, Pinacate,
November 1965. (Photo-
graph by Julian Hayden)

Sr. Bojorquez with a
seed jar owned by Juan
Caravajales, the last
Hia C'ed O'odham to
live in the Pinacate,
December 8, 1965.
(Photograph by Julian
Hayden)

Phoenician name, and he had other reasons for thinking that this was the case, but I don't know if anybody ever paid any attention to him. Paul believed it but didn't ever say anything about it, because it would have been professional suicide. I could go into that, but I don't feel like it.

Casa Grande and all those other structures, of course, were made from blocks but not in the usual sense. They made the wall sections so many feet long and so many feet wide until the mixture would begin to slump, and then they'd keep on going around or come back. I worked that out on Pueblo Grande and University Ruin and published on it. But it wasn't adobe brick per se, and I don't know why.

Celaya Crater is the site type-area for the Pinacate. I know that now. But those understandings don't come overnight. I've told you I was interested in geology, always had an interest in it. Geology and geomorphology are, of course, very closely related, whether you use the terminology or not. Your geomorphology is controlled to a great degree by geology, and it's all the same damn thing, just different aspects of natural processes of aggradation and degradation, which are constantly operating all over the planet.

And if those things become interesting, then you watch for evidence of their operation: alluvial fans, colluvial fans, arroyo cutting and sheet cutting, and all that sort of thing. In the deserts particularly, if you're dealing with human remains, then you're dealing with remains that are affected by geological processes. Now those are pretty general terms. Take fragile-pattern areas, for instance. Malcolm Rogers and I used to talk about that sort of thing but not using that terminology. We used to wonder about and discuss problems connected with collecting in areas in which the processes of nature had taken place and disturbed the remains left by man. If an Indian family had a camp in a dune area, and they dropped some potsherds and some burnt bones and some scraps and whatnot, then the winds come and the rains come, and eventually some of it's buried and some of it's lowered to a common plane, a common level. So, the problem arises how you're going to separate that particular family's debris from some other family's debris from a different time period. Everything is on the same plane.

Bunny Fontana and I talked about that the time I took him to Pinacate. He started digging up specimens, and I guess that's about the time I really began to clarify my thinking. And I said, "Bunny, what are you going to do with those?"

He said, "I'm going to take them to the museum."

I said, "What's the museum going to do with them?"

He said, "That's where they ought to be."

"Well," I said, in effect, "look, I'm doing the archaeology here, nobody else is. If you take that away, I won't have it for evidence. You're destroying a pattern here; there's a pattern here of some sort, and you destroy it by picking up anything."

Well, we didn't see eye to eye on it, so we had some friendly talk, and he eventually gave in because I was cooking the beans. And I got to thinking about it, again, and the upshot of it was I wrote that "fragile-pattern" paper. Originally it was submitted to Liz Morris, who was editor of the *Kiva*. But at that particular time salvage work was taking place in Libya and Egypt. The University of Pennsylvania and some other institution were arguing about the proper method to collect in the dune areas. Liz had read about it, and figured that was the appropriate place to inject the fragile-pattern idea. So she sent it off to *American Antiquity,* and Tom Campbell published it, just like

Desert pavement in the Pinacate near Tinaja Maria, May 8, 1965. (Photograph by Julian Hayden)

that [Hayden 1965]. It happened to be apropos. And I think it did some good. It's still referred to [see *Fragile Patterns: Archaeology of Western Papaguería*, 2008]. So that's how the "fragile-pattern area" concept came along, developed from just thinking about it over many, many years, you know, without really thinking about it. All of a sudden something crystallizes and you can see it.

And the same way with desert pavement. Pavement, as far as I'm concerned, is a deflationary process. You get climatic changes, you come into dry times, or you come into wet times, and vegetation grows and spreads, and everything is lush as we've seen in Pinacate in miniature in the years we've been there, you and I. Some years you can't even see the ground because the ground cover is so luxuriant. Then come the dry years, and plants die and blow away, and the rodents leave and quit disturbing the soil. Then winds blow away the soil, everything's dropped to a common level, a mosaic, and clay forms underneath the mosaic, the surface level. It is sterile, because it is so full of evaporite salts that seedlings can't take root, and you've got a permanent pavement, a permanent geomorphic surface.

When I really got involved in that in Pinacate, there was very little interest in desert surfaces. Geologists were not interested in desert pavement, since it's a short-term thing. Most geologists in those days were not concerned with the minutiae of geomorphology. They were more involved in taking a longer view of it. Obviously, though, it concerns the field archaeologist. Many of these pavements contain tools of several different periods in occupation, several different peoples, perhaps. And what to do with them, how to separate them? How are you going to tell?

San Dieguito tool at Celaya Crater, Pinacate, May 30, 1975. The lower left corner of the tool has been broken off and is lying beside it. (Photograph by Julian Hayden)

Rogers had worked it out to some degree, in what he called horizontal stratigraphy. He developed that first on trails, which is another question. It's necessary to know not only your technologies, or to work them out, but you've got to know the changes that can take place in the surface of stones through years or centuries or millennia of exposure. Oxidation, which Rogers used to call chemical alteration, or deposition of desert varnish, which was not known when I started working on desert varnish, is the key.

There had been a number of hypotheses: pollen, it was this, it was that. But there was obviously a real difference in the technology of tools carrying a very heavy varnish, those carrying a light varnish, and those carrying no varnish at all. And I was familiar enough with Amargosan technology and with San Dieguito I technology, from having worked at Ventana and from having worked with Rogers.

Here in the desert pavements around the waterholes at Pinacate, at Celaya, for instance, we found the lightly varnished or even heavily varnished stone tools embedded in the pavement. On the pavement were unvarnished tools of the Amargosan technology, and the technologies did not overlap. They were separable. So it seemed very clear, particularly after Ventana, where we had that hiatus between Pluvial and Altithermal, or the Altithermal hiatus between Pluvial and the San Dieguito occupation and the Amargosan occupation, which still continues.

We had a blank spot in there of drought when Ventana was unoccupied, and varnish had obviously formed to a certain degree on tools outside the cave, as at Celaya. So it seemed to me we had a separation. I was looking at this heavy varnish, this thick varnish, as I went along, and I found some tools down there at Emilia Tanks, at the foot of the mountain. They were polished, rounded ejecta which had had flakes knocked off the edges by man, so I thought, and the flake scars had very heavy varnish.

So one time I had a meeting here with the bigshots. Because it was a totally new concept, they didn't grasp that we might have these varnish-forming periods separating periods of occupation. The question kept coming up: what forms desert varnish? I didn't know; nobody knew. It looked very much like a coating of black epoxy, liquid, so for a while I even called it liquid varnish.

And I talked to Ronald Ives. I said, "Ronald, this looks just as if somebody had gone over these rocks with varnish. They've even got drips, in some cases, of varnish. Is it possible that we could have a natural polymer? A polymer could form naturally?"

"Well," he said, "I don't know. It's worth looking into. Look into it."

So I finally got a hold of a professor, Dr. Bartholomew Nagy, at the University of Arizona, who was one of the world's polymer specialists, authorities. And he was very nice to me, considering I had no degree and was just a green outsider. He said, "It's entirely possible. Look into it." Well, I appreciated that.

Then I was telling Tita Braniff about it, from INAH, from the Instituto Nacional [de Antropología e Historia] in Mexico. I'd met her down at a big convention in 1974 in Hermosillo. And she said, "Why don't you talk to Dave Snow in Santa Fe." He's an archaeologist. So I wrote him a letter, and he put me in touch with an organic chemist, who worked at Los Alamos and was a graduate of the university, named Rogers, and he got interested.

By that time I was suggesting that possibly the pollen of brittlebush, *Encelia farinosa*, caused varnish. It is certainly the dominant flowering plant in Pinacate, and when its pollen blows, it might accumulate on the surface of these desert pavement stones and tools, and with enough summertime heat it might develop to form a natural polymer.

So he experimented. I made several trips to Pinacate to collect blooming flowers, big bundles, bouquets of it, from various parts of the mountain, and out by Saguaro National Monument, and on the traffic islands on Alvernon. I kept them all separate and got several big boxes of it. He finally produced a natural polymer from brittlebush pollen. He separated out what he called a rabinose sugar, which means nothing to me, but it's one of the sugars in pollen, and he put it in an oven on a quartz petal, and by God he got a nice, very thin, black or dark, varnish. But it didn't have enough carbon in it, or it had too much carbon in it. The carbon in varnish is less than 1 percent and he was getting 3 or 4 percent, so that ruled that out. But it was a start.

Russ Potter got ahold of it when he stopped to visit Rogers one day. Russ was an organic chemist from Caltech, working on his bachelor's thesis, I think, and Rogers showed him what he was doing, so Potter got into it, with another man named Rossman, who may have been his adviser. And they started analyzing varnish. They found it had various types of clays, contained various clays, as well as trace minerals. So that was nice. He published it. I think he got his master's thesis on it, if not his doctorate, and he eventually went to work for a glass company in Ohio the last I heard of him.

Meanwhile other people got ahold of it. And some man, wondering about the origin of manganese nodules underwater in shallow seas, came up with the hypothesis that perhaps it was a bacterial deposition of manganese. Some bacteria and water were organizing manganese for energy and making a deposit. He sent me his paper, because by that time word was getting around that we were interested. I couldn't understand how it would work, but I sure as hell didn't discourage him. Who was I to discourage anybody? But it was an idea.

And then Ronald Dorn asked if I'd like to see his honors paper for his bachelor's. He was at Berkeley. So I sent him money enough to Xerox it, since he was a student and didn't have any. He sent it down and, hell, he carried all this even further. He and his principal adviser had determined the presence of manganese and iron and the various clays. The microbes that fed on manganese, and by oxidizing it derived energy from it, were bacteria! Microbes!

And they went into dormancy when conditions were *good*—that is, when there was moisture enough, enough organic matter around, for other bacteria to live and thrive. But then when times got hard—especially dry, either cold or hot—these bacteria were reduced to living on manganese, which they couldn't handle, so they disappeared. Then these varnish-fixing mixotrophs, so-called, came out of dormancy and just got fatter than hell on it, laying down layers of varnish. We find two different types of varnish, done by the same bacteria and under changing conditions of moisture and so forth.

So Ted Oberlander and Dorn were the two that really brought this to a head and analyzed it. They were actually able to isolate bacteria, mixotrophs, on varnish from the desert, from the coastal hills particularly, and cultivate it in the laboratory, and made red varnish. Just wonderful. But that's how I got into desert varnish. It couldn't have been done at an earlier time, because we didn't have the knowledge.

This is the gradual progression of increasing knowledge over a number of years, and, as far as I can see, it pretty well started in the Pinacate. We were trying to answer some problems down there, and it led us one way and another until we got where we got. It's a wonderful example of interdisciplinary cooperation. All starting with a busted-down, septic-tank contractor. Too, there's a correlation between desert varnish and caliche formation. Caliche is mainly a pluvial formation, particularly on the basalts. The basic basalts, like those in the Pinacate, contain a lot of calcium, sodium, and potassium. They're basic salts, and they leach readily. That's why you have stalactites on the under-side of basalt blocks in the rock heaps you've noticed. The upper ones have stalactites on them, because it's leaching out of the rock. If the rocks are buried or partially buried, you have increasingly heavy laminae of caliche underneath, which are actually harder than the basalts.

At Celaya Crater there are places where the basalts have completely eroded away and just left these caliche rinds on them. You've noticed that? That's why I call it shell caliche, because it looks just like seashells. But that takes you back to Pluvial times, and probably back into earlier Pluvial times, perhaps even back to the glacial times when there was water enough to put those salts into solution. And when they go into solu-tion they drip, just like the formation of any stalactite or stalagmite in any cave. So by observation, any stone that's buried or partially buried by man since Altithermal times, whether in the Pinacate or here, will have a relatively light dusting of caliche, a grain of caliche deposit under it but not a shell.

If you go back into San Dieguito I times, prior to the Altithermal, you may have a definite thin layer, but it won't be as hard as earlier caliche deposits. A Malpais deposit, which goes back into glacial and preglacial times, will be hard and is often laminated. If a San Dieguito man were to pick up a Malpais boulder or ejecta that's got a heavy crust on it, and then he put it into a windbreak or whatever, then by the time we come

JULIAN HAYDEN'S PINACATE CHRONOLOGY

Time Period	Cultural Horizon
40,000–20,000 BP pluvial period	Malpais
20,000–17,000 BP glacial advance; cold, dry period	Unoccupied
17,000–9,000 BP pluvial period	San Dieguito
9,000–5,000 BP glacial retreat; hot, dry period	Unoccupied
5,000–150 BP pluvial period	Amargosa/Pinacateño

Source: Adapted from *The Sierra Pinacate*, by Julian Hayden (1998).

along, that caliche coating will have pretty well dissolved, probably almost entirely. And it will have gone through the San Dieguito Pluvial, and through the Metathermal of the Amargosans, which lies on this side of 5,000. So, that caliche will be pretty well dissolved.

If you get back into an earlier varnish-forming period, that'll still be there. But it's very active because it's so hard. San Dieguito caliche will be gone, if it's exposed through the Altithermal and through the Metathermal. And the only thing you might notice is that the varnish of San Dieguito times, on the areas that were exposed, will continue. The varnish is not affected by time, but the areas that had been buried and had the light caliche of San Dieguito times, that caliche will be gone, and no varnish will have formed on it. You follow me?

So you can date that. You can say that that stone, if it had been made into a tool, or if it's a stone in a windbreak or in an alignment, was set by an Amargosan or was set by a San Dieguito Indian who picked it up, you can say it's a San Dieguito alignment. If it's got a dusting on it, it's Amargosan. But the surface may have an unvarnished portion or a lightly varnished portion showing, as contrasted to heavier varnish on another exposed surface.

You can date trails that way, too. You can walk along a trail which is very heavily varnished, and I know where there are several of them. If you take varnish along with Tindale's anecdotes about the kids running ahead of the families along the trails and stopping and digging out stones that their parents might stub their toes on, and throwing them off to one side, then you get a pretty good idea of what happened down in Pinacate. As you walk along a perfectly black trail, heavily varnished, over here will be a stone with Malpais caliche showing, lying with the caliche side up. And others with a later varnish showing, you know, lighter caliche showing.

You can tell that the trail has been used since Malpais times, since San Dieguito times. It's really not hard to do, because the stones are just where you'd throw one if you stubbed your toe. And it's the only way it can get there: thrown by man. That's the

A trail from Tinaja del Tule to Tinaja del Bote, Pinacate, April 1964. (Photograph by Julian Hayden)

Julian's sketch of Pinacate pot breakage.

sort of thing that upsets the theoreticians, but nonetheless, that's human nature. This figuring-out process probably isn't logical at all. It just comes to you. And I've stubbed my toe, damn it, more than once, and so have you. I know damn well these Indians weren't any less human than I am and possibly more so.

Talking about trail breakage of pots, I even drew a cartoon one time, and I've used it a few times in my slide show. In the background of Pinacate I've got a lovely slim lady walking along, and she's just very long, oh, she's a darling, and she's just dropped her water pot. Behind her here's the old man tearing his hair, jumping up and down. That's trail breakage. Malcolm Rogers pointed that out to me. And it's perfectly rational. That's all the logic there is to it. It's just common sense, having been out in the world a little bit instead of just sitting in front of a professor.

I got here at the right time. I followed the woodcutters from Sonoyta and San Luis by two years, so they had a few inroads which I could follow. But I preceded the *ejidos* and the cattle, which formed trails which many would confuse with ancient Indian trails or game trails. Cows and horses don't leave shell or sherd. Horse trails have sets of tracks like clumps, cows don't. Ann Woodin spent a lot of time down here; mused to me at one trail wandering, "Oh, I wonder how that ancient Indian felt at the time he walked and made this trail; what was on his mind when he formed this junction and that graceful curve through the desert pavement." "Oh, shoot, Ann," I said, "the graceful curve was just where he arced around a cholla cactus and the junction is where he peeled off to look for a waterhole on a thirsty day." She didn't like that.

And where they did drop pottery vessels, we never find all of the sherds. That's a curious thing. In the early days I found a beautiful, globular vessel just east of the Sierra Extraña on a trail. I didn't photograph it, but I wish I had. I collected it. The whole

Sunset Camp sleeping hollows, January 21, 1981. (Photograph by Julian Hayden)

equator is missing, and I have no idea where it could have gone. I've got all of this and this, but I don't have the equator. Malcolm Rogers commented on that, too. It is just a plainware vessel, and the ground was perfectly flat, so it couldn't have washed away. There's no reason for those particular pieces to be gone.

I was walking from Chivos down to Sunset Camp one time, the main trail in the early times, and here in the middle of the trail was a beer bottle. A green beer bottle. Broken. Somebody had dropped it. And I thought, ah, this is nice level ground, and now I'm going to see. You know, I couldn't find all of it. Part of the lip and part of the body itself were missing. Now, where'd they go? And why? It's impossible for them to have washed away. No one would have picked them up. And it was a modern bottle, probably just prewar. I don't know where those sherds went. You wouldn't think a pack rat would take the pieces. Why would they take a piece that might weigh as much as themselves? A good heavy beer bottle. Those are the puzzles.

I found a place at Sunset Camp where a family was doing nothing but making disks. And I've got a lot of them, all stages of manufacture, just around this one room. In another room some family made nothing but drum beads out of glycimeris shell. Just one family working, I suppose, where they dug out for a windbreak. But a lot of those answers that you are interested in? They don't come from rational thinking I don't believe, I think they come from observation over a long period of time.

When I hit upon the idea that the Amargosans, like the Uto-Aztecans, spoke Piman, I was driving home one night from the Pinacate. It was about midnight or one o'clock, and I was tired out, just thinking about this problem, and all of a sudden it came to me: of course, Amargosans were Uto-Aztecans and they spoke Piman. Because the

Pinacateños were a dialect group of Sand Papago, they all spoke Piman. The Piman speakers reach all the way into Jalisco and all the way up to Hopi country. The Spanish picked up guides, including some that could go all the way to Hopi country and speak the languages. This is just the Amargosan migration of the Uto-Aztecans. By the time I got home, I had it all worked out in my head, and I sat down and wrote it before I went to bed. I'd been figuring it for years, and didn't know it. See what I mean? As Isaac Asimov said one time, if he'd spoken Greek, he would have said, "Eureka!" Or vice-versa.

Why did I pay so much attention to the Celaya Crater Site? Why is the Celaya Site so important? It's the one site on the mountain which shows everything. Celaya is a broad but shallow crater with a high rim around three sides of it. On the east side the rise of the rim is very shallow; it's covered with ejecta, dating from the time the crater was formed. And most of those ejecta are oval, comparatively thin, rounded and smoothed in the throat of the crater before they were thrown out. They lie on that long gentle slope, like shingle on a shingle beach. And there they've been lying ever since they were thrown out, which is some time ago.

During that time they accumulated a very heavy coating of desert varnish. When you get away from that slope you get down into very, very broad *bajío*—which is a Mexican term for a broad drainage with no arroyo, almost a sheet-flooding drainage. There's a lava flow about ten or fifteen feet high, lying east and west, on the north side of the bajío. Going south from that wall of lava is a flat of almost a playa, and through it the water flows from the east in flood times. There's only a little trenching, no arroyo yet.

When you get off farther south, you get into greasewood, that creosote bush country with all the hummocks of sand through the loess, with soil around each greasewood. And in the bajío is a dense thicket of mesquite and palo verde and, in a wet year, all the annuals come up; it's just very, very lush. The rodents love it, and the birds love it, too. There's plenty in there to eat.

There is a major arroyo that comes from the north and separates the lava flow from the northeast wall of the crater, the high rim of the crater at that point, and that drainage comes from some distance to the north. It's cut a deep arroyo right down through the rim of the crater and gone down into the bottom of it. The floor of that arroyo, at one time, had tanks in it. But they've been eroded away, so they're now undependable and don't hold much water.

The San Dieguito I people, Pluvial people, who preceded the Altithermal prior to 9,000 years ago, lived in the area between the bajío and the crater. From the shingle slope, they used the stone for artifacts. There wasn't a really extensive San Dieguito I occupation, but their tools lie on the heavily varnished desert pavement which formed under the shingle or with the shingle. Those tools bear a comparatively light varnish as compared to the varnish on the shingle and the tools made by the earlier, the Malpais stages, the ancestors of the San Dieguito. They can be differentiated on the basis of technology and on the basis of varnish thickness.

Then the Amargosans, who came in after the Altithermal around 5,000 years ago more or less, reoccupied the area. They chose not the paved areas to live upon but the sandy areas and the dune areas, particularly up against the face of that north lava flow. They lived there a lot of the time. It was nice and sandy, you know, and soft. They also lived in the sandy floor of another, smaller arroyo that comes from the south. Those tools that they left there and scattered over the property have no varnish whatsoever. Also,

Julian at the mouth of the arroyo into Celaya Crater, Pinacate, March 1976. (Photograph by Ric Windmiller)

there are potsherds and plenty of seashell, along with all the imperishable material that the Amargosans usually left in their camps.

So we have a clear, three-stage occupation there. You've got the early, heavily varnished tools. You've got the much more lightly varnished tools of San Dieguito I times, tools which correspond to the bottom layer of Ventana Cave, which are 11,000, 12,000 years old, and older. They have a light varnish. There's also bifacial flaking on them. There are no projectile points at all, for they haven't come in yet. And the Malpais tools, the earlier tools, are all unifacial flakes, flaking only on one side, not from both sides.

I had first noticed something special at the place I call Horse Tank, which is just north of the road that climbs up the hill to Tinaja Emilia on the east side of the mountain. The pavement there, down below the tank, has the same ovoid ejecta lying in the pavement. I noticed that some of them were turned over, so that the underside, the so-called ground varnish, showed. Ground varnish contains a lot more iron than the black, manganese varnish on the top, which you are accustomed to. The contrast was so great between the overturned stones and the stones that hadn't been touched, that you could stand off at a good distance and photograph them.

So I got to wondering, and started looking at the overturned stones. Some of them had been cracked, broken, or flaked by people who were testing the stone to see if it was good tool-making material. I couldn't see any other reason for it. Some of them were flat pieces that had been broken by a blow right in the center. Mountain sheep couldn't do that stepping on a stone. They were overturned by a man. And when he learned what he wanted, he threw it down, and if it landed upside-down, why, here I come a few weeks later, or thousands of years later, and recognize it. They were probably turned over during Amargosan times, because the ground varnish was still bright, and no caliche had formed on the undersides. So, all the turnovers were post-Altithermal.

But some of these stones had flakes on them, and the flake scars were varnished. Particularly around the perimeter of a stone, the edge of a circular or ovoid stone would be flaked. Instead of bifacial flaking, it was a sort of hit-and-miss flaking, but if it were natural, why weren't flakes all the way around, here and there? And why weren't other stones flaked? They all landed at the same time, presumably, where they were.

So I began to think maybe it was something earlier. I was looking, of course, for heavily varnished, simple tools, like Rogers used to find in his deserts. He called these tools Malpais for a while. Then he discontinued the term and lumped everything into San Dieguito I. That, too, had me thinking. I brought them in and showed them to that gathering we had here, but I got no response because it was a whole new concept to everybody. Still, it interested me.

Then I came to a tank, whose site I call Tinaja Vereda, Trail Tank. That's north of Suvuk, north of the Romero ranch. It's up on a ridge or promontory above an arroyo with a tank in it, above Tinajas Figuras where the figures are. Blake Benham and Jim Sciscenti were with me. Blake had been learning how to flake tools from somebody, so he had an eye for things. He was standing on perfectly black pavement, and he bent over, picked up a stone, and turned it over. I'll be damned if it wasn't an end scraper, with a rounded end, a convex end scraper. It had a very heavy varnish on the exposed underside of it, and it was thoroughly embedded in the pavement, so it was coeval with the pavement. Even the flake scars were varnished, though somewhat more lightly. He looked at it and said, "Well, this was done with a soft hammer, a wooden baton instead of a stone hammer," and so forth, and we discussed it. It was a rather fine job of unifacial flaking.

Now that really got to me, so I began to watch for those things, and I thanked Blake for that. I would have found it eventually, probably, but this helped me a great deal. And then Jim Gutmann, the geologist, who did his work on the Elegante Crater, showed me a gizzard stone, or stomach stone, which was a perfect sphere. It looked like white quartz, actually. It's an accretion or concretion of carbonates, that forms in the stomachs of deer and other ruminants. He had found it at the Celaya Site. It was probably out of a medicine man's kit and had magical powers, ordinarily. And he said there was pottery there.

I had never stopped there. I had driven right by it, because it was only three miles off the highway, and I figured everybody and their dog knew all about it. So I went over there, and nobody had ever been there, except Jim. There was no trace whatsoever of any occupation by anybody except the Indians. Everything was just where they left it. The whole damn history of the mountain was right there to be deciphered. And that's why it's my favorite place, and that's why Fernando Lizárraga has protected it and told people not to go there. It's the key place to which we take people like Vance Haynes and Dennis Stanford.

There's a beautiful big Amargosan camp clearing there, about thirty or forty feet across. There are San Dieguito sleeping clearings there in the malpais. Over in the dunes are all the imperishable debris of Amargosan camps. There are graves there, pottery,

Peggy and Jim Gutmann at Papago Tanks, Pinacate, March 20, 1971. (Photograph by Julian Hayden)

metates, shell, arrowheads, whatever you like. It's all there within the area of about five acres, I suppose. That's why I like the place.

I've got a fireplace there, a natural fireplace, that Fernando Lizárraga says he's going to put a brass plaque on someday. He won't, but he talks about it. I took him there, and showed him what it was all about. When I was going down regularly, I always camped there at night if I was on the northeast side. He'd join me about eight o'clock in the morning, ready for breakfast. That's where Vance Haynes told me, after looking the place over for a whole morning, and digging some holes and whatnot, that he couldn't accept my great ages, because the dating technique had not been validated yet, but he would accept my sequence. And I told him, "That's fine, that's all I want to hear." Look at the dates later; sequence is what I'm interested in.

And I got some good news a couple days ago. A friend I've known for many years called. He'd been working up in southeastern Utah, with Dennis Stanford from the Smithsonian. My friend said they've got the same sequence up there that I have down here, Malpais and San Dieguito, with the various varnishes. All my friend lacks now is a dating curve.

So has Tony Andretta down in Alpine, Texas, because even though his is limestone and quartzite country, not volcanic, it's on the pathway from the Bering Strait to South America. It takes us right down through the Rio Bravo country, the Davis Mountains, and the Concho River, right down through the volcanics. So it's very interesting.

Of course, I had C-14 dates from Ventana Cave to which I anchor my sequence. One time [my son] Steve and I went down below Ventana Cave and found the San Dieguito I tools down there on the terrace where the Indians who lived in the cave had

E-mail message from Michael R. Waters to Colin Hermans, April 3, 2008 (used by permission).

Colin,

How odd it is that our paper on pre-Clovis culture in North and South America appeared almost ten years to the date of Julian's passing. I still recall the last day I saw Julian. It was very sad. I visited him whenever I could and was in town. I remember fondly all the wonderful trips to the Pinacate. I remember the backyard conversations. I remember the encouragement. Julian was just a great man. I have a picture of him that I keep in my office. I see his picture every day. I still have all of his letters.

I was trained by a Clovis-First guy (Vance Haynes), but was always profoundly influenced by Julian. He was my real mentor.

When we wrote the [*Science*] article, I wanted to put in the acknowledgments "Julian, you were right." But I do not think my co-authors would have understood. I am just tickled that Julian's ideas have been proven correct after all these years. It just took time.

Mike

been doing their heavy work of cutting, crushing, whatever. All those San Dieguito I tools had light varnish. We only found one heavy tool in the lower levels of Ventana. Everything else was small tools, "finishing tools," I call them. They were small scrapers, small knives, flake knives, and small disk choppers. In other areas around the cave are Malpais sleeping circles and Malpais cairns with a very heavy varnish. So we've got the whole damn sequence there, too. That takes us back damn near fifty years to the beginning of the work in there.

My discovery at Celaya was a good deal like my exhausted insight into the Pinacateño/Uto-Aztecan situation. You think about things and think about things, and then you're thinking about something else, and all of a sudden it pops into your mind. Then the gentle aggravation starts, because you can't expect these things to be accepted overnight, not in our conservative so-called profession. You're trying to get other people to see what you see so clearly. And admitting that you may be wrong, nevertheless you see it very clearly? Or I do. As a matter of fact, I've told more than one student over the years that the longer I think about it and the longer I've been in this country working on this stuff, the simpler it all gets. The less complex this early stuff is. And I think that's perfectly natural. I think people's way of life was a damn sight less complex than it became.

On one of my first trips to the mountain [Pinacate] I met the Romero boys. They had the ranch there and later the temporal to the west. Sometimes two crops a year. But then a seven-year cycle of drought ruined that. They were forced to move to Puerto Peñasco, and the old man died there—couldn't live in town. On the other side of the mountain, Pancho Begarán had a field in that fenced area south of the Grijalva ranch. It, too, dried up to nothing. Once I met a caravan of vehicles from some Mexican department, and citizens—they were going down to the dunes east of the Buried Range, somewhere near where Pozo Nuevo is now. They'd heard that the new power plant at Libertad was going to be nuclear and would deliver unlimited power to desalinize seawater. They thought the dunes would be flattened and turned to fields. They wanted to get their claim in early. Even these ejidos by the highway (Norteño, Nayarit) will revert to desert when the water table drops and seawater moves in to replace it.

I've made 160 or so trips down here over the years, most of them on two-day weekends. Longest one ever was four days. Usually I'd leave on Friday night and drive to the border and cross it when it opened at 8:00 a.m. Later, when Helen knew the business, I could leave on a Thursday night, and a few times I left on Thursday and didn't return till Monday night. But I couldn't leave her too long, too often because she had all those men to manage and there was forever something breaking down. Not uncommonly I'd spend the first day just sitting under a tree watching the countryside. The drives back and forth helped, too, because they gave me time to think and to unravel some of the knottier mysteries. I never climbed Pinacate Peak. When I was younger and able, I had too many sites to find; now, when I can hardly breathe, I don't have the energy.

There's a large intaglio near Suvuk, a figure of a man near Suvuk. I photographed it once in a rainstorm, and it filled with water, showing it well. I first saw it in low light. Ives had looked for Suvuk Tank but thought it was on the eastern end of this range. I was sucked into it by the trails. Suvuk Tank has a ledge of resistant basalt over loess; cut original bottom out of basalt tank, like one just above the ledge. Rains skim the tank bed with thin layer of silt, which pretty well holds the water, until some cow or coyote comes along to drink and punches a hole in that skin, and then it's like pulling the plug on a drain.

On one flat north of Suvuk are some circles. They cost me three or four trips. The earlier peoples had cleared those circles, as shown by the patina and varnish; then a later group came in and re-cleared the same circles. Boy, that really jumbled my theory for a

Julian with Pancho Begarán in the Pinacate, March 28, 1965. (Photograph by Colin Hermans)

Intaglio at Suvuk filled with rainwater, February 25, 1966. (Photograph by Julian Hayden)

while, until I figured out what had happened. There's a site to the west of there—maybe over one pavement tongue—which has a collection of sleeping circles and artifacts which I'd like to see again. There's a picture in Marc Gaede's book, but I haven't found my way back yet. It's a good excuse to come again.

13. Tracing Early Man

I think I told you, told a good many people, including some skeptics, one of these days there's going to be a breakthrough about Early Man. I've been prophesying that one of these days there'll be a breakthrough comparable to the breakthrough that occurred when the presence of Folsom Man was agreed upon because of artifacts with bison bones. There aren't many people who believe that man has been here prior to 12,000, or at least they won't admit it. I, along with a few others, have been arguing a different story.

Dennis Stanford, director of Paleoindian/Paleoecology at the Smithsonian, is a very good field man, one of the best. He gets all over the world, but he has to be a politician. Even if he were to see concrete evidence that man were here prior to 12,000 in the New World, and he might agree with the finder, as he did with me in Pinacate, he's not about to say so out loud yet, because he's got to live.

And, in Loren Eiseley's autobiographies, he tells about being pretty well started in his career as a paleontologist and anthropologist, when someone asked him to inspect a site in the West which had artifacts and the bones of extinct animals. He was advised by some of the biggest men in the country, "Don't go, because if you get involved, your career will be ruined. You'd be through, so stay away from it." So he stayed away, but he's always regretted it a little bit. All right, that's the sort of thing that Dennis has had to do: stay away from it. Or stay away from saying that there is anything more than a bare possibility.

But in recent years Tom Dillehay, with the University of Kentucky, has uncovered a site in Monte Verde in Chile, which has the foundation of some fourteen rooms, wooden foundations, timbers, pegged to the ground with the wood of a different species of tree. He has fragments of mammoth-hide covers, tents or roof covers, tied to the timbers with camel-hide thong. He has stone tools, contents of a mastodon's stomach, and at least eighty different species of plants, many of them medicinal and some of which come from as far away as the Chilean coast and Argentina. These people weren't Neanderthals, and they weren't Piltdowns, either. These were hunters and gatherers, but mostly gatherers, in *South* America 14,000 years ago.

So, in order to have thoroughly acclimated in southern Chile 14,000 years ago, it's obvious that man had to have been in the New World considerably longer than 12,000 years. That's 14,000 years as dated by accelerator mass spectrometer dating and C-14. And below that, or nearby it in a lower level, dating at about 30,000, are what those of us who have open minds will accept as tools, but the conservatives won't. Thirty thousand is not old in my book; I've been talking that for years.

But the important thing is that, at a meeting in Denver recently, in mid-April 1990, some linguists and others got together to discuss the proposition of a man named

Joseph Greenberg, who asserts that there are three language stocks in the New World: Amerind, the oldest, from which most languages have spun; and Eskimo-Aleut, which I think is the latest; and in between Na-Dineh, which is Athapaskan. Some linguists dispute that, so they had a meeting to talk about it. Dennis Stanford chaired the meeting, and there were archaeologists there, also.

It must have been a hair-pulling bee, a real session. The upshot of it was, according to Virginia Morell's beautiful three-page write-up in *Science*, twenty-seventh of April 1990, that Dennis Stanford said in effect, "Well, boys, we might as well face up to it: man was here prior to 12,000. He may have been here 20, 30, 40,000 years ago. Let's face up to it and work with it, because there it is. There's no arguing about it." When I saw that I, well, I actually grinned out of one side of my face. I promptly called Tony Andretta in Texas and told him about it, and he hit the ceiling with joy—he's still bubbling. So am I.

It's going to help the minds of the young students as soon as they get tenure or as soon as they get their degrees. I'll lay it five to one that Mike Waters will just stand up and whoop and holler because he's seen the evidence for earlier man. He was with me in the shell dunes in Adair Bay where we found used seashells older than 37,000, and probably 70,000.

Dr. David Meltzer, who told us off over in Texas, has no use for us at all, saying we didn't have anything. He said that Tony and I were just a couple of radicals, crackpots, who had nothing but some naturally cracked stone and no evidence of antiquity at all. He spread that all over Texas after he went back. Then he wrote an article [1989] bringing up the possibility of multiple entries, but he has been standing firm on the idea that Clovis was the first entry and the only entry at 12,000. In effect, he said, "Well, it's barely possible that there were multiple entries in the New World prior to 12,000, but obviously they all failed, because we have no evidence whatsoever that they were here." I read that as trimming the sails a little bit, getting ready for the day when he can say, "Boys, I told you so." And that's what he's probably doing right now. But more and more folks are coming around to thinking, "Why should it be the only entry? Maybe other people came in earlier." We've got to explain people living in Chile at 30,000. So it's a lot of fun. 'Course I wouldn't dream of saying I told you so in public, but nevertheless I feel good about it. I wish Malcolm Rogers could have seen this, and Morlin Childers, with his Yuha Man.

I told you about what Dr. Meltzer said about the Yuha Man, did I not? I met Meltzer there in Alpine, Texas, and he said, "You know, there is nothing to any of these claims for antiquity of man in the New World. Every time one is brought up it's disproven. Take an example from your part of the country, Yuha Man in Imperial Valley. Folks said that burial was 21 or 22,000 years old, but it was proven to be only 4,000 or 5,000. It's that way with everything."

So I didn't know what to say for a minute, and finally I said, "Dr. Meltzer, I don't think you know all there is to know about Yuha Man." And he looked at me. I said, "I was there when it was excavated, and I watched it come out. I inspected the details, and I think 21 or 22,000 is a modest age for it. It's a Malpais burial in my book."

And he stared at me and he said, "Well that's what you *say* you saw." He was very definite, and I stared at him, and I didn't know if I was being insulted or if I didn't hear him properly, but by the time I could catch my wits, somebody had taken him away. He

Julian Hayden, Huarache Tank, Sierra Pinacate, 1963.

might as well have stood up and called me a damned liar right there. People don't do that to me ordinarily. If they do I usually lose my vocabulary for a moment, and then it's too late. But the next day, then I can tell them. So you see I'm not very fond of some of these Bishop Usshers, these conservatives. They're not even polite, not only not to me but to people like Dillehay and others.

The Yuha Man supports my own theories. Before you can even begin to assess the possible validity of a man's statement, you've got to know something about him. I've known Morlin Childers a lot of years. Morlin was an Imperial Valley rancher with a lot of land. He'd been interested since he was a youngster in fossil seashells. So he began collecting and became a paleoconchologist. He had no particular education, certainly not a college education, but he became so expert that new species are named after him.

He came across Malcolm Rogers's work sometime in the 1960s or early 1970s when Rogers's book came out. So, Morlin got interested in the archaeology of the area. He noticed that Rogers had stated that there was nothing below about the 400-foot level, 400 feet above sea level. You didn't see any archaeology below that which was more than a couple of thousand of years old.

But Morlin had decided that possibly there were some very high sea levels in the Blake Sea, or Lake Cahuilla, whatever you want to call it. At the 440-foot level above sea level there were terraces and beach cobbles covered with tufa and all that sort of thing. So Morlin decided to look up at that elevation. And he worked out to his satisfaction, a seashore at 440 feet clear around an enormous area, clear up past Blythe. Pilot Knob had travertine on it, halfway up the pillar at about 440 feet. And above Truckhaven, which is a truck station on the west side of the Salton Sea on the road to Indio, at the 440-foot level is a beautiful terrace covered with heavily varnished stones, including a lot of artifacts, and a cairn, which he opened and found a human skeleton.

Childers was working with amateurs from the Imperial Valley Junior College, and he was an amateur himself. He took the skeleton out in a block and treated it with preservative. He lifted it out with a Marine Corps helicopter that came over from El Toro and took it down to the museum. But treating it with preservative made it impossible to date. However, they did examine it. So I went up there with Childers and with Paul Ezell. We looked at the site. It's a quarry site with a marvelous pink stone. It's metamorphic, fine-flaking stone that's spread all over the country. The Indians traveled with it, imported it or exported it.

And there were stones with the blackest varnish you ever saw, and some that were flaked just yesterday. As far as the cairn or the black varnish, I'm personally satisfied that it's a Malpais burial. Malpais means that the varnish was deposited during a dry time, probably toward the end of the Malpais occupational period which is prior to the last glaciation. So, we're going back 25 or 30,000 years.

West of Calexico is a hill that stands by itself, surmounted by a statue, I think of either Garces or Anza. There's a butte that stands up there and has a terrace, a beach terrace, around it at the 440-foot level, with sand dunes. In the little arroyitos leading down from this beach are the outlines of stones which Childers called fish traps. One might assume that as the sea level was lowered and the sea began to retreat, people were trapping fish in these traps. More modern fish traps on the west side of the Salton Sea were used by Yuma Indians. So that's known.

Morlin Childers at a fish trap at the Radar Site west of Calexico, California, October 23, 1971. (Photograph by Julian Hayden)

And at this Yuha site are some very interesting tools which are not found anywhere else, and they're varnished and sandblasted. And here's this cairn. The body's bones were encrusted with caliche, and the lower cairn boulders were encrusted with caliche, hard-shell caliche, not soft stuff, and it's from Malpais times. It's been through a pluvial period, or possibly more than one. Dr. Bischoff, with the USGS over in Menlo Park, dated the caliche on the bones at 21 or 22,000. I don't think he got enough collagen out of the bones to date them.

That, of course, caused a commotion. And I published his finding in my 1976 paper in *American Antiquity*, "Pre-altithermal Archaeology of the Sierra Pinacate," in which I was following Morlin Childers's lead and talking about a vast inland sea. This sea would have ameliorated the climate until it drained. Morlin has told me, but I've not seen it, that on the west side up against the mountains at 440 feet there is the stump of a delta dam thrown up by the Colorado River. And there is some evidence of a dam on the right side, too. It makes sense and it's plausible. There's too many coincidences here for this to be only imagination. So I wrote that up in the *American Antiquity*. I never got any kickback on it, probably because it was so far-fetched to most people.

And I described the burial there, too. The burial was sent over here to Walt Birkby to be extracted from the matrix and to be studied for the physical anthropology of it. Then local politics got into the act over in Imperial Valley, and Morlin Childers came over here and took the thing up before Birkby was through with it. It was sent over to San Diego where Rose somebody, the physical anthropologist at the museum there, presumably continued the work. Eventually it came back to El Centro. But then the earthquake hit and did so much damage to the building that the burial has never been seen since. In other words, those were the only dates we had on it, the only tests made on it.

It is an extremely controversial thing. Dr. Taylor and his protégé Louis Payen, University of California, Riverside, had come out in print and said that the damn thing was a fraud and that there was nothing to it at all. Other people said that American Indian Movement fanatics went in and stole it. Others actually said, and Meltzer implied, that Childers had stolen it himself and destroyed it so that nobody would disprove his statement. So you see what you're getting into.

Then somebody came up with Yuha's foot bones, in a box on the shelf. And it was claimed that the skeleton had had a foot tucked under the pelvis somehow, and those foot bones had been overlooked when the skeleton had been sent away. So, they worked on the foot bones and sent them to Bischoff. Bischoff wrote back and said that these are not the bones of the same skeleton that I worked on before. These are some other skeleton; there's something wrong here. But who could prove it one way or the other? Those foot bones dated at about 4,000 or 5,000 before the present.

There was an Archaic or Amargosan burial cairn, which I did not see, some distance from this Malpais cairn. I don't know whether it is even on the same island. It was Archaic, 4,000 or 5,000, and experts dated the skeleton as 4,000 or 5,000 years. So Payen and Taylor wrote an article for *American Antiquity* debunking the whole thing and saying the skeleton was only 4,000 or 5,000 years. It's been one of the foundation stones of the skeptical Bishop Usshers ever since. See how it all works together so nicely?

Nobody knows what happened to the skeleton; I don't. Childers didn't know. I know Childers well enough to know that he didn't destroy it, because he was a scientist, albeit without degrees. Then he died, which leaves me now as the only halfway competent one who saw the thing come out of the ground. Matter of fact, Paul Ezell and I were the only two. Paul was a professional with a PhD, and I had some experience. We were the only two other than Childers who saw it come out. I'm telling you this, because I think it's important. If nothing else, to give you an idea how the archaeological mind-set is in some cases, some places. And they call it science.

There are any number of similar situations in North America, and many more in South America. The prevailing attitude can be shown in something I read some years ago. An American archaeologist, whose name I've forgotten, was reviewing a book by a South American in which the man claimed dates of 20 to 30,000 at some sites in South America. This American said, "Well, these are impressive dates. And when the day comes that our South American coworkers can approach us in this country in skill and knowledge and instrumentation and all the rest of it, then we can pay a little attention to these claims. Until then, we'll have to disown them." Talk about chauvinism! My God, I was as insulted as the South American must have been.

So Dennis Stanford's coming right out in the open like that is one of the finest things that's happened since Folsom Man as far as I'm concerned. It might even make it possible in a few years for me to publish on the shell dunes, and Tony Andretta and I to publish on Trans-Pecos. I hope I live that long! Sure intend to, anyway, as long as the mescal lasts.

Now, Andretta's sequence is just as neatly laid out as mine is but much richer, because he has a different area than I have, probably much richer in foodstuffs and very much larger in area. He has twenty-two thousand square miles to work in, and we've only got six hundred down here in Pinacate. He can move from mountainous areas

Tony Andretta at a San Diego Museum meeting, probably in the 1970s or 1980s.

and find butchering tools and grinding tools, and then drop down into the lower lands of the mesquite country down toward the river where he gets his grinding stones, his gyratory crushers, his metates. They have the same varnish in both places. The stone tools common to both places are identical; you get identical key tools in both places, but the mountains are hunting areas, down below are gathering areas. We haven't got all those distinctions in Pinacate. We just simply don't have the area. I don't even have pre-Altithermal grinding stones there.

I think Malpais was the heyday, the richest occupation of the Pinacate. This Malpais occupation is basal to the San Dieguito; they were the first San Dieguitoans. At a guess, they were the first people that came over from the Old World. They came over a long time ago. Their tools went through at least two varnish-forming periods, though just when those periods took place, I don't know. One heavy varnish-forming period certainly took place during the last Wisconsin glacial advance, which peaked about 20 to 24,000 years ago. It might well be that that was a very rich time for the people there. The rainfall pattern would be different, probably less summer rains and longer winter rains, and it would be much cooler. The vegetation we know was different: pinyon and spruce and Joshua trees, big bear grass, no saguaro and probably no mesquite. The difference would include all the now-extinct fauna. Probably the flatlands were savanna-type flatlands, not boreal because it's too far south. But it would have been good hunting country.

What they used for hunting tools, I don't know, unless they used wooden spears with fire-hardened spear points. Maybe they didn't hunt big game; maybe they just

Malpais hearth in Texas, ca. 1980. (Photograph by Julian Hayden)

scavenged. But they certainly gathered, although in Pinacate there is no evidence of their having used grinding stones at any time until after the Altithermal.

I think probably that the Amargosan migration, probably from the north to south, dropped off bands of gatherers along the way. These included the Amargosan-Pinacateños, who dropped off into that area during the Medithermal when conditions were better than they are now. Probably they gathered seeds and small game and fish and whatnot. Others went on down to Jalisco and learned how to irrigate from folks down there, but they didn't have the gyratory crusher until 4,000 or 5,000 years ago. I thought it had been invented in Pinacate, but it hadn't been.

Just as the Pinacateño band lived in a different manner, other bands dropped off and settled down to became farmers. So, too, the Malpais who came down from the north and headed for South America eventually, might well have dropped off people in the same fashion. They must have, or else we wouldn't have had them over here in Malpais I and II times.

The concentration is north–south down the Rio Grande area. There we do have, in Malpais II times, gyratory crushers and metates and manos and all that sort of thing. They probably brought the metate with them. I'm not clear in my mind at the moment what the varnish is on the earliest metates that we've got over there. You get the first gyratories in Malpais II times, but they seem to have originated down south. Some of the people went on down and developed the gyratory, and then it filtered back up again. And it never did get over here in the boondocks. None of the grinding tools get over here into the boonies. That's the way I read it, anyway.

Tony's playing with the idea that the big-game hunters, the so-called Clovis people, were San Dieguito II, the second stage of San Dieguito I. First you get to Malpais; then

Maria Ruiz demonstrating the use of a gyratory crusher from the Pinacate, March 20, 1970. (Photograph by Julian Hayden)

you get separated by the varnish-forming periods, and then the Malpais II is separated by a long one, probably during the last glaciation. San Dieguito I is separated from San Dieguito II, over there in Texas, and here in southern Arizona to a lesser extent, and we don't get it at all in Pinacate. We get it over on the coast, and out in western Arizona, by a lesser degree of varnish, which would have occurred during the Altithermal.

The upshot of it is that over in west Texas and Trans-Pecos you've got grinding stones for tens of thousands of years. Then we get up into ceramics. I agree with Rogers that the Sulfur Springs is nonexistent: it's actually San Dieguito I. The development into San Dieguito I has metates, but it doesn't have gyratories. You only have to go fifty or a hundred miles east to find metates and the whole thing. Perfectly logical to me, but we have metates over in the San Pedro, where there are plenty of mesquite and other things to be ground. It never reached over into Pinacate until Amargosan times, post-Altithermal times, which are not San Dieguito at all. That's the way I rationalize the process of metates in early times in the eastern part of Arizona. I don't know that anybody agrees with me except Tony, but it suits me.

We did find Clovis points over here in Arizona. Out here in the Tucson Mountains someone got a big Clovis point with flakes surrounding it where somebody sat down and made one but "lost" it apparently. You go down into Mexico, down around the latitude of Tiburón and on the mainland at El Gramal, and you'll find large numbers of Clovis points and Clovis flaking. At La Playa north of Hermosillo is a beautiful Paleoindian site with Clovis. That's all varnished material. But they don't recognize it down there. Clovis-oid points, two of them, one of them locally made and one an import, were at Ventana Cave down in the 12,000-year level no less.

But I look on that as a matter of Clovis people wandering and picking out the game but moving on again without lingering or without having any effect at all upon the local people. I think they were safari people: they were wanderers, hunting, butchering, and moving on. I don't know if they had any effect on the people in Trans-Pecos, as far as that goes, but they were in there. The Clovis camps are very closely related to San Dieguito III camps; they're not in the same spots, but they're very closely related. We find Clovis-like points in San Dieguito III camps. And it may be that the San Dieguito people actually are the Clovis people. Perhaps they became Clovis people as times changed and emphasis on different ways of making a living changed with the changing climate. That's a possibility Tony is considering very seriously. As the SD II branched off and spread out, they were up in Nevada. They were up in Utah; they were up in Idaho. We know that they veered off with the changing climate and became the so-called Desert culture of the Great Basin, that we hear so much about. And they were in New Mexico and Colorado.

I've seen pictures of stuff from way up in eastern Oregon and eastern Washington that might be Malpais. If they were down here and varnished, they certainly would be. But you can't prove it up there. We don't have any skulls with dangling dog tags, so we're stuck on that. I don't know what we're going to do about it. We've got some old dates up in Canada, western Canada, but they're all subject to question. Either the deposition, the stratigraphy, is unclear, or the provenance isn't quite certain, or maybe it fell into the hands of some conservatives that didn't look at all the angles. I don't know.

But they certainly were developing in the Old World and were coming up northeast Asia, through Siberia, and across the straits. We're getting older and older material, and simpler and simpler tools, more like Malpais and San Dieguito. We're just beginning to learn what the Russians are doing up there, especially through John Olsen. His father, Stanley Olsen, was a bone specialist up at the university [of Arizona] in the Department of Anthropology. Anyway, we're just beginning to learn what the Russians are doing, and they're doing more and more work. We'll make a link one of these days.

Were there several crossings of the Bering Strait? Why not? Hell, the Athapaskans were some of the last ones to come across. The Navajos and the Apaches are the latest comers down here. They've only been around here for five hundred years, six hundred years. They're mutually intelligible to Athapaskans way up in the Yukon country. They can talk to each other for they talk the same language. And there were other entries too. There's a lot of argument on the linguistics because of the length of time it takes for language to change.

When my father went to Harvard, Wegener had already proposed continental drift but was put down by everybody, if you recall your history. So my father put it down, too, because he had learned differently—there could not possibly be continental drift. Of course, with me, I knew nothing about it, so I didn't say anything. But I never forgot it. While my father was still alive—he died in 1969—continental drift was just being talked about again. Coming back. Now it's accepted, improved upon, and refined.

They do the same thing in archaeology. A friend of mine was here yesterday. She's known Dr. Haury for many years, and she remarked that Dr. Haury's life has been very interesting from the standpoint of changing viewpoints. He originally thought in his early work that Hohokam were indigenous. And then he decided on the basis of Snaketown that the Hohokam were immigrants, who came in suddenly about 300 BC bringing the whole culture with them. Then, in recent years, he is turning back to his original viewpoint. Meanwhile, people in his own department and elsewhere are now saying that the Hohokam are an indigenous development with no immigrants. It all started here, developed here, and died out here.

I think my idea is better than either of them. There is no doubting that all these traits show up so suddenly, and they were brought in by immigrants, who aren't immigrants. They are people belonging to the same stock, who speak the same language as the Amargosans who were hunting and gathering around the valleys here. People had been traveling back and forth for thousands of years, traveling all the way from Idaho clear down to Jalisco.

And for whatever reasons, the Hohokam, who lived as a peaceful people down in the Rio Santiago in Jalisco country, came up and planted themselves in the Gila. The local Amargosans, who were their kinfolk, the same language stock, fell right in with them. Hell, probably half of them had been sleeping with each other, you know? That's much simpler to me than either the indigenous or the immigrant. As I said to my friend, "If a bunch of Texans come into Arizona, and teach us a new trick about raising cattle, are they immigrants? Or not?" They're not immigrants. We're the same culture, the same people with the same language. I don't know what you'd call them. But they're sure as hell not immigrants in the sense that they're people of a different stock.

I wrote it up in "Hohokam Origins" in *American Antiquity* [1970]. I haven't had any reason to refine it, and I haven't had any reason to retract it. I haven't been able to find any contradictions, linguistic or any other thing. It's never been rebutted, either because they can't rebut it or they don't think it's worthwhile rebutting. Dave Doyel at Pueblo Grande published a paper in which he said, "Maybe it's about time we went back and looked at Hayden's paper with his concept of a Piman ribbon corridor going north and south." That's the only time I've seen it mentioned, in years. But it answers some questions to him, or he wouldn't have mentioned it.

So Pinacate then is certainly a *type* area for a very wide geographical area. And the solutions I've found in Pinacate would apply from Idaho to Texas to Jalisco, except for Hohokam. It hasn't got anything to do with Hohokam particularly. They never got in there. It's all passing through to go down and collect shells. I don't think it has any bearing on the Hohokam question. Its importance is that it's an isolated area in which people have been pretty much by themselves since the Medithermal when they first settled there. They were pretty much unaffected by developments outside. Sure, pottery came in and that sort of thing, but they traded for it—they didn't make it themselves. All their pottery comes down from the Gila and the Colorado Rivers where it was made by the Yumans. The Yuma Indians learned it from the Hohokam and other pottery makers.

The interesting thing to me is that it's almost a pure culture. You've got pure Malpais I; you've got pure Malpais II; you've got pure SD I. And development stops at SD I. In Pinacate it didn't proceed into SD II and III, whereas it did in Texas and it did in California. Some parts of western Arizona came into SD II, but in Pinacate it stayed right at SD I. Even Clovis has no effect on it. They're coeval. Late SD I in Pinacate is the same age as Clovis is elsewhere, as Clovis is, 11,000.

That's what makes Pinacate such a nice place to work. Your controls are so definite on your desert pavements, which lie up on lava flows. With no arroyo cutting, no overflowing by other debris from the mountains, it's all right there just the way God made it. I haven't seen any Pinacate Sites with stratigraphy. Down at Chivos Tank, there's some places with two or three feet of fill and loess in that terrace above the tank itself, but it's so churned by rodents and people that you can't do anything with it. It wouldn't help at all.

There is stratigraphy along the Sonoyta River, but the river has been affected so seriously by climatic change, by drought and by torrential floods which have cut like hell—twenty feet deep in places. And then, in equitable times of proper moisture, the river builds up its beds. As Ives pointed out more than once, the present Hohokam metate is twenty feet below the present surface. In other words, the Sonoyta River was cut twenty feet deep in 1100 AD, and it came back up to grade and now it's cutting down again. That's the way it is all over the Southwest. You'd be lucky as hell if you found anything there that you could use.

Other problems which perplex me these days in the Pinacate? Mostly dating. The other thing is not a problem to me, but it is to other people: the relationship of the volcanic eruptions, volcanism, to human occupation. For example, Dan Lynch claims Tecolote Cone erupted about 2,000 years ago. He bases this on a C-14 date from varnish on the lava slope above our camp. He walked up on the lava flow there, got some samples which came out at 2,000. But meanwhile, I was working down below, picking up ejecta from the same flow they were embedded in. These have caliche of at least Pluvial age on the underside, so there I'm talking about 20,000 again.

But we have a C-14 of 2,000, and that cost me a liter of damn good tequila to Dan Lynch, which I'm going to re-collect with interest if and when I can prove that it's too young. But I can't imagine these Amargosans sitting around and saying, "My, isn't that a pretty sight?" when that thing erupted. Two thousand years ago? With Amargosans all around and no legends? Everybody knows what a volcano looks like. The Hopi remember the 1066 eruptions, so I don't know why the Papago-Pinacateños wouldn't remember one 2,000 years ago.

And I've never seen any evidence of any volcanism cutting a trail, or having any effect at all upon heavily varnished areas. All this varnishing took place since any real volcanic activity. I can't prove it, yet. There are only igneous and metamorphic rocks in Pinacate, no sedimentary. The metamorphic ranges—the Hornaday Range and the Sierra Blanca—are older than Pinacate. They're granitic and metamorphosed sediments, the schists and so forth.

The seashells in the Pinacate help date antiquity. You've got to go afield, down to the coast to Adair Bay, and you'll come across very old food shell, shell not deposited

E-mail message from James T. Gutmann to Bill Broyles, May 17, 2008 (used by permission).

If only Julian had lived at least a bit longer. Dating geologic events and surfaces can be tricky business but understanding and technology advance steadily. Less than five months after he passed away, the age of the Tecolote lava flow beside which Julian camped was determined via the widely tested $^{40}Ar/^{39}Ar$ isochron method to be twenty-seven thousand years, plus or minus six thousand years. It occurred to me as these numbers appeared on the computer screen that Julian had won his bet after all. And although he was perplexed, I think he knew he would win some day, the only question being when. He also knew "there's time enough for countin' when the dealin's done." But he surely did want to collect that tequila, and it better be good stuff!

As for people witnessing Pinacate eruptions, that could well have happened, but evidently not in the last two or three thousand years: the youngest eruption age we have obtained so far is that of La Laja, which yielded a date of 12,000 years ago, give or take 4,000 years.

by birds or waves but shell hauled up in great quantities by people. These people carried them up to the top of aeolian (wind-formed) dunes, where they cooked and ate their shells and their fish. Now that shell, lying exposed, has made a pavement, and acid rainfall has corroded the shell surfaces. As the rains channeled them, they turned gray and formed a pavement, which is impervious to erosion, like a desert pavement. That shell gives me a date of 33,500 years, which actually is a young date, because of radioactive contamination by fallout.

Immediately under this shell pavement, just ten centimeters below the surface, is other human-used shell that is beyond the range of C-14, so it's older than 37,000. And as you go down, it's progressively older, obviously, but you don't know how much older because 37,000 is the limit. So far.

Shell midden camp near Adair Bay, Sonora, Mexico, March 29, 1970. C-14 dates of greater than 37,000 BP were obtained from the lower midden horizons of this dune.

Then we go up in the Pinacate to the old sites, like Tule Tank. You don't see so much shell on the east side, but you find a lot on the west side, where shell was more conveniently carried. The heavy shell, dosinia shell, has been made into scrapers, knives, gougers. Superficially it's identical to the shell on the surface at Adair Bay—it, too, is channeled by erosion, it's gray, it's ancient shell. So I assume, for the purposes of argument, that it's at the same age as the food shell I see down in the dunes. And it's found only in association with very heavily varnished Malpais tools or pavements.

So the problem now is to get better dates on the shell from the dunes. Once we have dates on them, then we can say something about the sea level stage at the time when people were harvesting those shells. If we go back to the height of the Wisconsin glaciation, sea level in the Barbados was as much as one hundred and twenty meters lower than it is now, according to a report I just got. That's three hundred and sixty feet lower. I don't know where sea level was in the Sea of Cortez, but even if you say fifty meters lower, then according to the hydrographic maps you've got to go thirty kilometers from the coast at Gustavo Sotelo to reach the beach where you could collect chione, or get to deep water where you could collect rock oysters. Nobody's going to walk thirty kilometers and haul tens of cubic yards of seashells back to climb a dune and eat it.

Of course, I don't know how much the bay has filled in with sediment, either, in those 30,000 years. But at any rate there wasn't live water around those dunes at the height of the glaciation when the sea level was so low. You've got to go back to the interstadial. And I personally think we've got to go back to the Sangamon, which is 80,000 to 120,000 before the present.

Sea levels are a damned important thing when it comes to determining the age—relative age at least—of Pinacate occupation by working through the shells and their habitat. It makes a big difference whether they're estuarine mud dwellers, or whether they need live water. There are ridges of pure white turitella shells, clear, pure species from the Cerro Prieto estuary north of Rocky Point. At Gustavo Sotelo, the coastal cliffs were pure chione shell underneath that hard overcapping. It's coquina, and it's just as clean and fresh as what they put in there yesterday. It's just very lightly cemented together. I've got a sneaking suspicion that it's an old estuary. Gustavo Sotelo sits on an extinct estuary, as you may have noticed. If we can get a date on those shells, we might be able to tie it in with the sea levels, because that shell is sorted somehow, just the way the turitella was by storms. It's holding up there in that pure deposit of coquina shell, of chione shell. And overlying that is carbonate, with broken shell and gravels and sands, and then the present sand. That used to be the floor of an estuary, like at Tres Ojitos. I think we can get a relationship there of dating that would be damned important to our problems of trying to date human occupation.

Somebody was here, and we were talking about it the other day. He said, "Damn it all, it's moving a little too slowly!" And I said, "What's the difference? The next generation's going to do it anyway; we're not going to live long enough to see this accepted. It'll either be proved or disproved in the next generation." I've got all the patience in the world.

14. New Trends

The new trends in archaeology, compared to the old trends, can be put pretty simply, I think. Tony Andretta's the only one who would agree with me . . . and a Frenchman named Paul Courbin. No, I think even my father would agree with me.

Archaeologists up until twenty, twenty-five, thirty years ago used to employ the scientific method as religiously as possible. They went out in the field to gather evidence, all the evidence in the field that our knowledge and ability would permit us to gather. Even though much of it didn't seem to be pertinent to what we were looking for, we nevertheless collected it because we were destroying it. Archaeology is purely destructive, as you know. So the big ones like Hodge and Harrington and my father, in his own way, all the great ones recorded all the possible information they could see. Even if they didn't understand it, someone, someday, might.

Out of the information they gathered, they put together hypotheses which occurred to them, and then they'd test them, to use a term that I don't like, but that's what it amounts to. They tested the hypotheses by hunting for evidence which would refute the hypotheses. And if they found refutational evidence, they took roundance on it—went around about—and possibly dropped the hypothesis entirely. You're familiar with the scientific method, as familiar as I am.

Then Paul Martin of the University of Chicago, David Clarke of England, and some others, and also James Deetz, I think, was one of them, they got it into their heads that this was a waste of time to do all this digging and collecting all this evidence that would never be used. And they came up with this idea: formulate your hypothesis, then go out in the field and excavate that which supports your hypothesis, and any evidence extraneous to your hypothesis, ignore it. It's a waste of time collecting stuff you'll never use.

I remember vividly a note in "Current Research" in *American Antiquity* [Riddell 1968:413] twenty-five years ago. Martin had a school up at Vernon where the students were working on the Mogollon culture. Martin used this field school to proselytize his idea of archaeology, which became the New Archaeology. The note in "Current Research" said precisely what I've just said. Do not collect extraneous information. Formulate your hypothesis at home in the library, go out in the field and collect that which supports it, and ignore the rest of it. And I couldn't believe it. I looked at it three or four times. I came in and I read it to Helen. She was horrified, and so I wrote the editor of "Current Research," a man named Francis Riddell, a Californian. Eventually, after a lot of prodding I got a little note back saying that the note in "Current Research" was poorly edited. Well, sure.

I remember the Pecos Conference was held over in El Paso one year [1968] just for the convenience of the Vernon School, and the Vernon people did all the talking.

I went up. Some New Archaeologist put forth a very learned talk on the reasons why there was a sudden burst in population in a place called Hay Hollow, where suddenly the population just skyrocketed. When he got through, Al Schroeder, who likes to puncture balloons once in a while, got up and said, "Have you considered the possibility that a new hybridized corn might have come in, a new strain of corn might have come in with a shorter growing period, which would make it possible for more people to live there?"

And the speaker stared at him and said with great indignation, "That's not fair, that's not in my hypothesis!"

So Al said, "Well, you can prove the earth is flat that way, can't you?"

And the man said, "That is not fair!" And he turned and ran off the stage, and all of the Vernon School left the conference and went back to Hay Hollow. And that really happened.

A man was doing salvage archaeology on I-19, coming out of Nogales, on those terraces. I'd been working on the missile sites down there, and I knew those terraces pretty well. I spent a lot of money on them because I several times let things get away from me while I was hunting for artifacts, which cost me. There is nothing that impresses a man more than to have something cost him on a contract.

Anyway, he and I were old friends, so he invited me down, and I walked around with him on these terraces. I'd pick up a tool and say, "Here's a nice San Dieguito chopper."

"Bah," and he'd throw it away.

"Fine," I said, "what the hell do you want?"

And he said, "I'm looking for projectile points."

And I said, "There aren't any."

He said, "How do you know?"

"Oh," I said, "Malcolm Rogers spent thirty-five years looking, and I've been looking for somewhat over a longer time than you've been born, and I've never seen one, neither of us."

"Well," he said, "you just haven't looked in the right places, you don't recognize them."

"All right."

And then I realized it was his job—he'd been assigned to find them and he "would"—so I shut my mouth and didn't say anymore. Then one day I went down to the museum, and he called me in and showed me his table full of artifacts. I said, "Where are all the metates?"

"Oh," he said, "I didn't collect them."

I said, "Where are the manos? Where are the Papago-style arrow points?"

"I didn't collect them."

I said, "What the hell did you collect?"

"Well," he said, "we just haven't discovered them yet. I'm looking for early projectile points."

He had a lot of tools lying out, as well as some stones that were not tools, which were naturally flaked, and all of which were oxidized. And I said, "Well, you've got a lot of good San Dieguito tools here, with all the proper oxidation on them."

"Oh," he said, "I called a geologist in and he said those were all flaked, all broken that way in streams." That was the end of that whole program, all that evidence thrown out. But I had a good collection myself of good San Dieguito material. So that's the New Archaeology.

Dr. Courbin from one of the distinguished French institutions got so fed up with this that about eight years ago he wrote a book called *What is Archaeology?* just now translated beautifully by a man who got all Courbin's wit and his sarcasm and his puns and everything else into English. I promptly bought a copy, read it straight through all in one night. I ordered another copy for Tony Andretta, who is a scientific method nut. He stayed awake nights reading it. We love it, because Courbin says what we've been saying.

So that's the situation. That's New Archaeology for you, with all kinds of ramifications. I can't even remember the lingo. I don't even want to remember the lingo they use. They've changed the whole English language around to fit their completely false and fabricated philosophy, to me. They're talking about ultimately not doing any field work at all, and just looking at collections at hand. That's what it boils down to if you carry it to its logical extreme, what they're told, what they say. Good field men, you know?

I've read a couple of salvage reports, big ones, by good people who've been misled, of course, by the New Archaeologists, and they've criticized me loudly because they can't determine my research design for the Pinacate. Well, of course not. I never had one. I'd never worked in the Pinacate before. Rogers never had one when he hit the desert. He didn't know what he was going to encounter. He collected everything he could see, all the evidence he could, and formulated his hypothesis. He changed his mind for forty damned years. And I've changed mine damned regularly, too, and I'll do so again. And that's archaeology, I think. Or the important part of it. That's a lecture I didn't want to get into, but I feel strongly about it.

Lay it on the table, look at it yourself. You're the man doing the work. Write your notes. I've got notes on every conceivable subject in the Pinacate. I've done the best I could. I could have done better if I were smarter or better trained, perhaps. I notice everything that I can, and someday it might come in valuable.

The same goes for archaeology. And there's lots of things that I know I haven't seen. I may've seen them but haven't recognized them. It took me a long time to recognize varnish to the point where I could talk about it. I even called a meeting here one time with Dr. Marie Wormington of the Denver Museum. She's the grand old lady of Early Man in the New World. She was a guest lecturer at ASU, some years ago, while Helen was still alive. And I was beginning to feel pretty strongly that I had not only Malpais, which is preglacial, but I had a Malpais I, of possible earlier stage. I didn't know it at that time but I thought it might be what I call now Malpais I.

So I called her, and she came down here and stayed with us a couple nights. Everybody came to the meeting: Bill Robinson, Paul Ezell came over, and Morlin Childers came over, everybody but Dr. Haury. I didn't invite him because he was not in sympathy and because he was so impressive a man that the other people wouldn't feel free to speak up. So we looked at things all afternoon out there in the lab. Helen and I blew our bankroll—took them all to dinner at the Club 21 and had a wonderful time. When I brought up Malpais II and Malpais I, there was dead silence. So we demonstrated the varnish on the flakes, and the cortical varnish and so forth, changes in technology. There was complete silence. And nobody said anything later, either. Probably because it had never occurred to any of them that there was such a thing. They had to have time to think about it, but at least I got it out.

Paul began to think about it, and Childers began to think about it. Marie was open-minded, and we had a good visit. How in the hell could I put that in a research design? That changed everything, changed the whole focus of the studies down there. That and the observation that it appeared that during varnish-forming periods, which presumably would be either hot or cold, and certainly very dry, vegetation was dying, the roots in the soil there, and the rodents, would, of course, be gone, and nobody could live there. That took a lot of observing, too. And noting. And digging holes in the ground, testing the structure of desert pavement in the subsurface. That's what I call the scientific method, or an application of it. And then I write up my reports, present my evidence, and draw my conclusions. You can look at my evidence and do what you like. Disagree with me. That's all right. Maybe you know something that I haven't known.

I recently read the program for a southwestern symposium on archaeology at the university. I read it three or four times. And then I got out my dictionary, but it didn't help me a bit. I threw the whole thing in a pot and boiled it for twenty minutes, and I still couldn't understand it. I'm not going to the symposium. That's the way I feel about it. One reason this is bunk—it all depends ultimately on the quality of the field man who did the actual excavation and wrote the actual report. If he or she didn't know what they were doing, that misstates the whole thing clear at the top. So why waste my time, when I know that some of the field work was lousy. Some of these people soon to graduate couldn't tell the difference between a lava flow and spilled talcum powder, because they'd never been taught it. I feel very strongly about it, not that it makes any difference to anybody except me. There: I got my say-so.

The New Archaeologists are getting away from corroborating their evidence with geology and meteorology and the other basic sciences. I think a lot of them have done that, but I think it's going to swing back now. Otherwise, Paul Courbin probably couldn't have published his book. I think it will swing away from it when the universities retire their archaeological faculties who were hired at the peak of the fad and are tenured. Maybe in another twenty or thirty years we'll have some professors in there who know what the scientific method is. I'm not talking personalities. I'm talking discipline or whatever the word is.

How in the world could they be skilled in securing basic tangible evidence when they've never been in the field? Or, if they've been in the field, they've been collecting only that which they were instructed to collect, that which fit their research design, their hypothesis. How could they see anything else? And what would they do with it if they did see it?

Jane Rosenthal is one very sharp young lady. She worked with me in Pinacate, and she worked in our lab out here. I helped her get through grad school. She wrote her doctoral thesis on the stone tools of Pinacate, and she developed a computer program so that she could computerize the bloody thing, which was fine so long as she used it as a tool. She got her doctorate. Later I said to Jane, "Look, kid, you did a beautiful job, and you worked like hell on it, and you didn't tell me a damn thing more than any competent field man could have told me in four days in the field."

"Yes," she said, "I know that, but I certainly quantified it, didn't I?"

And I said, "Yes, you did." And she did. She did a good job of quantifying it, but she didn't teach me anything.

Julian at camp in the Sierra Pinacate with his International Travelall El Chapulín Chancanquero *(the lubber grasshopper), so named by Pinacate cowboys.*

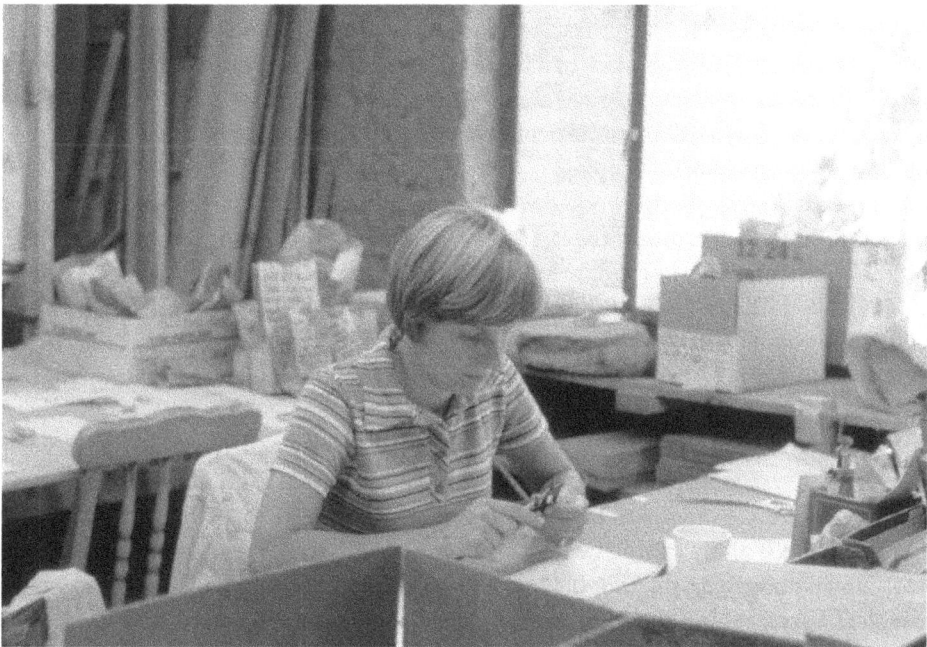

Jane Rosenthal working in Julian's lab, Tucson, ca. 1973.

Another grad student was trying to find a way in which she could look at a map, and by using random walks and all the other techniques of New Archaeologists, you could decide that it's more likely a site will be here than it is there, so you can go out in the field and waste as little time as possible. Tony Andretta and Malcolm Rogers did the same thing by eye, because they had worked in the field so long that they knew where the prehistoric people, where the Indians would have lived. Tony can even tell you the elevation of a site, from a map; he can say, "Now there will be San Dieguito I there." And you can go out in the field and, by God, that's where it is, because he knows that particular area so intimately. Rogers could do the same thing.

One thing that's bothered us a long time is the tendency, the effort, of professional archaeologists connected with academia to turn archaeology into a science to make it respectable. They've adopted all kinds of scientific jargon and fitted it to archaeological work. It's all in this book by Courbin; he takes them all apart. I'll just content myself with saying something my father said many years ago and I believe thoroughly: "archaeology is an art, it's not a science, and it can never be a science."

You can't make a science out of people, in any way, shape, or form unless you have them in the mass and you apply statistics to them. You can't apply statistics to Joe Blow and Benny Roanhorse out there because you've only got two people. They're just as different as people can be, and you can't do anything with them at all. And the only way you can do anything with them is by knowing as much about people as possible, either in the flesh or in their names. How in the world can a man understand a prehistoric people who hasn't even done a hitch in the army, let alone go out and work on a construction job? Or do anything other than hit the books and repeat what his professors told him? What does he know about the world? And after all, we live in the world.

Al Olson once remarked that he learned more about anthropology helping me dig sewer ditches and lay sewer pipe than he'd ever learned in class. Meaning that he learned more about people, including more about me, I reckon. And I'll stand on that. That was one reason so few, academics particularly, have any knowledge, practical knowledge, quite aside from knowing people.

My CCC boys whom I worked with in the field a number of years were wonderful diggers at sites. They came off the farm, they came out of the coal mines, and they came off the streets, and they knew how to work and how to use their hands. They knew how to think about things because they had hit problems. I'd explain to some of them, this is the way you make a chopper and this is the way a chopper works. "Ah," they knew exactly what I was talking about. That's true of any man who uses his hands. They've got "hand sense."

Paul Ezell came over from teaching archaeology in San Diego. He hadn't been teaching for very long, but he was astonished and half disgusted because he'd lay out a tray of stone tools, and say to his class, "Handle them and tell me what they are, how they were used." Only one or two out of twenty would walk up and start picking the tools up and bouncing them in his hand to get the feeling of them. The others would put their hands behind their backs, figuratively, and look just as dumb as a chicken at Christmas time.

I said to Paul, "If you're in a culture in which a city boy can't even remember how to mow a lawn because he doesn't have to, and there isn't anything that he has to do, how do you expect him to know how to make a tool or how to use a tool? Or how to even tell you what a tool is? Or what it was used for?" Paul was complaining he had to go to the dime store and buy a plane, buy a hoe, buy a bit, a borer, so he could show the kids what tools were, show them how to hold it in your hands. He thought it was terrible.

But these CCC kids of mine, my God, they were sharp. Emil Haury would bring his master's class, all four of them, down once a week, to University Ruin, in the afternoon, out there, to see how to sort pottery and to see how things were going. And my boys delighted in taking them stone tools and saying, "What's this?" And it was damn seldom anybody could tell them. My boys knew how to make them. They also knew the stratigraphy. They knew the difference between salt erosion debris and rain wash. But the M.A. candidates didn't because they'd never been taught it, never been exposed to it. These folks didn't know the difference between andesite and obsidian.

You can't make archaeology into a science. You can't make anything into a science as long as you're dealing with people in limited numbers, as far as I'm concerned. And the more hand sense you have, and I'm going to take credit for that phrase at least, within our limited circle, because I said to Paul, "How do you expect these kids to have hand sense?" I feel sorry for people who can't do things just because they've never learned.

The New Archaeologists are trying to apply statistics to artifacts, but then they miss the connection between the artifacts and the people who used those artifacts. I've argued that for years, too. A man came over here, a doctoral candidate from the University of Riverside. He wrote me, wanted to come over and go through my lab. Said when he'd be here. Well, he didn't come and he didn't come and he didn't come, and all of a sudden he showed up one evening expecting a bed and board. All right, some people prove that they particularly don't have manners, anyhow.

But I took him out in the lab and showed him the San Dieguito tools. I left him there. And he came in the next morning, after working all night. So I fed him, and then I said, "Now what did you learn last night?"

"Well," he said, "I went over every stone tool that you laid out."

And I said, "What did you do?"

And he said, "I measured the beta angle on each one."

I asked, "What's the beta angle?"

"Well," he said, "I don't know exactly, but I know how to do it. I measured them all, we always do it."

And so I said, "What does it tell you?"

He said, "I don't know, but we always do it." You think I'm exaggerating? I'm not. So he went off and never even said thanks or go to hell or anything else and went away.

Later on I understood he wrote a little note to the effect that I didn't know what the hell I was talking about and didn't have any artifacts because the beta angles all told him differently. Beta angle, as far as I know, would be the theoretical angle on a tool. If it's too obtuse, it's made by nature. If it's acute, past a certain number of degrees, then a man made it, something of the sort. Frankly I never really understood it and I never really cared about it anyway, because beta angles and any other angles are controlled so largely by the material. You get an entirely different angle with andesite than you do from basalt.

That's one of the things that was challenging Don Crabtree, the finest flintknapper we ever had. He was a pioneer. That's one of the things that got him interested in the basalt tools in Pinacate and Trans-Pecos, because he'd never flaked basalt. He wanted to work out the physics of it, the forces required and the angles that would result and all that sort of thing. When he died, that was the end of it. No one continued his work in basalt.

There are lots of people who are good flintknappers and say that these San Dieguito and Malpais tools from here and Texas are naturefacts. George Carter was absolutely correct when he said that many of his tools were manmade. Folks laughed at him then, and they still laugh at him, but he was right for many, many reasons. One simple reason is you don't get, in my experience, consecutive flaking along an edge in nature. That has to be deliberate, one blow after another.

People say, "Well, that went through a rock crusher." I've probably crushed more goddamn rock to make a living than most archaeologists have ever seen. One day I picked up an end scraper, in what we call the dust palliative here, out at Davis-Monthan on a taxiway. The whole thing was in gravel, and each side of that pavement had gone through an inch and a half screen, crushed. Yet, I went to it just as straight as an Indian going for a drink of water. I picked up an end scraper with a very obtuse angle on the face of it. It was an exhausted end scraper. At one time it had had an acute angle, between the bottom plane and the facial plane. And the man kept resharpening it until he'd worked it back to the point where it was no longer usable. Then he threw it away. And by the grace of God, it was picked up in a power shovel in the gravels out here in the Pantano. San Dieguito, in my opinion. It went through this crusher, wasn't damaged, went through the screen, because it fit, and I picked it up. I showed that to I don't know how many experts, and most of them said, "Hmm."

I showed it to Norman Tindale and he looked at it and he said, "An exhausted end scraper, so what?" Norman Tindale was accustomed to that sort of thing. I have looked at more rock, crushed rocks, on some aspect of my work over my life, and I'll wager I haven't seen three or four that could be mistaken for manmade. The difference? For all kinds of reasons, some subjective, most of them objective.

One sample I have is a San Dieguito chopper. It was exhausted. He was taking off flakes around the perimeter, and the one hit a hinge fracture, so he couldn't do anymore and threw it away. It lay out there all through the Altithermal and developed a nice, heavy cortex of oxidized phenocrysts, which contain iron. Then when the area was reoccupied, some Amargosan came along and picked it up. He hit it a damn sight harder, and he made a new chopper. He reduced the size of it and had new flakes with the old cortex showing in between. So, it's a two-generation tool.

Malcolm Rogers used to tell me when he was up at Santa Clara, the Indian pueblo, he went out for a walk with one of the Indian boys one day. The boy had a rifle, and he shot a deer. Malcolm turned around and came back to the pueblo, and pretty soon the boy came in with the deer all skinned and dressed out. Quartered and all. Malcolm said, "How'd you do that? You didn't have a knife."

"No, of course not," he said. "I knocked a flake off a cobble and used that."

"And what did you do with the flake?"

"Why," he said, "I threw it away, why carry it home? Make some more of them anytime."

Tom Dillehay, down at Monte Verde in Chile, has some wooden structures and all that sort of thing down below his 14,000-year level. Some distance below that and a little distance away, he's got tools. Very simple tools, but they're exotic. They are broken cobbles, and they don't belong there. They don't belong in that region. Somebody carried them in, broke them, and used them. Yet you can't convince a lot of people that that's even thinkable. I think most anything is thinkable: at least you've got to look at it, and analyze the situation, before you condemn it.

People don't recognize them as tools, you see. They're not recognized as tools, therefore they're not tools. But someone else with experience might. A man like Tindale, who knows what the Aboriginals use over in Australia, will recognize tools that none of our people in Arizona would recognize, because they had not seen them used. These links with cultures such as the Aboriginals that still use tools are crucial for our own understanding. They're the only way we're going to find out how stone tools were made and how they were used in different cultures. They're very important. Now, just because I talk about the ways that the Aboriginals made tools, it doesn't mean I think these people were the first people over here, or even second cousins to them—that's not the point. We're all human and use tools in similar ways.

Perhaps you want to go so far as to say that people in the New World, as well as the people in Australia, come out of Southeast Asia somewhere with a common ancestry. That's entirely possible, but it isn't something you write much about, because that's pure speculation. That's what you talk about over the campfires, as Tindale and Paul Ezell and I used to do. Only at that time we talked about people living here 35,000 years ago, and now I'll talk about 100,000.

Archaeology is a part of anthropology. Archaeology technically begins with the material culture, the imperishable material culture, and some perishable. But it seems to me that if all you know is what's imperishable, how are you going to know what was perishable?

J. P. Harrington, ethnologist, prepared an exhibit for the Pan-Pacific exposition in San Diego, Balboa Park, 1915, I think. He went up to the Mojave Indians on the Colorado River and collected examples of all of the perishable artifacts that he could. Some of them were already going, for only the oldest people remembered how to make them. Harrington put on an exhibit, all labeled and catalogued. But in my time, they were discovered up in the attic of one of the old buildings, some of them half rotted away. And, if I recall, there were some thirty-five hundred artifacts—different tools, different objects—that these people used! Harrington had collected them, gotten the uses, gotten the Mojave names, but all that's forgotten now.

And those tools have now all fallen out of use, because of changes of life in the Mojave since the advent of the white man. That's where the ethnology comes in. People sometimes call it archaeo-ethnology, which might be all right. But a good many people simply don't recognize the propriety of moving from archaeology to ethnology anymore than I was when I first used the Pima Creation Myth in the article on Hohokam origins to suggest that there was an actual historic foundation for the myth. I was criticized severely for that because "one does not do that." I'm an archaeologist, not an ethnologist. That's one reason; the other is the pretentious notion that no Indian can remember more than ten years, so many experts contend. As time goes on I feel better and better about it.

Deni Seymour, who worked on her doctorate over in the San Pedro on the Sobaipuri, had a piece in the *Journal of the Southwest* a while ago [1989], very nice. It boils down to the same thing: archaeology, ethnology, history, the Spanish encountered the Sobaipuri, the Sobaipuri were trading with the Hopis, the Jeddito Black-on-yellow, and all that sort of thing. They were fairly accustomed to traveling up to Hopi country and back, right over here in the San Pedro. And that seems to have been true in prehistoric times, too.

According to legend and according to some archaeological evidence, the Sobaipuri apparently were the people who came from the east and whipped the hell out of the Hohokam sometime after 1400 AD. If the Hopi can remember the eruption of Sunset Crater in 1066, I think maybe the so-called "dumb beaneaters" could remember an invasion and driving out their oppressors, the Hohokam, in 1450 AD. And I'll say so every chance I get.

These stone tools just sort of leap into your hand. You know this one here. It's a lefthanded tool. Some of them are distinctly right, and some of them are distinctly lefthanded. Helen was lefthanded, and she always picked this one up. People get fixed in their ways, and they get ideas in their heads. They believed in flakes. They contend the only purpose this exhausted disk chopper had in life was to serve as a source for large flakes, which could be used as tools. Flakes were reshaped or used as they were, and when all the flakes had been taken off that were possible, they threw the core away. They called this a core. I call it a core *tool*.

Sure, they may have used the flakes. I would have, certainly, and I know damn well the Indians did. But this core tool is what they made the shape for. They wanted to make a chopper. I've got one in there on the shelf that has the flake glued back on it, just for demonstration. I found the flakes around it up there in the foothills at San Dieguito. This is a beautiful chopper from a cobble of rhyolite. Some ancient split it. He knocked off some flakes and made this chopper. You could cut a tree down with that, or do anything you like.

I've taught enough people. Remember the big bomb scare, when people were putting in bomb shelters all over the country and the next day an atom bomb was going to fall on Tucson? I'd be working up in the foothills with my operators on a big trenching machine. While the machine was doing the job, I'd be wandering around picking up tools. Sooner or later one operator or another one would come down off their rig and say, "What are you doing, Hayden?"

"Well, I'm picking up stones."

"What are you picking them up for? It's just a cracked rock, isn't it?"

"Well, I'll tell you. When that bomb falls, if you survive, this may be what you use to make a living with."

"What do you mean?"

I'd show them. "You see, here's a chopper. You may find yourself in a situation someday when this is all you have, to kill an animal with it, or to drive off an attacker. And this is how you make it." And I'd show them how. And, having hand sense, they all caught it instantly. Sooner or later one of them would come up to me, weeks later, maybe, and say, "Damn you Hayden!"

"Why?"

"I was showing my kids how to do that, and I smashed my thumb!"

That's the way the Aboriginals did it in Australia. I've read in Tindale that there is one cliff on the south coast, a high cliff, where the rock was of such quality that an Aboriginal up on top of the cliff could pick up a big cobble and drop it on the boulders

An Escondido Malpais tool from Texas, ca. 1982.

way down below to make tools. The cobble would shatter in such a way that he'd get a whole handful of usable flakes to bring home. He could hammerstone on them, and he could reshape them into anything he wanted. I've got pictures of it, in a book you ought to read called *Down among the Wild Men* by John Greenway.

Finding all the evidence? It's purely a matter of chance. You've got a scattered population, wandering population, of a few thousand people or a few tens of thousands, over North America, so it's just sheer chance that you might find a campsite. Look at all the Clovis points that have been found. We've got half a dozen kill sites, and we've got only about two Clovis campsites. And to hear tell, there were more Clovis people out here than there are Eastern dudes.

But why don't we find some bones? Why don't we find their bodies? We only have two or three Clovis skeletons that I know of. And the one big criticism of anything earlier is that we don't have any bones. We haven't got a skull with a dog tag clenched between his teeth with his date of birth. We don't even know how they buried their dead—maybe they exposed them.

Then you get into the Middle West, Iowa, where my friend Kay Simpson works. There you have anywhere from five to fifteen to twenty feet of loess over the Clovis horizon. Imagine trying to find burials in that situation. And look at all the vicissitudes of time on the terrain, on the topography over the length of time that we have to consider if we go back just as far as 12,000. If we go through the Pluvials, if we go through the glacial periods, if we go through the Interstadial, then God knows how the topography has changed in those times. It's changed tremendously. *Quaternary Research* is full of specialized articles on the changing topography of the late Quaternary and the early Holocene. Talk about finding a needle in a haystack! I'm surprised we get as much as we have.

Usually we get it only in our southwestern deserts, where we have pavements which are essentially permanent. And they have to be volcanic at that, because the stone itself doesn't break down within our time frame. Once the pavement is established, it's permanent as far as we're concerned, whereas pavements on metamorphics and detrital pavements are constantly losing stone: rocks decay, and more stuff comes down on top of them, plus they're undercut, which you don't get in lava. In lava flows, you get pavements.

Tony Andretta has got marvelous evidence of that over in Trans-Pecos where they have beautiful pavements and underneath are many, many feet of volcanic clays. Those are subject to erosion, and the areas are trenched, so the pavements roll off. They roll down into the arroyos, and you get a hell of a mixture of stuff. But over here in Pinacate, we have lava flows underneath the pavements, so they're permanent. They can't go anywhere. That's the only place you're going to find the very early stuff.

Then you've got to sort it all out, because it's all in one area. That's where your varnish comes in. If these pavements were up north where we don't have varnish, it might be that you couldn't say much about the relative ages of the various tools, stones incorporated in the pavement. And you certainly couldn't in a cave, where no oxidation takes place at all. That's why I think, here and in Trans-Pecos, we have some hope. On other volcanic and paved areas all the way down to Tierra del Fuego we've got the same situation . . . once people become willing to look and learn to look.

15. Why Archaeology?

You asked about archaeology and politics. They are, of course, mutually exclusive. There are no politics in archaeology. No archaeologists are politicians: they're all sincere, honest-to-God, dyed-in-the-wool scientists. If you believe that, I'm made out of green cheese.

We were talking about the Harris Site. As you recall, I left a CCC job over in Pueblo Grande at Phoenix in the summer of 1938, took a team, and went over to the San Dieguito River north of San Diego by Escondido. I worked for Malcolm Rogers, the archaeologist of San Diego Museum of Man. Malcolm had a Carnegie Foundation grant to do some work there, to run some trenches into a post-Pleistocene terrace. Nowadays we would say it was late Pleistocene, but in those days we didn't know what it was. Malcolm thought the San Dieguito River had aggraded. To put it another way, the river had cut the grade, the hardpan, during the wetter parts of the later Pleistocene. And it had built up this bed and filled the entire valley with alluvium, and then cut again. The cut took place, probably sometime in the last 11,000 years, maybe even before 5,000 years and perhaps at the onset of the Altithermal, as far as that goes. That's when streams cut, maybe 8,000 or 9,000 years ago.

But at any rate, there was a broad streambed cut again through hardpan with terraces on each side. There was a fill which had once filled the valley. There were Phase III San Dieguito complex flakes and tools coming out of the cut bank of the terrace face. Now, Rogers in those days thought that that had all taken place since 4,000 or 5,000 years ago—he was very conservative. We now talk happily about 30,000 years, when he spoke of 4,000. We're getting close to politics now, of course.

So we ran trenches into the right angle to the stream bed, and we got stratified deposits of gravels and sands, which clearly contained artifacts, the debris of hunting camps from the San Dieguito Phase III period. We now place them about 8,000 or 9,000 years ago. There were workshops, not where they fabricated tools from the raw material at all but where they brought the blanks that were preformed at the quarries up in the mountains. They completed their manufacturing in this camp, and also resharpened lance points; we had no projectiles. Spear points which had had their tips broken off. We got the debris of all of that, and we also saw where men had sat on convenient stones, boulders, and dropped their debitage, their flakes, and every once in a while we'd find half of a blade and sooner or later we'd find the other half where he'd thrown it away in a rage . . . if he's like me, anyway. Very human.

We also found there stone scrapers of an earlier period, San Dieguito I, and San Dieguito II phases, which we now put back, oh, 18, 20, 25,000 years. But at that time Rogers thought they might go back 4,000 at the most. These had been oxidized, and the surface cortex, oxidized cortex, chemical alteration as Rogers called it—some people called it patina, but patina's the wrong word. These had been washed down from hilltops in the vicinity of the river and lodged in the same deposit that we found the later stuff in.

The earlier people characteristically lived on knolls, high ground, probably because of wet country and wet climate. Then above all of this was a sterile layer of sand, obviously from a flood, and then a La Jollan layer, which is local, coastal people, who used extremely crude flaked-stone tools, far simpler and far rougher and far cruder than anything the San Dieguito people used. Obviously, these had no relation to the material we found below. [The La Jollan layer] included grinding stones and basin metates, which have never been found in the San Dieguito layer nor even in California or anywhere else at that time. Above that, I believe there was another sterile layer and above that was Diegueño of the present, showing the people who lived in the region when the Spanish came.

So we had a sequence there, a nice sequence of three occupations, three different people. Rogers wrote a brief report for Carnegie, and that's about all the attention that was ever paid to this site. Rogers never wrote the thing up properly. The war came. And everything had happened.... The San Diego Museum was taken over by the Navy. The mosaic of the trench wall was put away downstairs, in the basement. Rogers left the place until the war was over, and he just simply never got back to working on it. He retired. And nobody at the museum paid any attention to it, so all that was lost, essentially.

Then he came out of retirement, eventually. Helen and I talked him into going out in the field in this country. He worked on his San Dieguito complex in the Harris Site in the Rillito/Pantano, here in Tucson. Also, he went down to the Willcox Playa and so forth, and published on it in *Kiva* [Rogers 1958], which got the whole thing back into circulation.

I might also say that in the late 1930s, he wrote a report called *Early Lithic Industries of the Lower Basin of the Colorado River and Adjacent Desert Areas* in which he laid out all the stages that I mentioned—all the San Dieguito stages, and the Malpais stage, which he said was earlier than the San Dieguito I, II, and III. But later he incorporated the Malpais into SD I, which caused problems for me later on. We'll come to that.

But the politics comes in because nobody in those days believed in the antiquity of man in the New World. Six thousand years was the absolute maximum, according to Hrdlička, and he was the arbiter of everything concerning archaeology for a great many years. For anyone to propose artifacts older than 6,000 years was enough to run a man out of the profession.

But Rogers nevertheless was a damned good geologist and a damned good observer and a damned good archaeologist, so he kept on working. His notes were good and his collections were excellent. Before he died, he had partially edited his first draft report on the San Dieguito complex throughout the Southwest. Unfortunately, he had no illustrations. The report was written right here in the house here and in San Diego. My wife, Helen, edited it as she typed it, and she typed all of it. She cleaned it up but didn't do the final editing.

And then Rogers died, 1960. After that Paul Ezell went in to the Harris Site and ran a trench; and Claude Warren, from UCLA I think it was, ran a trench. Paul never wrote his up. But Claude did, and he went back some years later, and ran another trench. But Claude insisted, and I guess still insists, that San Dieguito complex per se was, as Clem Meighan said, a "figment of Rogers's imagination." He said that San Dieguito culture was a single-phase culture, as exemplified at the Harris Site. And it was not a type site, as Paul Ezell liked to say, because only one aspect of the Phase III culture was represented, the hunting camp, not knowledge of food gathering or anything else. Now, that's a fair statement.

But when Clem Meighan came out in the review of a book, *Prehistoric Man in the New World*, and said that the San Dieguito complex was a figment of Rogers's imagination and the three phases was a complete fabrication, he made me unhappy, so I wrote a rebuttal to *American Antiquity* and restored San Dieguito Phase I of the Harris Site to its proper place in the San Dieguito sequence. It had a long fancy title, and it was printed [1966]. Unfortunately, the editor took out some of my harsh words for Meighan, but it was very clear what I meant. I've never spoken to Meighan, so I don't know what he thought about it. Last I heard he still stuck to his guns. But I could identify the three stages. Well, so, one of us is wrong. It turns out that Rogers was correct, though he was off on his dating. His sequence was right.

As I've been saying for years to people like George Carter and others, let's worry about sequence, establish that, and then the dates will come. We'll get new tools, new methods to date material: then we'll know. I fired George Carter from the Harris Site in 1938. He lasted ten days. He was a brash young redhead who wanted to run the dig. I told Rogers, "Get that SOB out of here or I'll pull my crew." Ezell later commented on him, "Wouldn't it be ironic if we prove Carter right for all the wrong reasons?" Carter went on to write *Earlier Than You Think*. And it's turned out that way, as you know.

I got a letter from George the other day. That pleased me, because he said that—you know, it's always nice to be told you're right, particularly by a man with whom you've argued over the years—he said, "You were absolutely right, insisting on sequence first." He said he could never see that; he was hipped on 200,000 years, and that's all he could see, and that's what he fought for. He made lots of enemies and got laughed at, and may have set the whole damned study back a generation. But now, he said, we have the tools; we've established the sequence, and now that we have the tools, we're finding out that man has been here whatever you like, 50, 70, 100,000 years, long time. And that makes me feel good.

M. R. Harrington had worked with my father at Madisonville, Ohio, in the mounds, on Long Island, and upstate New York back between 1905 and 1909, somewhere in there. . . . Harrington had dug in southern Nevada, at what is known as Lost City on the Muddy River, when he was working for the George D. Heye Foundation of the Museum of the American Indian. And he collected Pueblo I potsherds up there, which he brought down to Doctor Hewitt or Mera, at the Laboratory of Anthropology in Santa Fe. He laid them on the doctor's desk. The professor asked, "Where did you get these?"

Harrington replied, "Southern Nevada, Muddy River valley."

"But there's no Pueblo pottery in Nevada."

"But here's this."

"Oh, they're nonexistent," and he swept them into the wastebasket. Period. He essentially called Harrington a damned liar. Lost City is a state park now, a big complex with contiguous rooms, all Pueblo I.

Look at the conflicts these geologists have had. I forget their names, but it's all in the literature. A man had proposed that stratification in rocks meant a great lapse of time, and he was told no. I've been arguing for many, many years that Pinacate is a beautiful classroom, if you like, or a beautiful exhibit of all the stages of man's occupation. He's been there a long time, as shown by the desert pavements. And I've argued that heavy varnish is indicative of a very long time; even though I didn't know what made varnish, we had the differences. We had the difference between heavy varnish, medium varnish, light varnish, and no varnish. Each one was accompanied by, or fit, a certain typology of stone tools. So we couldn't have coevolution. Impossible.

I remember when we had our big conference here with some of the bigshots. I proposed that sequence, and I got blank stares, because it was a new thought. Clovis was the oldest in the New World then. And it's just now beginning to be accepted by more people that he's not the oldest. I didn't have any tools to prove it. Nobody knew how to date varnish, and nobody paid any attention to it. Emma Lou Davis, in her giant report for the American Philosophical Society, I think in the 1950s, on the giant ground figures of the California desert, pointed out that varnish can form within thirty years, because she found numerals, which white men had laid out, in the desert pavement, 1926, or whatever it might be. All were beautifully indented and beautifully varnished.

What she didn't know or didn't occur to her was that people have a certain aesthetic sense, and if you're going to lay out a date or your name in a nice dark brown or black desert pavement you're not going to put the stones down wrong side up, the white side up. The Indians did. Even modern children putting their names up on top of Falcon Cone in the Pinacates always properly set these stones just the way they have been found when they were picked up. She didn't know that. Also, wind and rain had pushed light cinders up against the stones and they of course had all varnished over the years anyway. So, she said thirty years will varnish them real good.

When she published her report on the survey of the southern Panamint Valley, in Nevada, she collected stone tools and debitage of all the phases of occupation there. And she actually listed the various degrees in weathering: heavy varnish, light varnish, and so forth, right down to no varnish whatsoever. She gave the number of tools in each category, but she never described the tools. If she had described the tools within the categories, weathering categories, she could have had it laid right out there for her, because all the technology was different in every one.

And I compliment again the three editors of *American Antiquity* who published my papers describing varnish in connection with archaeology. They allowed me to suggest that 40,000 was possible, and didn't censor me. There have been times when I couldn't have published those, before and since.

American Antiquity is the only one that everybody in the country gets. It's the authoritative journal. Was. Now there are a couple of others, like the *Journal of Field Archaeology*. Most journals are highly specialized, though. And *American Antiquity* is still the one you want to publish in if you can. But there again, styles change, so we get editors who are theoreticians, who love theory, or who love the Mayans, and who are not interested in publishing anything on the Southwest. Those things happen, common to all editing, I suppose.

But in recent years, I doubt that Tony Andretta and I could publish a paper, easily, on the stuff that we're working on in Texas, which ties right in with what we've got in Pinacate and throughout the Southwest deserts anyway. I think we'd have a problem. I know it. When I wrote up something with Tony for a Don Crabtree memorial volume,

Gladys Sayles and Emil Haury at Snaketown, March 1935. (Photograph by Julian Hayden)

the manuscript went out for review ["The San Dieguito Complex and the Trans-Pecos, Texas," 1982]. We got some very favorable reviews. And some that just tore the skin off our backs: we were damned fools; we were dreamers; we were liars; we were everything under the sun. We had no evidence, fabricated the whole thing—people said that.

They were all anonymous reviews. And presumably these people, these reviewers, were reputable and authoritative archaeologists. So that's why we didn't publish that paper. We couldn't get it accepted. The editor loved it. Actually, they did us a favor, because within two or three years we knew so much more about the area than we had that we would have been out of date by the time the book appeared. Since then Andretta and I wrote another one, for an international conference ["Early Man in the Far Southwestern United States and Adjacent Sonora, Mexico," 1987]. It was sent back to me for certain changes, which I didn't think were justifiable, so I didn't do it, and so it's still sitting. Now that may be my fault. Probably is.

There's an old-boy network of archaeologists. Absolutely. I remember Emil, Dr. Haury, for whom I worked in 1934 and '35 and worked with ever since. He was given a lot of flack, because he came up with such things as a Mogollon culture when the word was that everything was Anasazi. Gladwin and Haury came up with the Hohokam. And then Haury later came up with the Mogollon, lying in between the Hohokam and the Anasazi. Now those are all accepted now, no question about them. And Harold Colton came up with the Sinagua, lying to the southwest of Flagstaff. That's in between Hohokam and western Anasazi. And that's a valid one, too.

But 1934, '35, there was a lot of doubt about the existence of the Hohokam. Puebloan. Surely the Anasazi you know. They were just beginning to believe that was possible, beginning to get around that maybe there was something there, the Red-on-buff Culture. Haury was sputtering one day about some folks, including me, who contradicted him. "Damn it," he said, "that can't be the case. That's the way it is!" And I said, "Emil, you've noticed, I know, but you're not thinking about it, that in every generation the young bucks come up. And the young bucks always fight the old apes. I say they throw the old bull ape out of the nest. And they get seated there, and they get comfortable, and they're looked up to and they're fed bananas by the young ones. And the ladies and the other old bull apes, they all hang together. But there's another generation of young apes coming up. Don't you remember when you were a young ape? When you were a rebel? And now by God, Emil, now here comes another generation, of which I'm one. Paul Ezell's one."

This was some years ago, of course, when I was working at University Ruin. Some happened to be locked into the academic machine, but I never was and never will be, so I talk. I said, "I'm one of the young apes. And if I were in academia, if I stayed with it, I'd probably get locked in just the way you have. Then someone would come along and roust me. That's the nature of the beast and that's the way they make progress, Emil. Quit bucking it."

Well, Emil still bucked it. He's teutonic, of German descent, and he's just as stubborn as any damned, square-headed Teuton I ever heard of or ever encountered, as we all are in our own ways. So what are you going to do? Aleš Hrdlička was wrong. He admitted before he died that maybe man had been here three thousand and *one* years, or whatever it was.

The description of scientific method needs very few words. You go into a field of any kind, with no preconceived ideas, no beliefs, an open mind. You encounter certain evidence and make certain observations. Then you collect those observations and you look at them. And you duplicate them. Later you begin to arrive with hypotheses to explain those observations of apparent facts. And if you make even a single observation that contradicts your fact, then you've got to backtrack and find out what the problem is.

That's why I've been traveling in Pinacate so many years. And why we've been so fortunate down there, because most people don't have a chance in archaeology to go back a second time. It's no wonder there is so much misinformation, and probably one reason that people cling to their beliefs so tenaciously, even though further work might completely disprove them. That's the size of it, you try to keep your personality out of it, and you try to make matter-of-fact observations. If they suggest others, why, you check those, and eventually you arrive at some idea as to why all this takes place, and then you have to put that into sensible English, and sensible thought, and go back and check some more. And maybe before you die you'll find something that disproves it. Then somebody else picks the challenge up in the hope of. . . . Well, that's another very literate way of describing the scientific method, and damn it all, that's what it amounts to.

That's why Tony Andretta is such a good man: he operates solely on the scientific method. And what little dreaming he does is around the campfire, just the way I do, the way many of us do. He doesn't expose his ideas to academia because they laugh at him. They laugh at me, too, but that's all right. Time will tell. They laughed at George Carter for forty years. Paul Ezell said once that he was shocked that George turned out to be right for all the wrong reasons; that's a nice wisecrack, but George is probably a damn sight more right than wrong. And so am I in Pinacate and in the deserts. I don't know

Geosciences professor Paul Martin, U.S. Geological Survey botanist Raymond Turner, and Julian near Sykes Crater, Sierra Pinacate, November 10, 1990. This trip, sponsored by the University of Arizona's Desert Laboratory (of which Martin was director and Julian served on the advisory board) was one of Julian's last to the Pinacate. (Photograph by Mary Peace Douglas)

about other archaeology. And now you see Dennis Stanford coming out in a three-page feature in *Science* saying precisely what I've been trying to talk about, which is satisfying in some ways. Now the real work begins.

People come here and want me to justify my extreme dates, so called, but what's the use of talking about it? You've never been there; you don't know what desert varnish is, and I can't explain it to you, because you have your mind made up. You've never seen a desert. You'd be surprised how few people will accept desert pavement who've never seen it. Even Greta Ezell would never accept it. I had two tools from Malcolm's collection, two end choppers. One was a Yuman I, the other was San Dieguito I. The Yuman I had a little ground stain on it; the other one was heavily sandblasted, and heavily oxidized, not varnished, as it happened. They lay within six feet of each other on the pavement over the carrizo in the Imperial Valley. They're almost identical choppers. The Yuma I were using very crude, primitive, very simple tools, just as San Dieguito I did. There are drawings of them, I think, in *Ancient Hunters of the Southwest*. Greta could never believe that. She couldn't accept it; she just couldn't visualize it.

Logistics have more to do with it than anything else. Until fairly recently, how in the world could you get most people to the Pinacate? Very difficult, you know that. Now people go pretty near everywhere in their four-by-four Blazers. But your professor, at the university, say, in California or Pennsylvania, what is he going to go down there for? He's going to pick up a text, or a paper I write, and say, "Why, the man doesn't know what he's talking about. Varnish. Garnish."

I'm constantly astonished at how few academic archaeologists, professors, and assistant professors, people in the business, read the journals. They don't read *Quaternary Research*. They don't even read *Science*. I'll bet you three-quarters of the archaeological section at the university never sees *Science*. That surprises me. Or how many of them ever see *Engineering News Record*?

I know this to be a fact, because I encountered it. You feed back what I teach you, and don't argue. Paul Ezell came over one time horribly disturbed, because he was fed up with teaching, which is reason enough for a man to get out of San Diego. He said, "You know these undergraduates, wet behind the ears. They always want to argue, they want to ask me questions they're not competent to ask. I've had it. I tell them"—and this just horrified Helen and startled me because we didn't think Paul would do it—"Now look, I'm the PhD here, I'm the doctor, I'm Dr. Ezell. I'll tell you what you will feed back to me. I don't want anything else until you've got your degree. Get your union card, then call and ask me questions and we'll talk. Face-to-face." That really shook us up, but I think most professors of archaeology feel that way.

I find myself puzzling over these kids. Students come over here, and those who come back several times are apt to be rather thoughtful people, who either go back and ask their professors or try to check out the validity of what I tell them here. If they can't find any information, then they're up against the same question that I often pose myself when a man makes a statement to me: "What's his background? What's his experience? Is he dependable or is he a crackpot or what?"

I probably get along with students because I'm excited. I'm interested. And every day is a new day. I'm just like a damn goose, you know. My Okie cousins used to say, "Every day is a new day." And I'm not locked into anything . . . that I know of. I suppose I am, but I don't know it. I don't know any more about Pinacate than any graduate student sitting out here. I've been there; I've seen a lot; I've recorded a lot; I've collected a lot. But he's just as apt to go down and take one look and come up with something that might knock me galley-west and make me have to rethink everything. That's exciting.

Mead Kemmer was a grad student, then a professor back East. Bill Robinson wanted to bring him along one time, bright guy. I think Bill was on Mead's doctoral committee. So I didn't know Mead very well except he was a sharp-faced young fellow, and obviously very sharp-witted, too. We went down. And he said, "What are these cleared circles?"

And we're not talking about sleeping circles, we're talking about these circular openings in rough pavement that are paved with fine cinders. "Well," I said, "I don't know what they are. Paul Ezell and I thought the first time we ever saw them that they were sleeping circles, but they're clearly not. So many of them are where a person would never go for any of them. I've got half an idea that maybe they're where trees blew down and died out, I don't know."

Paul Ezell at Organ Pipe Cactus National Monument headquarters, April 5, 1958. (Photograph by Julian Hayden)

"Well," he said, "have you examined your parameters?" He was a grad student, after all.

I said, "Why don't you chop it up and boil it awhile and tell me what the hell you're talking about."

"Why," he said, "have you looked at all of the angles? Possibilities?"

"Well, I've never paid much more attention to it, why?"

"Well," he said, "these are trees, obviously dead and gone and fallen over. All around it is the same rough pavement. A few overturned, uprooted caliche-coated pebbles, or stones, otherwise there's no difference in texture."

"Well," I said, "you're correct."

"Well," he said, "damn it, now you've got me upset."

And I said, "You've interested me, I'm going to have to come back and look." So I made three or four trips just to look at that. And I trenched some of them. And I found out what caused them, simple enough. I just hadn't thought of it. They are depressions in the underlying lava flow. And the mantle of ejecta that covers all the lava flows normally is irregular, and the loess lay in and settled and filled that depression up. It covered the coarse ejecta, and then light cinders washed over the top of that.

I saw a nice example of it that made me chuckle later on. Down west of Tule Tank I saw two badger holes about fifty feet apart, and I stopped to look at them. This badger started a hole in coarse ejecta, but he hit hard caliche and caliche-covered ejecta—it was just plain hard digging. He went down about two feet, gave up, and moved over to one of these clearings where he had himself a mansion down there. I thought, "Well, the old badger, he must have been smarter than I was." But I think that's why I get along with these kids. Besides, I haven't got any dignity. That helps too, maybe.

And I don't have a fancy office down at the U of A. No, as far as I'm concerned, I'm in the same fix as the students. I'm no better and no worse than they are. If they're interested, I'm interested. We have that in common: an interest. Whereas a good many professors I know have got it all worked out . . . and no further interest.

Also, if you're in class and you're subject to the professor, you say, "Yes sir." I remember Haury one time, at Snaketown II, held the staff over after dinner, and I stayed on to see what it was all about. He was lamenting the fact that none of the staff members felt as though they were members of a family. At Snaketown I we had worked all hours of the evening, and we had had one aim: to do the job. Here they worked eight hours and in the evening played their guitars or looked at TV or did something else. Jonathan Yellow Hair was the only one who worked after hours.

And Haury said, "Well, understand that if anybody had any trouble at Snaketown I, they'd come up and talk to me. They'd tell me about it and we'd work it out. Here, nobody ever comes to me."

So I stood up and I said, "Emil, I'm going to go outside, and when you're through come on out, I want to talk to you." So he came out after a while and he said, "What do you want?"

I said, "I'm going to gnaw on you, goddamn it." I've always been able to talk to Dr. Haury that way because I'm not obligated. I said, "Look, Emil. You're comparing apples and oranges. At Snaketown I, nobody on that job was obligated to you, or in your debt, or afraid of you. We didn't give a damn who you were. We knew that you were running the job. We were doing the job. We were all there for the job. And we worked

Julian watches as Al Lancaster and Emil Haury attempt to witch a Hohokam well under excavation at Snaketown II in the winter of 1964–1965. (Photograph by Helga Teiwes, courtesy of Arizona State Museum, University of Arizona)

all hours, it made no difference. We loved it. And we all got along because we loved it. We all had the same aim.

"Now," I said, "here, we've got about ten fine people, and only two of us that aren't indebted to you. The rest are all your doctors, or they're candidates, or they're working in the state museum with you. They're all obligated to you. Al Lancaster and I are the only two that aren't, and Al Lancaster's scared to death of you because you know so much about these Hohokams. I know a little bit about them, too, but I don't scare Al because we're both on the payroll. So that leaves me. And you don't scare me a damn bit. You complain about us working only eight hours? You know in ten years you'll be lucky to get five hours in paid work. You just don't know how damn good you got it. Relax, Emil." Next time I went up, a week later, he was playing softball with the gang outside. So he catches on. I saw his point, and I sympathize with him.

I can't give—I don't give—people advice, you know that pretty much. If they learn anything from me, they pick it up, without my trying to teach them anything. And that advice, my friend, is worth just about what it cost you, nuthin'. Possibly another can of beer.

About how to survive? I remember Al Olson, a grad student who worked for me on weekends to earn a little extra money. My men didn't work on weekends, so he and I'd go out and dig sewer ditches and lay pipe and do this, that, and the other thing. I never thought I was teaching him anything, why should I? He was a doctoral candidate. But his widow told me that Al used to go around telling his grad students some of my *dichos*. And one I remember he told all his students: Al said, "One time after I left Julian, I was working on a pipeline surveying up in northern Arizona. Conditions were bad. It was a bad situation. I said to Julian, 'I think I'm going to have to quit. Would you quit under those conditions?'

"And Julian just turned and glanced at me and said, 'You signed on, didn't you?'"

I don't remember that at all, but he thought about that and he stayed in that job and he taught all his students to remember that. And I probably have said this before: "You're the only one. There's only one of you. But you've got a dozen students out there. They all remember you, you don't remember them. They'll remember every word you say. You don't remember what they say." By the same token, if you wind up down at the police station you'll remember all those cops, but they'll not remember you. The shoe's on the other foot.

Times have changed a hell of a lot, of course, for archaeological jobs for those who didn't get their big degrees. Before World War II, there was very little work. I imagine that the Southwest had not more than half a dozen non-degreed field men. Earl Morris was a shining example. Al Lancaster, an old bean farmer, had no degrees; Earl didn't either. And, of course, I never had any schooling [in archaeology] at all; I never took a course in my life. I learned mine in the field, and so did the others. Nowadays you've got to have your degrees before you can even work in the field. That partly reflects the educational establishment.

I tell kids, "Look. There's a hell of a lot of competition in archaeology nowadays. You've got contract archaeology, yes, but you've got to have a bachelor's in order to be a laborer. You've got to have a master's to get any higher, to be a crew chief and so forth. And now that the Society of Professional Archaeologists has come into being with all its damn bureaucracy, you're going to have to pass examinations; you've got to be certified even to work on a contract job in any position at all, and that means you've got to have a doctorate, or will before long. So, if you want to go and get your degrees and spend five or ten years getting your degree, waste your youth and your energy and your interest, well, spend it that way, and go ahead. You may not have a job when you get out. Or you may get a job in academia. Then you've got to out-wait the tenured ones, but by that time you'll be burned out. Your wife will be unhappy and your children will be unhappy, if you've got any. I'd look for something else."

Personally, I wouldn't have anything to do with academia or an advanced degree. But then I can say that. If I were your age, I don't know what I'd do. I think I'd take enough anthropology and archaeology to allow me to become an "avocationalist." They're so-called in Texas; I and other people call them amateurs. I'm an amateur, because I have no degree. And I'd join the local clubs. And more and more of them are conducting workshops, excavations, trips, tours. You can do all sorts of things.

I had a friend in Phoenix, who after the war went to work for the Associated Press, running a teletype machine. That's how he earned his living. But in his spare time and on weekends, he developed his photography skills, and he became an archaeological photographer. He had the time of his life. That's one way to do it. If you've got a job that doesn't consume all your vitality and interest, put your time in and raise your family . . . and be an archaeologist on the side. Then work up.

There are journals now for amateurs. Some of them are damn good. The *Kiva's* one. You don't have to have a degree to publish in the *Kiva*. You've got to be juried, but you don't have to have a degree. You can make a reputation. Look at Don Crabtree, flintknapper. I don't know whether he had any more than a high school diploma, which I have. Matter of fact, we have very similar backgrounds. He was an old country boy from Glen's Falls, Idaho, but he always liked to collect arrowheads. When he was small, he got to wondering how they were made. By the time he died, he was the top authority on the physics of flintknapping in the world. And you can do the same thing if you find something that intrigues you.

You can photograph fragile-pattern desert areas, and you can describe and note, but eventually you've got to collect. It's a quandary. You encounter it and pick it up and put it back where you got it, and then the next person along, they take it home with them. And the only knowledge that you'll ever have of it—that anyone will ever have of it—is in your notes and photographs.

You salvage some information that we wouldn't have had otherwise. Someone else would have picked them up and taken them home. Just the way the people did who found that pot in that cone right in the center of Moon Crater. Someone found and left it there, but some Californians came the next week and took it home. Now we know nothing about it, except for the pictures.

Academic people need a more practical outlook on field things. One academic was writing about charcoal from an ironwood-tree fire but, as any desert camper knows, ironwood simply burns down to dust. He was trying to disprove the Snaketown chronology by arguing, in his paper on Snaketown, that Haury's C-14 dates from hearths in Snaketown were undependable and too old because people had used old wood. He pointed out that ironwood can be extremely old when you pick it up and burn it. But he didn't know that ironwood burns to an ash, white ash. It wouldn't occur to him to ask anybody.

We used to find all the Hohokam firepits—Snaketown, Grewe Site, and so forth—filled with white ash. White flour ash. So, we used to wonder about it until I was here at the University Indian Ruin. I found some nubbins of corncobs; they were dry fill, with adobe-sealed, filled rooms. They were little tiny things, each two inches long, scrappy little things. And I knew damn well the Hohokam raised corn, because I had just seen a cache jar from the foothills, and it had cobs in it ten inches long. Beautiful stuff. I was talking about it with Old Man Eichoff, who was one of the foremen at the C camp in Tucson. I was writing the report, and he said, "Well, did you ever burn corncobs?"

And I said, "No, I never did."

"Well," he said, "we burned them all the time up in Nebraska when I was a kid," and he was a man going on seventy born in Niobrera, you know, Mari Sandoz's country. Niobrera River. You know Mari Sandoz, *Old Jules*, and all that? Anyway. He said, "That's what we burned. I'll just bet those Indians burned their corncobs."

And why not? By golly, I'd never thought of it, so I came home and I told Helen about it, "Well," she said, "of course. We always burned corncobs in Virginia when we were living there in the summertime, you know." So, some of those insights are serendipitous. Even Emil didn't know about it.

I don't do my own welding. I see no point in my trying to arc weld, because we have so damn many alloys, and you've got to know them all, and you've got to work with them all the time. I go down to a welding shop. I go to a specialist. And I expect someone to come to me here if he wants to talk about how to dig caliche: that's my business. I could hire welders, but I can't hire people who know caliche or the geological structure and mechanics of it. That you learn by doing. Hard work. So I don't know how you teach students, they'd have to pick it up. Take them out in the field; let them watch. Comment once in a while on what you see. Ask for comments. Say, "If you don't understand, holler." After a while they'll ask.

We need field camps. That's where you learn, is in the field. It's where I learned. You don't learn how to use a trowel, you don't learn the textures of soils, from a book. My CCC boys from Oklahoma and from Pennsylvania, Fish Town, Philly and so forth, made wonderful field men. They were in a strange country, but they were interested. We introduced them to something new that turned out to be fascinating once they found a potsherd. And I made a point of explaining soils to them . . . and *why* we're interested in soils. Rain wash. Salt erosion debris. Puddle caliche. Water-deposited caliche that sets up harder than hell.

I had one good example when Dean Cummings dug a room beside one of the mounds out there. He got down to the floor and backfilled it, but my men and I opened it up just for fun. We realized he hadn't reached the walls. So then I showed them, "Well, you can see the laminations." This caliche was just harder than hell. Caliche washed from above, you know, and poured down. So we went in, with picks, and we just peeled it off, and found the most beautiful smoked plastered wall behind it about two inches. Dean Cummings or his students didn't know soils. The kids never forgot that.

A Korean girl came here, and I taught her the rudiments of silversmithing. She could use her hands; she had good eyes; she had talent. So, we introduced her to the tools and materials, the silver and brass. We explained a few things to her, and finally she said to her husband one night, so he told me, "Why Julian always watch me so much? I don't need him. If I need help, I call him." When I heard that, I was pleased. She wouldn't tell me, but she told her husband. After that I stayed away . . . unless she asked me. And she made rapid progress. She turned out to be a damned sight better smith than I am, which may not be saying much, but she turned out to be a good one. I was very proud of her. It would be a hell of a note if our students didn't come out better than we are.

The importance of archaeology to society? That's been argued about for a long time. When we were working at Snaketown in '34, Frank Lloyd Wright was working at Taliesin West. My Helen had two schoolmates, the Braithwaite sisters, who were students at Taliesin West. They got together, and the next thing we knew, we all were invited over to Taliesin West: Haury, the staff of the Snaketown expedition, my father, Gladwin, Sayles and Erik Reed, and so forth. So we went over and had a wonderful time. We met that character Frank Lloyd Wright.

So Haury said, "Mr. Wright, I'd like to reciprocate and invite you and your crew over to Snaketown, to pay us a visit, and see what we're doing and the excavations we're conducting." Wright drew himself up, looked down his nose at Dr. Haury, and said, "Dr. Haury, when you can prove to me that archaeology has ever contributed one whit to the welfare of humanity, I'll come over." That left Haury sucking air, you know? My father, very tactfully, kept his mouth shut. But Wright never did come over, and I haven't got any better answer than that myself.

I've remarked more than once that archaeology never put a dime in a peon's pocket, which is just another way of saying that we are on the fringe of what is necessary. In hard times archaeology goes down the drain. And in good times, when people have some wheat in the storehouse and a few shekels somewhere, there's money to spare. Why do people do archaeology? Because there is money for it, but if there isn't, you darn well don't . . . unless you've got a welfare society and you put people doing archaeology to feed a few of them. That's the important thing, what pays for archaeology. And the why. To give people work.

That's what the CWA [Civil Works Administration] work was in 1934, where we excavated sites all over the United States. WPA did the same thing, you know. It was relief work, makework. We learned a lot about the prehistory that way. But, if it hadn't been that they wanted to make work, there would have been very little of it done, because it was mostly privately done before that time by the Gladwins and the Sessions and many others.

They invested money because they were interested. Oh, there was a certain amount of vanity in all of it, of course—it's nice to be a patron of an expedition. Also, if you're fascinated by archaeology and you've got the money to satisfy your curiosity, it's a good way to do it. Our work for Gila Pueblo was entirely financed by Gladwin and his wife's private funds. They were wealthy people. They bought that ruin up in Globe and rebuilt it, a Classic Salado Site of the fourteenth century. Room by room they excavated it, restored it, and that was Gila Pueblo. Now it's homes and offices and the museum and everything else. It was a great satisfaction to all of them.

It certainly adds to the interest of life. And without it I certainly wouldn't have talked with so many interesting people in this world. People come to me, and they say, "We want to be archaeologists; it's so interesting."

"Well, go ahead."

"But we can't find any work in archaeology."

"All right, go to your local archaeology society and join up, get acquainted. If they've got courses, take the courses, and eventually you'll become a certified amateur. They're coming up all around the country. And then you can actually go out on excavations and work . . . in your spare time. If you can't make a living at it, play at it." That's what I do.

I never made a nickel at it from the time I finished the University Ruin. Helen and I spent money on it, of course, but our lives would have been a damn sight poorer if we hadn't done so. It's kept me fascinated for sixty damned years. If I'd been a millionaire, I'd have probably had my own expeditions. And so would you. That's not a very good answer, but it's the best I can come up with on the spur of the moment.

Over here, we didn't use to call in the other disciplines. An archaeologist up until 1920 or 1925 had to know it all himself. He had to be a Victorian naturalist, in other words. You knew enough about every subject that you could not only discuss it, you could employ it. When Norman Tindale wanted to become an archaeologist at the age of seventeen or so, in Australia, he went to college. They had no courses in archaeology, although there were two fine anthropologists, Spencer and Gillen, at the University of

Melbourne. Although it didn't have any courses per se, there were interesting subjects which people could take.

So they set up a special curriculum for him, and he had to take everything under the sun: climatology, geology, mineralogy, entomology, nutrition, osteology, why good lord almighty! [Tindale completed his bachelor's degree in science with the University of Adelaide.] He had to know everything that he might encounter in the outback in his travels. He had to be able to answer any question, or at least recognize and record what he saw so that it could be answered by somebody else somewhere. And that's what he did. They sent him to Oxford, on scholarships, and they did the same thing for him there. As a result, his reports are absolute masterpieces. He has worldwide fame as an authority on moths, one of the outgrowths of his interests.

He's a linguist who spoke I don't know how many Australian dialects. An expert on Aboriginal religion, he also could knap flint and make his own tools. He could live in the desert by himself with no clothes or supplies, no nothing, just the way an Aborigine did. So, he had to know his entomology. He had to know his mammalogy, herpetology, and all the rest of it. Nowadays, nobody has got a whisker of a chance to do that. Everything is so damned specialized. And if you did undertake to do it, you couldn't get a job, because you're not specialized enough to be an authority on anything, you see?

Malcolm Rogers had the same problem. He was a Victorian naturalist. It was possible in those days to think that you could know all there was to know about everything under the sun. Or at least enough of what was under the sun, so that you could cope with it. And record it. Now you chase the decimal point down to the far corner of the room, going nuts doing it, and that's all you know. Now we call in every discipline that might be required. It's all really joint efforts now. And that's the way it ought to be, the way it's got to be: the world is so damned complex, and so many people know so much about so many things.

I'd give anything if I could get some specialists in to help me down at Pinacate, but the specialists are all busy. Once in a while I find a good one. Students? They're the people we want to reach, because they're the ones who've got to carry this work on. I'm going to die one of these days, Tony Andretta's going to die a little after me, maybe. Paul Ezell's already gone. And if we don't have young folks to carry it on and understand what we've been talking about, and understand what we've written, that'll be the end of it, see. That's what it's all about.

Really, we've scarcely started. There's so much archaeological material and we don't know anything about it. That's what makes it so bloody fascinating. We've got thousands of sites around here. People living all over them. But the important thing is that we don't know what we should know about them.

My brother was a good man. He used to come over once in a while and tell me how to run things, and then he went home with a burr under his tail—it was good for him. I was eating regular. I remember he came over once. He said, "Damn it, Julian, you just dress up—put on a white shirt and a pair of clean slacks, and shine your shoes the way I do. You could have more jobs around this town than you could shake a stick at." I said, "If that's what it takes to get jobs—slacks and a white shirt instead of know-how, then I'll just do without the jobs." So he went home again a bit irritated.

Once I, too, thought I could expand the business and add crews. And yes, I could have, but I resisted that temptation. It wasn't hard. I had always had it in my mind that I'd never get in any deeper than a certain point. I always looked ahead to see how I could get out. If I bought a piece of equipment, I knew how I was going to pay for it. I checked what my resale value would be if I had problems, and I never took a job so big I couldn't recover if I lost my shirt on it. After all, I had Helen and four kids. And I had no use for a million dollars. My friends in the contracting business are either dead from overwork or they're broke, maybe a couple of them retired. They didn't get to go to the Pinacate on weekends. They had no other interests.

I kept my hands on things. I didn't want to be just a manager. And besides, what if I had pulled an Ashton and worked all over the country? What the hell would I have gotten out of it? I wouldn't have any more than I've got now. Or have had. Sure, Helen and I didn't go anywhere, never took vacations, but that was my fault because I got into a service business, so we couldn't get away together. I think we got away together only two, three, four times in thirty years. Nothing can be done about that. That was my fault, but there I was. We did put four kids through out-of-state colleges and I think they're all fairly successful people.

And we had an awful lot of fun. I haven't any regrets. I had lunch with Helen every day of the month except one, and usually every night, too. I didn't get married to go out and join service clubs or go out and pal around. Hell, no.

I've got more damned notes that have no bearing on anything except that they're interesting. I've always kept notes. I've kept a diary from the time I was fifteen or sixteen or so, just for my own amusement. My father wrote newspaper articles and columns, and once had his own paper. Sometimes I notate my archaeology. I was raised with it. I don't know why. I never had any courses in it, but I just learned. And I always understood that if you're going to study something or experience something, put it all down. It might come in handy some day. And it does. I write a journal every morning in as much detail as I feel like making it. I've got all kinds of things in it. I don't know what good it'll be. A hundred years from now it might be of interest to a sociologist if we have such things. And if somebody's already burned it, why that's all right, too, what the hell.

My archaeological notes are divided into two parts: first I write my general notes, my gossip and all the rest of it, whatever I experience and observe on a trip, whether it fits anything or not. If it caught my eye—birds and lizards and battleship turret brassieres—it all goes in. And then the other half is the technical notes which are perfectly impersonal descriptions of the archaeology, and whatever happens to strike me as pertaining to archaeology.

I formed the habit after Helen died. Before that, the only notes I kept that amount to anything were the Pinacate, archaeological notes. Since then, I sort of write letters to her every day. I put all this in. I put down a lot of what intrigues me. I don't know who the hell is supposed to go through my letters to Helen. I feel sorry for those who have to, and I hope nobody does. My intention is to burn them. They've gone on now over ten years, daily letters. And they're long ones, some of them are two or three pages of all these things that occur to me. Then, if I am not too worn out and exhausted by thinking about it, why, I write them down on another page and put them in another file.

Pinacate and people and so forth and so forth. God knows I hope nobody ever knows what I think, but I don't give a damn. I won't care if they're read.

You see how my piles are stacking up on my desk here. Everything is in that. It works for me, that's all I know. Another reason I do it is that I've always thought that the things that enter into the changing of a man's approach or of his opinions and so forth, through time, are worth having.

I was criticized many years ago because, as Dr. Haury told me, he said, "You know the big trouble with you, Jules, is you change your mind too often."

"Well," I said, "whenever I get evidence that causes me to change my mind, I'll change, if I have to do it every day."

"Well," he said, "you'll never get anywhere doing that. You've got to work with what you've got. Stay with that."

I said, "What good is it, if it's not valid?" So we went at it, and had a pleasant talk.

And I have no pride about being fixed in my mental habits. If I said God has pink whiskers on Friday, I'll change it to blue whiskers on Monday if I see they're blue. But Haury wouldn't, because he was conservative. A lot of people won't do that, partly because their jobs depend on their being consistent. Consistency is a crock, in my opinion.

But I can go through my notes, and anybody else can someday if they want to, and take what I was thinking when I first went into Pinacate, and go through all the steps by which I arrived at what I think right now. If someone wanted to, if they had the patience, they could follow my mind. It's all there. And the reasons, too.

There's a hell of a lot of information in there, I'll tell you. Particularly in later years, as I got more accustomed to doing what I'm doing, you know. Probably it's one reason I don't write any more than I do, because I tell Helen about it and then, what the hell, I go about my daily business.

I had a wonderful experience a couple weeks ago. Aggie Lockwood was at Snaketown II, a volunteer worker in the lab. She was a dear friend of Helen's and mine, and of Dr. Haury's and others. She called a while back and asked if I'd be at home around eleven o'clock and I said yes. So, she showed up. And she had Dr. Haury in tow. And I was surprised to see him and pleased because he hadn't been here in years. He handed me an envelope and he said, "There's a communication in here concerning Pinacate that you'd better read." So I wondered what in the world this was all about.

I opened it. They were both watching me very carefully to see my reaction. It was a marriage license issued that morning to the two of them! Doc Haury's wife's been dead for several years, and Aggie's husband died several years ago. And all I could think of to say was, "Why you goddamned wonderful kids!" which seemed to fit. Probably one of the happiest marriages I've ever encountered.

Emil, of course, was beaming, and said, "Do you remember that round, clay figurine, fake Aztec figurine that I planted on your father at Snaketown I?" Emil had hidden it in the ballcourt, so my father would think it came from Mexico. I remembered. Dad had let out a yell and shut the job down; we all went over. He photographed it, he noted it, he described it, he brought it in. And we all looked at it, and finally it came to me and I sniffed it and said, "I don't know, but it smells like plaster of paris," which I suppose it would have anyway. Of course, Emil, the prankster, wouldn't commit himself.

Later Dad gave it to Helen and me as a wedding present. We called it Billikens and it sat by the telephone forty-two damned years. By the time Emil got through asking me if I remembered it, I had it in my hand.

I said, "Here he is, Emil. He's done a good job for Helen and me all these years. Now he's ready for another assignment and I guess he's got it. Here!"

He said, "Do you mean it?"

And I said, "Certainly, I mean it." So they went away with the household god. I think that's a nice story. And I said, "Emil, I'm going to get that in the archives somehow."

"Well," he said, "I think you should."

And I said, "Here it is."

Oh, this field man has had a king's life.

The so-called Billikens figure that Emil Haury had planted at Snaketown I for Irwin Hayden's benefit. Irwin gave it to Julian and Helen as a wedding gift; Julian later gave it to Emil and Agnese Haury when they were married.

Letter from Emil W. Haury to Julian Hayden, November 5, 1986

Dear Julian:

I do indeed know something about the effigy that your Dad did a lot of stewing about. Although I'm sure I have told you the story, I'll mention it again in some detail. During one of the periodic trips I made to Gila Pueblo from Snaketown I had a little interlude of target practice with Tom Gladwin, using a 22 rifle. Harold Gladwin had cleaned out a lot of fake Mexican pots and thrown them on the junk pile. Tom and I saw these as good target materials and so we carried the stuff up a little gully to our "target range." Amongst the collection was a small red seated figurine in the Aztec style which we decided was too good to shoot up and con-

cont. on next page

nived right then and there that it would go to Snaketown and be planted in the ball court that your Dad at the time was working. Tom was to leave for Snaketown early the next morning and I was to come in about noon. After Tom's arrival, he talked to your Dad about the work in the court where he would be focusing on the digging for the rest of the day. At lunch-time Tom slipped out and stuck the figurine in the ground in a place where your Dad said he wouldn't work the rest of the day. For some unknown reason, your Dad changed his mind and did work there and shortly the Pimas came up with the figurine. Just as I was driving into camp from Globe, discovery had been made, and your Dad, carrying his pith helmet in front of him cradling something beneath it, was motioning for everybody to come into camp. Usually such circumstances meant that a big discovery had been made. My simultaneous arrival with this event gave me reasons to be suspicious about the discovery, particularly after I saw it. I pointed out to him that the figurine was in the Aztec style which long postdated the ball court in which the figurine was found. This explanation did not satisfy him at all because he swore that the Pimas found it in a bonafide context. The whole staff was involved in trying to figure out some rational explanation. Erik Reed's inquisitive nose smelled the figurine and it had the aroma of plaster. I said that was not proof of its recency because if you go out and smell the ground in which it was found, that it would have a plaster-like odor, namely, caliche. Erik did go out to smell the ground and came back reporting that was, indeed, true. At any rate, the enigma went on for a couple of days, your Dad believing in the authenticity of the object. I being a party to the prank had to take a more skeptical view. Finally, word leaked out that it was indeed a plant and we had some fun about it.

. . . Your father pulled one on me which I didn't exactly appreciate. As was customary when anybody made a major discovery of goodies, they would be sacked and handed to another person to inspect. One day your Dad passed such a sack on to me, presumably sheltering some choice find, and upon opening it I saw a dead rattlesnake!

You should know all about this figurine because, as you recall, it was given to you upon your marriage to Helen as a wedding gift. You should have it among your memorabilia, and I have had to think of it many times as an example of a prank of which there have been many played on archaeologists while in the field.

Epilogue

Steve Hayden

My father handed me a thick, spiral-bound book. A typed label read "Conversations with JDH—1991." I was just leaving the house in Tucson, heading for the airport and back home to Port Townsend, Washington, after a good, if too brief, visit.

"What's this?" I asked.

"Don't know if it will be of any interest to you, but take a look anyway," he said gruffly. "Let me know if you think it's worth keeping. Something Broyles and Diane put together."

After my mother died, in 1977, my father and I had gotten close—become good friends, in fact—and I treasured the annual, sometimes bi-annual visits to our old adobe in Tucson, when we'd sit for hours in the patio catching up on each other's doings, swapping stories and memories. If it was winter, the patio caught the sun, and we were warm enough—if it was summer, the big mesquite provided shade. Often there were visitors—grad students from the university, friends up from Mexico, or down from Canada, or from God knows where, folks from around town—an eclectic bunch, reflective of Dad's wide range of interests. The patio was well known as "la mesquitería"—a place where hospitality and a good conversation could always be found.

I began reading the book as soon as the airplane lifted off. It was a rough transcription of interviews with Dad, made over the prior couple of years by his dear friends, Bill Broyles and Diane Boyer. Almost immediately, my eyes watered, and I wanted to cry. My God! These were the stories I grew up with! Some were the same stories I heard over and over, and loved to hear, whenever I visited. Many stories I'd forgotten, and had wished I could remember—and here they were!

Memories flooded back. Nineteen forty-six, maybe it was '47. A summer storm was building up to the east, the rapidly growing thunderclouds lit bright by the late afternoon sun. Everything had a kind of orange glow, the mesquite and greasewood and eucalyptus seemed to brighten in anticipation of the coming downpour, the smell of rain. I was three or four years old, youngest of four. That calm period before the wind and rain hit, Dad would gather us kids on the foundation wall of the house he was building for us, just outside the two army tents we were living in, and tell us stories. Good stories, too, with pirates, and Indians, and Old West cowboys, and gunslingers—he brought them to life, with dialect, and turn of phrase, and the storyteller's gift for drama and tension. He had the knack for hitting the punch line just before the big lightning strike that would knock us off our perches and send us scrambling for cover under the big dining table in the living room tent, wind and rain hard on our heels. Hard to forget a story told with special effects like that!

When I got to Port Townsend, I called Dad to let him know that yeah, this book he'd so casually handed me was of surpassing interest, and he should send copies to my brother Julian and my sisters Mary and Serena. Right now, actually. Of course, I didn't want to break down and cry on the phone, but I did manage to thank him for this incredible gift, a true family treasure, with enough dignity to avoid being sentimental. I think.

Bill and Diane continued with their interviews, the last of which were transcribed by Diane after Dad died, in 1998. This volume, so lovingly extracted from the pages and pages of those transcriptions, is, I reckon, Dad's big story for us, at least the story he chose to tell, in his late seventies, early eighties.

Like all his stories and, for that matter, all his instruction to us kids as we grew up, he doesn't draw conclusions, particularly, nor are there any lessons or morals spelled out. He tells the story, raises one eyebrow, and it's up to you to draw your own conclusions. Maybe there's a good laugh, certainly some strong opinions, but, thank God, a preacher he weren't. He was a storyteller.

This is not his complete life story—to be true, that would have to include too much of the hard and painful parts of his life, and, although he shared that with some of us kids, it was so we could better understand our own family, and our own lives, and "it's nobody's damn business but our'n."

Even though Dad obviously had a powerful intellect, and appreciated that in others, I think the thing he most admired in men (and women) was the ability to make things. He had what he called "hand sense," the ability to use his hands to understand and create. He was such a talented craftsman himself, easily moving from laying adobe to carving fine silver jewelry, from designing and building innovative septic systems to building cabinetry. He was a teacher (though he'd never refer to himself with that term). He taught me (and every man who ever worked for him) how to shovel all day without killing myself. I learned from him how to use and care for tools, from pick and shovel to micrometer. How to work wood, how to carve silver, how to fix plumbing— how to tackle just about anything that needs doing. He taught by demonstrating, and emphasized observing body movement, and imitating that. And he delighted in his students' successes, always.

Dad (and Mama) always encouraged us to go exploring—climb a tree, dig a hole, take a walk or horseback ride out into the desert, go spelunking—it didn't matter what. He'd send us off with a reassuring "we'll wait a couple of weeks before coming to look for you—you'll be nice and dried out by then, and easier to carry out." Poor Mama! What we learned was the self-confidence to follow his own father's instruction to him: "Follow your own stick." That wouldn't be a bad epitaph for him, would it?

Okay, this is supposed to be an epilogue, not a reminiscence. So here's the last story:

After Dad died, my late wife Jeneen and I were staying at the house in Tucson, post–memorial party, and feeling pretty melancholy. One morning, we were sitting at the patio table, and a disheveled mourning dove ambled over from the birdbath. To our astonishment, he hopped up on the table, then onto my knee. I'd seen Dad feed cheese to the spiny lizards, but the birds always kept their distance. Jeneen brought some birdseed, which the dove readily ate out of her hand. Jeneen laughingly said, "What's he going to do next, jump up on my head?" Which he promptly did! Well, that dove stayed around the place for a week, visiting us every day, cheering us up considerably. We could easily spot him in the flock of doves that came every morning—he was the one with feathers sticking out every which way, like he wasn't used to the new duds. He even went into the house, walked right in through the patio door, and strolled around inspecting things like he owned the place, calm and confident. The eight-week-old kittens we were raising tried to stalk him—he just elbowed them out of his way with a snort. And if you can imagine a mourning dove snorting, then you can understand this wonderful last gift from my father.

Shortly after graduating from Pomona College with a degree in history, Steve Hayden joined the Peace Corps and served on Onoun Island in what is now known as Chuuk State, Federated States of Micronesia. For three decades he worked in cooperatives in Washington and Alaska. When he retired he returned to live in Tucson in the adobe home his parents had built following World War II. He has assisted archaeological surveys in Arizona, Sonora, and Baja California, and he has returned three times to Chuuk. His current interests include gardening, kayaking, and assisting his island friends in meeting the challenges of the twenty-first century. He serves as a volunteer Ranger at Navajo National Monument, stationed at Keet Seel, an Anasazi site excavated by his grandfather and father as part of a Civil Works Administration project in the 1930s.

The Background of This Book

By the late 1980s, Julian Dodge Hayden, then in his late seventies, was a man we had separately come to know as a friend, mentor, and confidant, a role he played in the lives of an exceptionally diverse and far-ranging company of people. With his tall stature, thick gray hair, bright eyes, strong opinions, and formidable intellect, his was a powerful presence. As we each came to know him, we saw more of the human inside, the introspective artist and self-taught silversmith, the *patrón* of many a hard-working but down-on-his-luck *peón*, the foreman and owner who labored side-by-side with his trench crews, the blue-collar scientist who jousted with ivory-tower academics but slipped money and encouragement to struggling students. And the stories he could tell of days gone by, of people worth knowing, of life as a maverick amateur archaeologist . . . why, they could fill a book! While we don't recall exactly what first sparked the idea, we came to realize that his stories should be recorded. And while other people were better qualified for the job, we were at least willing to try. One of us (Bill) had previously recorded a few interviews with Hayden, but the focus tended to be on someone else, a Ronald Ives or a Paul Ezell. Getting him to talk about himself loomed far more daunting.

Before we even approached Julian with the idea of recording *his* story, we contacted his adult children: would they endorse such an idea? We called his youngest son, Steve, whom we had both met at "Lunch Bunch," an informal gathering of mostly older men with an interest in regional history and issues. Julian was a regular at these Wednesday repasts and, like many of the other regulars, brought along guests from time to time. Steve, who lived in Port Townsend, Washington, supported the idea wholeheartedly, and expressed his gratitude that we were willing to take on a project that he had long hoped would happen. This is a book born of friendship among multiple generations.

Julian was less enthusiastic, at least on the surface. At our first interview, held on January 15, 1990, at Julian's adobe home in Tucson, he began by proclaiming his objections. He snorted,

> Well, I'm going to register a protest right off. This project, from any sensible standpoint, is a waste of time and money and effort, and the only good it can do is to entertain me because you two are here. Now how the hell could I put it any more nicely than that? And I haven't even practiced today. But those transcripts, well, I can't imagine them being condensed any less than ninety-eight percent, and then there's nothing left, so why do it? And I've made my brag now. I'll shut up. Get with it. See what you can get out of the old man.

And he then launched into two hours of nonstop stories. He later came to relish the interviews, and sometimes we would find him pacing by the door, too anxious to wait for the recorder to be turned on before he began. Over the course of five years, we conducted a total of twenty-one interviews. Diane handled the exacting task of transcribing them.

This memoir is a consolidation of those interviews, to which we have added some material taken from a 1989 recording made by historian Peter Booth. The original tapes and transcripts are now on file with the Arizona Historical Society in Tucson. Julian reviewed many of the interviews before his death in 1998, but the editors accept final responsibility for accuracy and organization. While we have made some minor corrections of fact, we have left most of the details as Julian told them. Although his memory for minutiae and names was remarkable, some of the tales were decades old, and some of the details may have shifted in the telling. However, comparisons with his original notes or documents reveal an uncanny accuracy. In a few instances we have substituted passages from his letters, notes, or diaries to give a fuller or more accurate account than we harvested on the tape recording. Steve Hayden supplied the photos and his father's jewelry-design sketches, which illustrate many of the sidebars. Diane Boyer, Steve Hayden, and Bill Broyles all contributed to the annotations collected in the people and places subsection at the back of the book. Numerous friends helped us track facts.

This is a memoir of Julian's world told from his memory, as you would have heard it sitting on his brick patio under the arching limbs of a stately mesquite tree that he himself planted.

People and Places

See also the Selected Readings section in the Bibliography.

Allen, Joshua Albert (1877–1957). Cook on the 1934 Keet Seel stabilization project; resident of Taylor, Arizona. Allen's colorful turns of phrase greatly influenced Julian in his formative years as a storyteller.

Amargosan. Occupants of the lower Colorado basin and lower southwest desert, 5,000–500 BP.

Andretta, Antonio A. "Tony" (1927–1994). Amateur archaeologist in the Trans-Pecos region of Texas. Director of Southwest Federation of Archaeological Societies based in Alpine, Texas.

Arizona-Sonora Desert Museum. A mostly outdoor, "living museum" showcasing the region's plants, animals, ecology, and geology. Located west of Tucson, it was founded by William H. Carr and Arthur N. Pack and opened in 1952.

Arizona State Museum. Established in 1893 by the territorial legislature at the University of Arizona in Tucson, it is the oldest anthropological museum in the Southwest.

Ashton, Harold (1915–2003). Founder of Ashton Construction Company, which specialized in homes and major public buildings and bridges in Tucson and the Southwest. See Kimmelman, *Harold Ashton: Reflections of a Proud Family Patriarch, Gentleman, and Master Builder*.

Astorga, Victoria. Seri Indian woman living in Sonora, Mexico. See Julian's January 1942 article in *Arizona Highways*.

Audish, George (1905–1982). Owner of a Tucson welding shop; fabricated concrete forms for Hayden Excavation Service as well as the frame for the table in the Hayden patio.

Bailey, Wilfred Charles (1918–2008). Professor of anthropology at the University of Georgia.

Barnett, Francisco and Miguel. Seri Indians. See Felger and Moser, *People of the Desert and Sea: Ethnobotany of the Seri Indians*.

Basich Brothers Construction Company. California contractor specializing in highways and large buildings.

Billikens. A doll, patented by Missouri artist Florence Pretz, that was extremely popular in the early 1910s. The doll featured pointed ears, a pointed head, a wide grin, and a round belly, quite different from the statuette so-named by Julian and Helen Hayden.

Birkby, Walter Hudson. Forensic anthropologist at the Arizona State Museum, University of Arizona, now emeritus.

Bisbee, C. A. "Biz" (d. 1944). Boulder City, Nevada, resident who wrote a newspaper column from the perspective of Hoover Dam workers entitled "Bunkhouse Bunk," published in the *Las Vegas Evening Journal* and the *Boulder Journal*.

Bischoff, James L. U.S. Geological Survey geochemist, now emeritus.

Blackwater. A Pima Indian village along the Gila River south of Phoenix, Arizona, about halfway between Sacaton and Coolidge.

Boardman, Harry L. Philosophy instructor at Riverside Junior College; managing secretary of the Riverside Chamber of Commerce.

Bolen, Jean Shinoda. Psychiatrist and Jungian analyst; professor of psychiatry at the University of California, San Francisco. Author of *The Tao of Psychology: Synchronicity and the Self* (1979).

Bowen, Thomas "Tom". Archaeologist. Author of many papers on Seri Indians and book *Unknown Island* (2000).

Braniff Cornejo, Beatriz "Tita". Influential Mexican archaeologist who championed the study of Gran Chichimeca. Associated with Universidad de Colima, Instituto Nacional de Antropología, and Museo Nacional de Antropología de la Ciudad de México.

Bryan, Kirk (1888–1950). U.S. Geological Survey hydrologist and soils expert, professor at Harvard University. Author of many papers including *Water Supply Paper 499: The Papago Country, Arizona: A Geographic, Geologic, and Hydrologic Reconnaissance with a Guide to Desert Watering Places* (1925).

Butler, Smedley (1881–1940). Major general in U.S. Marine Corps. Served in several foreign campaigns and was awarded two Congressional Medals of Honor.

Calles, Plutarco Elías (1877–1945). Founder of the National Revolutionary Party in Mexico; served as governor of Sonora (1917–1919) and president of Mexico (1924–1928).

Camp-Fires on Desert and Lava (1908): classic book on the Pinacate region, by William Temple Hornaday.

Carr, William H. "Bill". Co-founder (with Arthur Pack) of the Arizona-Sonora Desert Museum near Tucson.

Carter, George F. Archaeologist. Proponent of Early Man; see his book *Earlier Than You Think* (1980).

Casa Grande Site. Major Hohokam settlement east of Casa Grande, Arizona. Casa Grande Ruins National Monument was established in 1892.

CCC. Civilian Conservation Corps, a New Deal work program (1933–1942). Julian was attached to camps SP-4, SP-3, and MA-2, all in Arizona.

Celaya, Alberto (1885–1962). Guide and friend to Hayden, Ezell, Ives, and Lumholtz, among others. See Ives, "In Memory: Alberto Celaya," and Ives, "Alberto Celaya, 1885–1962."

Chamberlin, Thomas Chrowder (1843–1928). Geologist at University of Chicago who studied cycles of glaciation (he described himself as "born on a moraine"), climate (greenhouse effects), and origin of the Earth ("planetesimal theory"). Proponent of scientific method of "multiple working hypotheses."

Childers, W. Morlin (1918–1987). Discoverer of Yuha Man in 1976 at Yuha Pinto Wash in southeastern California. Worked at the Imperial Valley College Museum.

Children's Shrine. Shrine of Children's Sacrifice, near village of Santa Rosa, Tohono O'odham Nation.

Clarke, Leonard David (1937–1976). British archaeologist who emphasized analytical techniques. Credited with being a founder of New Archaeology.

Colton, Harold S. (1881–1970). Trained as a zoologist; published on zoology, history, archaeology, and geology, mostly of northern Arizona. Together with his wife, the artist Mary-Russell Ferrell Colton (1889–1971), founded the Museum of Northern Arizona in Flagstaff in 1928.

Conn, Margaret Shreve (1918–1983). Daughter of plant scientists Forrest and Edith Shreve; she worked for archaeologist Malcolm Rogers for many years.

Conrad, Charles "China Baby". Michigan contractor; visitor and volunteer at the Casa Grande Site. Married Dorothy "Dottie" Gay, with whom he leased the Linda Vista Ranch near Portal, Arizona.

Coolidge, Dane (1873–1940). Naturalist and author, who wrote numerous western novels as well as nonfiction, including *The Last of the Seris* (1939).

Costa Rica Ranch. Cattle ranch between Hermosillo, Sonora, and Seriland. See McGee, *The Seri Indians of Bahia Kino and Sonora, Mexico.*

Courbin, Paul. French archaeologist; author of *What Is Archaeology? An Essay on the Nature of Archaeological Research* (1988).

Crabtree, Don E. (1912–1980). Archaeologist known for flintknapping and experimenting with ancient technologies. See his *An Introduction to Flintworking* (1972), and Plew, Woods, and Pavesic, eds., *Stone Tool Analysis: Essays in Honor of Don E. Crabtree.*

Cummings, Byron "Dean" (1860–1954). Dean of Arizona archaeologists and professor at University of Arizona. Pick a Southwestern site—Kayenta, Kinishba, Pueblo Grande—or archaeologist—Haury, Ezell, Kidder, Douglass—and you'll likely find some connection with Cummings. See Bostwick, *Byron Cummings: Dean of Southwest Archaeology.*

CWA. Civil Works Administration, a New Deal work program, part of the Federal Emergency Relief Administration (1933–1934). Julian worked for CWA Camp 6 at Keet Seel, Navajo National Monument, Arizona.

d'Autremont, Hubert Hart (1879–1947). President of Southern Arizona Bank in Tucson, Arizona state senator. Married Helen Congdon (1889–1966), noted for her civic and philanthropic work.

Davis, Emma Lou (1905–1988). Southwest archaeologist based at San Diego Museum of Man. Co-author with Sylvia Winslow of "Giant Ground Figures of the Prehistoric Deserts" (1965) and co-editor with Christopher Raven of *Environmental and Paleoenvironmental Studies in Panamint Valley* (1986).

Davis-Monthan Air Force Base. Military base established in Tucson in 1940. Julian acquired the dirt used for making the adobe blocks for his house from base runway construction overburden.

Day, Charles (1879–1918). Son of pioneer and Arizona Territorial legislator Sam Day; operated the Bill Meadows Trading Post and also served as custodian of Canyon de Chelly and Canyon del Muerto.

Death Comes for the Archbishop (1927): a novel by Willa Cather about a cleric assigned to a mission in New Mexico.

Deetz, James F. (1920–2000). Professor of historical archaeology at several universities. Closely identified with New Archaeology.

DeVry, Louis. Owner of Louis DeVry and Sons brickyard in Tucson.

d'Harnoncourt, René (1901–1968). A noted Austrian-born artist, museum director, and authority on Native American and Mexican art. Was an administrator in the Indian Arts and Crafts Board (Department of the Interior), and later director of the Museum of Modern Art, New York.

Dighton, Edward M. With backing of the Ku Klux Klan, was elected mayor of Riverside, California, in 1927, serving in the office 1928–1929.

Dillehay, Thomas D. A leading archaeologist; professor of anthropology at the University of Kentucky and later at Vanderbilt University. Author of *The Settlement of the Americas: A New Prehistory* (2000), about an Early Man Site at Monte Verde, Chile.

Dobyns, Henry F. Anthropologist who published widely on Indians of the New World.

Dodge, Horace Elgin, Jr. (1901–1963). Son of Horace E. Dodge of Dodge automotive fame, who decided to apply the technique of mass production used on automobiles to his line of speedboats, the Dodge Watercar.

Donaldson, Edward Mortlock "E. M." (1912–1992). Royal Air Force pilot and wing commander, decorated veteran of the Battle of Britain, assigned as liaison to U.S. Army Air Force in spring and summer 1942.

Dorn, Ronald. Chemist who studied desert varnish; professor of geography at Arizona State University.

Doyel, David. Southwestern archaeologist, formerly with the Pueblo Grande Museum.

Drachman, Oliver (1903–1996). Tucson businessman and civic leader.

Early Lithic Industries of the Lower Basin of the Colorado River and Adjacent Desert Areas (1939): by Malcolm J. Rogers.

Eaton, Calvin A. A surgeon in Yuma, Arizona.

Eckhart, George Boland (1897–1978). Historian; author of *The Missions of Sonora* (1961).

Eggleston, Julius Wooster (1875–1945). Anthropologist who received his A.M. from Harvard in 1901, and his PhD in 1924; died in Riverside, California.

Eiseley, Loren C. (1907–1977). Anthropologist, and author of *Darwin's Century* (1958) and memoir *All the Strange Hours* (1975). Inscription on his tombstone reads: "We loved the earth but could not stay."

Epstein, Jeremiah Fain "Jerry" (1924–2005). Professor of anthropology at University of Texas.

Epstein, Yale. Tucson home builder, one of the founders of the Southern Arizona Home Builders Association.

Ezell, Greta June Sarrels (1914–1991). Anthropologist. Married to Paul Ezell.

Ezell, Paul H. (1913–1988). Archaeologist whose early research was done in the Pinacate and Papaguería. See Broyles, "Desert Archaeology: An Interview with Paul H. Ezell, 1913–1988," and Broyles, "Paul Ezell in the Papaguería."

Felger, Richard Stephen. Botanist specializing in desert plants of the Southwest. Author of *Flora of the Gran Desierto and Río Colorado of Northwestern Mexico* (2000), co-author of *People of the Desert and Sea: Ethnobotany of the Seri Indians* (1985).

Fell, Howard Barraclough "Barry" (1917–1994). Professor of invertebrate zoology at Harvard Museum of Comparative Zoology, and controversial proponent of epigraphy regarding pre-Columbian contacts between the Old World and the New World. His books included *America, B.C.* and *Saga America*.

Fewkes, Jesse Walter (1850–1930). Began his career as a marine zoologist and became a pioneer southwestern archaeologist with the Smithsonian's Bureau of American Ethnography. Followed Frank Hamilton Cushing as leader of the Hemenway Southwestern Archaeological Expedition. Early advocate for preservation of sites.

Floyd, R. A. Corps of Engineers captain and resident engineer at the Yuma Army Airfield construction project.

Folsom Man. Early North American people characterized by the use of Folsom spear points, a type first found at Wild Horse Arroyo west of Folsom, New Mexico.

Fontana, Bernard L. "Bunny". Eminent cultural anthropologist and field historian of Arizona and Sonora. His books include *Of Earth and Little Rain: The Papago Indians* (1981), *Tarahumara: Where Night Is the Day of the Moon* (1979), and *A Gift of Angels: The Art of Mission San Xavier del Bac* (2010).

Forman, Harrison (1904–1987). Journalist, photographer, explorer; author of *Through Forbidden Tibet: An Adventure into the Unknown* (1936).

Freeman, George K. Riverside county superior court judge.

Frenchman Flat. Location within the Nevada Test Site near Las Vegas, Nevada.

Gaede, Marc. Photographer. Served as curator of photography for Museum of Northern Arizona. See Gaede, Gaede, and Ambler, *Camera, Spade and Pen: An Inside View of Southwestern Archaeology*.

Gargantua: First of a connected series of five books written in the sixteenth century by the French writer François Rabelais about two giants, Gargantua and his son Pantagruel.

Gell, Jonathan. Historical archaeologist, now retired; formerly with the New Jersey Historic Preservation Office.

Gila Buttes. Prominent twin buttes along the Gila River where it is bridged by Interstate 10.

Gila Crossing. Location along the Gila River in Arizona where the Butterfield Stage Road crossed the river at what was called Morgan's Farm in 1935.

Gila Pueblo. The type site for Salado culture. Located on Pinal Creek near Globe, Arizona, and a mile upstream from Besh-Ba-Gowah Archaeological Park. Active AD 1225–1340. See Woodward, "Cremation-Pit 'Shrine Area,' and Other 'Rubbish-Heap History': Revelations of the Oldest Known Culture of the Gila Valley, Arizona."

Gillen, Francis James "Frank" (1855–1912). Self-taught Australian anthropologist who specialized in Aboriginal culture.

Gladwin, Harold S. (1908–1992). Wealthy stockbroker from New York who, with his wife Winifred, established Gila Pueblo Archaeological Foundation at rebuilt Gila Pueblo.

Goldwater, Barry M. (1909–1998). Arizona senator (1953–1965, 1969–1987); namesake for Barry M. Goldwater Range.

Gollob, Stefan "Steve". Croatian-born Tucson real estate developer and philanthropist.

Grabe, Bill. Owner of Grabe Brick Company in Tucson.

Gray, Robert and Henry. In 1919 Robert Lee "Bob" Gray established a ranch at what is now Organ Pipe Cactus National Monument. His nine children included son Henry.

Greenberg, Joseph Harold (1915–2001). Eminent linguist known for his language classifications. Professor of social sciences at Stanford University, author of *Language Universals with Special Reference to Feature Hierarchies* (1966).

Green Mansions: A Romance of the Tropical Forest (1890): novel by W.H. Hudson set in the Amazon jungle.

Gregory, Herbert E. (1869–1952). Geologist; educated at Yale, where he later taught; also worked for U.S. Geological Survey. Authored many volumes, including *Geology of the Navajo Country, a Reconnaissance of Parts of Arizona, New Mexico and Utah*, USGS Professional Paper 93 (1917).

Greth, Gary "Red". Tucson Newspapers, Inc., advertising salesman for forty-four and a half years, and drag racer of famed Speed Sport Roadster campaigned by Lyle Fisher, Don Maynard, and Greth from 1956 to 1964. He reports that frequently Hayden delivered the "Hayden Says" ads late, but the newspaper editors, concerned about libel, always wanted to read them before going to press. Sometimes the ads required a fast rewrite, but Greth notes that Hayden usually just said the same thing in different words, outsmarting the editors (personal communication December 29, 2008).

Grewe Site. Exceptionally large Hohokam Site extending a mile eastward from the Great House at Casa Grande Ruins National Monument, Arizona. Extensively excavated by Northland Research in 1996–1997.

Gutmann, James T. Geology professor emeritus at Wesleyan University, with a special interest in the volcanics of the Sierra Pinacate. See his "Geological Studies in the Pinacate Volcanic Field."

Gypsum Cave. Prominent archaeological site at a cave in the Frenchman Mountains east of Las Vegas, Nevada.

Halseth, Odd Sigurd (1893–1966). City archaeologist for Phoenix, Arizona, and director of Pueblo Grande. Married to Edna May Scofield (1879–1956), a sculptor who trained at the Art Institute of Chicago. See Downum and Bostwick, *Archaeology of the Pueblo Grande Platform Mound and Surrounding Features.*

Hamilton, Montana. Small town thirty-five miles south of Missoula. Seat of Ravalli County. Julian's birthplace.

Hanna, David C. Anthropologist. His 1982 San Diego State University master's thesis was "Malcolm J. Rogers, the biography of a paradigm."

Harlow, John M., Sr. (1905–1974). Founder and owner, with his wife Mary Louise, of Harlow Gardens landscape nursery in Tucson.

Harrington, Edna L. "Endeka" Parker (1882–1948). The cook at Mesa House; sister of archaeologist Arthur Caswell Parker, wife of archaeologist M. R. Harrington.

Harrington, Gwyneth (1894–1978). Born Gwyneth Browne, she was an ethnologist who worked with the Pima, Papago, and Seri Indians, among others. She married three times and divorced twice: first to Eugene Saudrey Harrington, second to Juan Xavier, and third to Frederick Wulsin. She had two children, Alan and Josephine, with her first husband. See Harrington, "Juan and Jack: Memories of a Desert Town, 1949."

Harrington, John Peabody "J. P." (1884–1961). Eminent ethnologist and linguist active during first half of twentieth century. Worked for Bureau of American Ethnology. Responsible for major collections and preservation of American Indian languages.

Harrington, Mark Raymond "M. R." (1882–1971). Collected ethnological and archaeological artifacts for the Heye Foundation; also associated with the Southwest Museum in Los Angeles. Conducted research on sites such as Gypsum Cave and Tule Springs, Nevada. See Harrington, *On the Trail of Forgotten People: A Personal Account of the Life and Career of Mark Raymond Harrington.*

Harris Site. Archaeological complex along San Diego River, near Escondido, California. First excavated by Malcolm Rogers and type site for San Dieguito culture.

Harter, Tom. Watercolorist; taught at Arizona State University in Phoenix. Julian traded silverwork for his paintings.

Hathaway, Gregory O. "Greg". Superintendent of Arizona Highway Patrol from 1950 to 1966.

Haury, Agnese Nelms Lockwood Lindley. Philanthropist, editor, and author; worked for the United Nations, Woodrow Wilson Foundation, and the Carnegie Endowment for International Peace. Her philanthropic foundations have supported work in archaeology, education, court interpretation, the arts, human rights, and the environment. Her marriage to Emil Haury is described in chapter 15.

Haury, Emil Walter (1904–1992). Archaeologist and professor of anthropology at the University of Arizona and director of the Arizona State Museum. Provided major support for the Department of Anthropology, Arizona State Museum, and Laboratory of Tree-Ring Research at the University of Arizona. Author of many publications, including *The Stratigraphy and Archaeology of Ventana Cave* (1950) and *Hohokam Desert Farmers and Craftsmen: Excavations at Snaketown 1964–1965* (1976).

Hayden, Carl Trumbull (1877–1972). Arizona politician who served as both a U.S. representative (1912–1927) and a U.S. senator (1927–1969).

Hayden, Helen Botler Pendleton (1910–1977). Julian's wife. Born in Pittsburgh, Pennsylvania, she was a graduate of Smith College, where she studied literature. In addition to raising four children and keeping the Hayden Excavation Service business running smoothly, she also proofread and edited archaeological papers written by Julian, Irwin Hayden, and Malcolm Rogers.

Hayden, Irwin (1881–1969). Julian's father. Born in Winthrop, Massachusetts. Received a master's degree in anthropology from Harvard in 1909; was Frederick W. Putnam's protégé. Married Mary Abbey Dodge in 1909.

Hayden, Jessie. Julian's sister.

Hayden, Julian Dodge, Jr. Julian's son and oldest child.

Hayden, Mary Abbey Dodge (1881–1963). Julian's mother. Born in New Boston, New Hampshire. Studied art with John Singer Sargent.

Hayden, Mary Pendleton (1937–2007). Julian's oldest daughter, married marine biologist Colin Hermans.

Hayden, Nan (1914–1997). Julian's sister.

Hayden, Perez M. (d. 1896). Irwin Hayden's father.

Hayden, Perez Morse "Perry" (1917–1984). Julian's brother. Married Marjorie Braman.

Hayden, Rosanna "Rose" Etherington (1849–1942). Irwin Hayden's mother.

Hayden, Serena Catherine (1941–2000). Julian's younger daughter; married pilot Joseph Camacho.

Hayden, Stephen Dandridge "Steve". Julian's younger son.

Hayden, Thomas A. (d. 1940). Chief assistant engineer for the Salt River Valley Water User's Association in Phoenix; Irwin Hayden's cousin.

Haynes, C. Vance. Quaternary geologist with an interest in Paleoindian archaeology; professor at the University of Arizona, now emeritus.

Heuett, Mary Lou. Contract archaeologist based in Tucson.

Hewett, Edgar Lee (1891–1946). Archaeologist who founded the Museum of New Mexico and what is now called the School for Advanced Research. Key figure in the passage of the 1906 Antiquities Act.

Heye Foundation. Museum of the American Indian in New York, now part of the National Museum of the American Indian of the Smithsonian Institution.

Heye, George Gustav (1874–1956). Electrical engineer by education and wealthy son by birth, he collected American Indian goods and artifacts, and founded the Museum of the American Indian in New York. His collections now form part of the Smithsonian.

Hill, Jesse Terrill "Jess" (1907–1993). Longtime coach and athletic director at the University of Southern California.

Hiss, Alger (1904–1996). A prominent U.S. attorney who helped establish the United Nations. He was later charged by the House Un-American Activities Committee as a suspected communist, and was jailed for espionage. Hiss maintained his innocence for the rest of his life, and while never vindicated, was eventually readmitted to the American Bar Association.

Hodge, Frederick Webb (1864–1956). Anthropologist. Editor of the original *Handbook of North American Indians*, secretary for the Hemenway Expedition at Los Muertos, and director of the Southwest Museum in Pasadena.

Horr, Ila (1910–2003). Self-taught anthropologist, historian, and artist. Married Luis Alvarez. Her daughter, anthropologist Anita Alvarez Williams, was a close friend of Julian's.

Hrdlička, Aleš (1869–1943). Smithsonian Institution physical anthropologist. Author of *Physical Anthropology* (1919), founder of *American Journal of Physical Anthropology*.

Hunziker, Phil. Tucson excavation contractor.

In Darkest Africa (1890): classic adventure book by Henry Morton Stanley on the Emin Pasha Relief Expedition.

Iowa scoop, Number Two. A shovel with a 27-inch D-handle and an 11 x 15-inch scoop blade.

Ives, Ronald Lorenz (1909–1982). Geographer and Pinacate expert. See his book *Land of Lava, Ash and Sand* (1989).

Jacobson, L. C. "Jake". First hired as a timekeeper by the Del Webb Corporation, he ultimately became vice-president and later president of the corporation.

Jaeger, Edmund Carroll (1887–1983). Biologist and naturalist who wrote extensively about the southwest deserts and their ecology.

Jennings, Jesse David "Jess" (1909–1997). Professor of anthropology at the University of Utah. Conducted seminal work at Danger Cave and defined Great Basin Desert culture. See his *Accidental Archaeologist: The Memoirs of Jesse D. Jennings* (1994).

Johnston, Mundey (1896–1986). Banking executive and community leader in Tucson. Served as area manager for Valley National Bank in southern Arizona.

Judd, Neil Merton (1887–1976). Archaeologist at the National Museum, best known for his work at Betatakin and Chaco Canyon; he was also a member of the 1909 "discovery" expedition to Rainbow Bridge. Nephew of Byron Cummings.

Jurgen, A Comedy of Justice (1919): widely read and influential novel by James Branch Cabell ("Tell the rabble my name is Cabell.").

Keet Seel. Largest cliff dwelling in Arizona, near Kayenta. Part of Navajo National Monument. Occupied off and on from about 950 to late 1200s. Last occupation was in the Tsegi phase of Pueblo III Anasazi, 1250–1300.

Kelemen, Alex K. Born in Hungary and served with the King's Guard. Worked as a forester; also an excavator at Avila and Casa Grande.

Kelley, John Charles (1913–1997). Archaeologist who specialized in northwest Mexico and west Texas. Served as director of the University Museum at Southern Illinois University–Carbondale.

Kino Bay. Town and former Seri village on north shore of Kino Bay, Sonora; east of Tiburón Island.

Korn, Lewis J. Archaeologist; participated in 1934 University of Pennsylvania–Columbia University expedition to the Guajira Peninsula in Venezuela and Colombia, on which Gwyneth Harrington was a participant.

Laguna Prieta. An intermittent artesian lake set among sand dunes about fifteen and a half miles southeast of San Luis Río Colorado, Sonora. Important prehistoric site.

Lancaster, James Allen "Al" (1894–1992). Archaeologist. See Adams, *Pinto Beans and Prehistoric Pots: The Legacy of Al and Alice Lancaster.*

Lizárraga, Fernando. One of the first rangers at the Pinacate Biosphere Reserve.

Lord & Taylor. A signature New York firm and the oldest department store chain in the United States, founded in 1826 and specializing in high-quality merchandise.

Lower California: A Cruise. The Flight of the Least Petrel (1932): Griffing Bancroft's account of an expedition to the Gulf of California, Mexico.

Lumholtz, Carl (1851–1922). Norwegian ethnologist and naturalist, who explored and wrote about Australia, Borneo, and Mexico. Author of *New Trails in Mexico* (1912).

Lunch Bunch. A group of old-time Tucsonans, originally all men, who met for lunch every week ostensibly to talk about history of the region and the West.

Lynch, Daniel J. "Dan". Geologist, now retired. Conducted his University of Arizona dissertation research in the Pinacate.

Machita, Pia. Tohono O'odham chief of Hickiwan District. See Blaine, *Papagos and Politics,* and Flaccus, "Arizona's Last Great Indian War: The Saga of Pia Machita."

Malpais phase. Julian Hayden's name for the earliest peoples who lived in what is now the desert Southwest, from west Texas to eastern California, perhaps an earlier phase of the San Dieguito I culture, 40,000–20,000 BP.

March Field. Military air base near Riverside, California.

Martin, Paul Schultz (1928–2010). Professor of geosciences at the University of Arizona, co-editor of *Quaternary Extinctions: A Prehistoric Revolution* (1984), and pioneer of dating processes, including packrat middens.

Martin, Paul Sidney (1899–1974). Curator at Field Museum in Chicago, closely identified with the Vernon field school and Mogollon culture.

Mason, John. Owner of a precast septic tank company in Tucson, which Julian purchased, probably in the 1950s.

McGee, W J (1853–1912). Ethnologist and field researcher for the Bureau of American Ethnology. Author of many papers and books, and an early voice for conservation. See McGee, *Trails to Tiburón.*

Meighan, Clement Woodward "Clem" (1925–1997). Professor of anthropology at University of California, Los Angeles. Author of many publications, and co-editor of *Chronologies in New World Archaeology* (1978).

Meltzer, David J. Professor of anthropology at Southern Methodist University. Author of *Search for First Americans* (1993) and *Folsom: New Archaeological Investigations of a Classic Bison Kill* (2006).

Mesa House Site. A Pueblo ruin near Overton, Nevada, excavated by Irwin Hayden in 1929, under the direction of M. R. Harrington, for the Southwest Museum. See Hayden, *Mesa House* (1930).

Mindeleff, Cosmos (b. 1863) and Victor (1860–1948). These brothers were archaeologists for the Bureau of American Ethnology, specializing in Ancestral Puebloan sites and culture. See Longacre, "Why Did the BAE Hire an Architect?"

Mittry Brothers. A large Southern California construction company specializing in highways, industrial buildings, and military facilities.

Morris, Ann Axtell (1900–1949). Artist and archaeologist. Married to Earl Morris. She wrote *Digging in Yucatan* (1931) and *Digging in the Southwest* (1933).

Morris, Earl H. (1889–1956). Pioneer southwest archaeologist. Married to Ann Axtell Morris. See Morris, *Archaeological Studies in the La Plata District,* and Lister and Lister, *Earl Morris & Southwestern Archaeology.*

Morris, Elizabeth Ann "Liz". Archaeologist and retired professor at Colorado State University. Daughter of Ann and Earl Morris.

Morrison Knudsen. Major construction company, based in Boise, Idaho, that worked on both Hoover Dam and the Golden Gate Bridge.

Mortensen, Jesse P. "Jess" (1907–1962). Coach for many years at Riverside Community College, then at the University of Southern California.

Motz, Alice Pendleton "Pen" Scully (b. 1906). Helen Pendleton Hayden's cousin. She married J. C. Fisher Motz in 1932.

Motz, John Christian Fisher "Fish" (1908–1991). Cartographer who drafted maps of Wupatki, Pueblo Grande, Awatovi, and Snaketown.

Muñiz, Pete. Longtime Hayden Excavation Service employee, skilled backhoe operator.

Muroc Air Base. Now Edwards Air Force Base and Air Force Test Flight Center, located in Southern California desert.

Nagy, Bartholomew (1927–1995). Organic geochemist at the University of Arizona.

Nelson, Nels C. (1875–1964). Master of stratigraphic studies. See Woodbury, "Nels C. Nelson and Chronological Archaeology."

Newman, T. H. "Pete". Sheriff of Yuma County, Arizona (1935–1944, 1955–1960).

New Trails in Mexico (1912): classic book by Carl Lumholtz on the Pinacate region.

Nichols, Edward Tattnall, IV "Tad" (1911–2000). Photographer who lived in Tucson most of his life and was especially interested in geology, anthropology, and the American Southwest. See his *Glen Canyon: Images of a Lost World* (1999).

Oberlander, Theodore M. "Ted". Geomorphologist; professor of geography at the University of California, Berkeley, now emeritus.

Old Kino. Historic portion of town at Bahía Kino, Sonora, Mexico.

Olsen, John W. Professor of anthropology at the University of Arizona, specializing in central and eastern Eurasia Pleistocene prehistory.

Olsen, Stanley John (1919–2003). Curator of zooarchaeology at the Arizona State Museum and professor of anthropology at University of Arizona; author of *Osteology for the Archaeologist* (1979).

Olson, Alan Peter (1926–1978). Archaeologist. See Morris, "Obituary: Alan Peter Olson, 1926–1978."

Oquitoa. Site of the San Antonio Paduano del Oquitoa mission, established by Eusebio Kino at the confluence of the Altar and Magdalena rivers in Sonora, Mexico.

Osbourne (Haydentown). Located east of Yarmouth in the Ragged Islands on the southern end of Nova Scotia.

Parker, Bertha (1907–1978). Anthropologist and actress. Daughter of anthropologist Arthur Caswell Parker and his first wife, Beulah Tahamont. Bertha, who was often called Bertie (or Birdie) was married three times, first to a Yuma Indian named Pallan, with whom she had a daughter, Wilma (Billie); after she and Pallan were divorced, to paleontologist James Edward Thurston, who left her a widow; and third, to actor Espera Oscar DeCorti, better known as Iron Eyes Cody, who survived her.

Payen, Louis A. Opponent of early dates for Yuha Man. Anthropologist at University of California, Riverside. Co-author, with Carol H. Rector, Eric Ritter, R. E. Taylor, and

J. E. Ericson, of "Comments on the Pleistocene Age Assignment and Associations of a Human Burial from the Yuha Desert, California."

Peale, Charles Willson (1741–1827). Prominent colonial-era painter.

Pecos Conference. Annual archaeological conference focusing on southwest archaeology, started by archaeologist Alfred V. Kidder in 1927. See Woodbury, *60 Years of Southwestern Archaeology: A History of the Pecos Conference.*

Pendleton, Hugh Nelson (1875–1953). Helen Pendleton Hayden's father; superintendent of the Rolling Mills at the U.S. Steel National Tube Works in McKeesport, Pennsylvania.

Pendleton, Isabelle (1911–1998). Helen Pendleton Hayden's younger sister. Drew the illustrations for Julian's Vikita report (Hayden 1937, 1987e). Married to Samuel S. Schiff (1911–2000), a veteran of the Abraham Lincoln Brigade in the Spanish Civil War.

Pendleton, Serena Dandridge. Helen Pendleton Hayden's mother.

Phillips, John (1887–1983). A California state senator, 1936–1942, then a California representative to Congress, 1943–1956.

Pinkley, Frank "Boss" (1881–1940). Director of southwest monuments, some of which he helped create, for the National Park Service. Eventually he supervised twenty-seven monuments across four states.

Pleasants, Frederick R. (1906–1976). Curator of primitive art at the Brooklyn Museum and lecturer in anthropology at the University of Arizona.

Point Mugu. Coastal point near Oxnard and Port Hueneme, California. Now a U.S. Navy missile test facility.

Point of Pines. Important site of Mogollon culture settlement on the San Carlos Indian Reservation, Arizona, and site of University of Arizona Field School, 1946–1960.

Potter, Russell M. Geochemist who received his PhD from the California Institute of Technology, later working for Owens Corning Science & Technology Center in Granville, Ohio. With George R. Rossman, authored "Desert Varnish: The Importance of Clay Minerals."

Prehistoric Man in the New World (1964): volume edited by Jesse D. Jennings and Edward Norbeck.

Pueblo Grande. Major Hohokam Site along Salt River near Phoenix International Airport, Arizona; proclaimed a Phoenix city park in 1924.

Pumpelly, Raphael (1837–1923). Mining engineer and world traveler. Wrote *Across America and Asia* (1871) and *Reminiscences* (1918).

Putnam, Frederic Ward "F. W." (1839–1915). One of the earliest anthropologists in the United States. Harvard professor and curator of the Peabody Museum of American Archaeology and Ethnology. Later directed World Columbian Exposition of 1893 and laid foundations for American Museum of Natural History in New York City and the department of anthropology at University of California, Berkeley.

Rancho Costa Rica. Cattle ranch between Seriland and Hermosillo, Sonora. See McGee, *The Seri Indians of Bahia Kino and Sonora, Mexico.*

Randolph Park. Large city park in Tucson, now known as Reid Park.

Ravalli Republic. Hamilton, Montana, newspaper for Ravalli County since 1885.

Reed, Erik K. (1914–1990). Archaeologist who worked for many years for the National Park Service.

Riverside, California. City along Santa Ana River east of Los Angeles, California.

Robinson, William J. "Bill." Dendrochronologist at University of Arizona, now emeritus.

Rogers, Frederick S. (1865–1942). Anthropologist and photographer, designer of the first electrically driven boat in America, and founder of Rogers Machine Company of Rochester, New York. Married to Nellie Jennings, Malcolm's father.

Rogers, Malcolm Jennings (1890–1960). Pioneer desert archaeologist and Hayden's first mentor in desert archaeology. His first wife was named Ethel, his second, Frances Grace. See Hayden, "Malcolm Jennings Rogers, 1890–1960."

Rosenthal, E. Jane. Archaeologist; her dissertation at the University of Arizona was on the manufacture of percussion-flaked shell tools from Sierra Pinacate.

Rossman, George R. Professor of mineralogy at California Institute of Technology.

Russell, Frank (1868–1903). Harvard anthropologist specializing in the Crees, Eskimos, and tribes of southern Arizona; author of *The Pima Indians* (1908).

Saguaro National Monument. Park east of Tucson created in 1935; later expanded to include land west of Tucson and redesignated as a national park.

Salisbury, Rollin D. (1858–1922). Geologist at University of Chicago; co-authored *Geology* (1904) and *Introductory Geology: A Textbook for Colleges* (1921) with Thomas C. Chamberlin.

San Dieguito phase II. The early occupants of the lower Colorado basin and deserts of eastern California and Arizona during the pluvial period 18,000–9,000 BP. See Rogers, "The Stone Art of the San Dieguito Plateau."

San Dieguito River. A small flowing river that rises in the mountains near Julian, California, and empties into the Pacific Ocean near Solana Beach, north of San Diego. Humans have lived along its banks for millennia.

Sandoz, Mari (1896–1966). Historian and author of books about the American West, including a biography of her father, *Old Jules* (1939).

Santan. Pima Indian village along Gila River south of Phoenix.

Santa Rosa. Village in eastern Tohono O'odham Nation.

Sasabe. Arizona community on Mexican border, southwest of Tucson.

Sayles, Edwin Booth "Ted" (1892–1977). Archaeologist best known for his work on Clovis and Cochise cultures. Long associated with the Gila Pueblo Archaeological Foundation and the Arizona State Museum. See Huckell, Creel, and Jacobs, "E. B. 'Ted' Sayles, Pioneer Southwestern Archaeologist."

Scherer, James Augustin Brown (1870–1944). Former director of the Southwest Museum (now part of the Autry National Center).

Schroeder, Albert Henry "Al" (1914–1993). Archaeologist for the National Park Service, expert witness in Indian Land Claim Hearings, and author of many articles and books, including *The Hohokam, Sinagua, and the Hakataya* (1975).

Sciscenti, James V. Archaeologist; owner of Archaeological Survey Consultants in Roswell, New Mexico.

Scrugham, James (1909–1996). Site laborer at Mesa House, Nevada. Son of James G. Scrugham (1880–1945), at various times Nevada's governor, congressman, and senator, and acquaintance of M. R. Harrington.

Sells. Town in southwestern Arizona and capital of Tohono O'odham Nation.

Sessions, Mr. and Mrs. C. H. Funders of excavations at Gypsum Cave and Mesa House through the Southwest Museum.

Seymour, Deni J. Research archaeologist with special interests in the Protohistoric and Historic periods of the southern Southwest.

Shelby, Carroll Hall. Race car driver and designer.

Shreve, Forrest (1878–1950). Plant ecologist with the Carnegie Desert Botanical Laboratory in Tucson. Co-author of *Vegetation and Flora of the Sonoran Desert* (1964).

Sierra Pinacate. Volcanic shield in northwestern Sonora, site of extensive human occupation. See Hayden, *The Sierra Pinacate*.

Simpson, Kay. Contract archaeologist; now with the Louis Berger Group.

Smith, William Neil, II "Seri Bill" (1920–2010). Trader with Seri Indians of Mexico.

Snaketown. Major Hohokam settlement along Gila River near Chandler, Arizona. First excavated by Gladwin, later by Haury with Sayles, Reed, and Hayden in 1934.

Snaketown II. Reexcavation of Hohokam Site at Snaketown, directed by Haury in 1964.

Snow, Milton S. "Jackie". A talented photographer who worked for the Soil Conservation Service and the Indian Service.

Solosth, Robert E. Phoenix orthoptician; founding chairman of the executive board of the Arizona Anthropological Association, which was based at Pueblo Grande.

South Mountain Park. Largest city park in America, south of Phoenix. Archaeologically and historically rich.

Spencer, Walter Baldwin (1860–1929). English biologist, who became a professor of biology at the University of Melbourne. Developed a strong interest in anthropology of Aboriginal culture. See Mulvaney, *"So Much That Is New": Baldwin Spencer, 1860–1929, a Biography*.

Spicer, Edward Holland "Ned" (1906–1983). Anthropologist at the University of Arizona. Author of *Potam: A Yaqui Village in Sonora* (1954) and *Cycles of Conquest* (1962). His wife, the anthropologist Rosamond Botler Spicer (1913–1998), was Helen Hayden's cousin.

Spier, Leslie (1863–1961). Anthropologist and ethnologist, professor at University of Washington and later at University of New Mexico.

Stanford, Dennis. Eminent paleoarchaeologist and anthropologist; at the Smithsonian Institution he is curator of several major paleolithic and archaeological collections, director of the Paleoindian/Paleoecology Program, and head of the Division of Archaeology. He is co-editor of *Paleo-American Origins: Beyond Clovis* (2005) and an early proponent of the "Solutrean Solution" theory of stone-tool technology distribution.

Steen, Charlie Rupert (1908–1997). Close friend of the Haydens. Worked for the National Park Service. Specialist in stabilization and restoration of archaeological sites who worked at Wupatki, among other locations.

Sunset Camp. Ancient campsite southwest of Tinaja de los Chivos in the Pinacates, Sonora, Mexico.

Supernaugh, William R. "Bill" (1905–1981). Superintendent of Organ Pipe Cactus National Monument (1939–1942, 1943–1954).

Taylor, R. E. Anthropologist; director of the radiocarbon laboratory and chair of the Department of Anthropology, University of California, Riverside. Opponent of early dates for Yuha Man.

Tecomate. Seri camp on northwestern corner of Tiburón Island, Sonora, Mexico.

The Spot. Tourist stop along Highway 80 between Gila Bend and Yuma, Arizona; now Spot Road exit on I-8.

Throckmorton, John J. "Old Dad" (probably 1865–1958). Educated in Missouri; worked as a muleskinner in Death Valley before becoming a laborer on archaeological sites, including Avila and Casa Grande.

Tiburón Island. Large island in midriff of Gulf of California, Mexico. Seri Indian homeland.

Tindale, Norman Barnett (1900–1993). Australian anthropologist, archaeologist, and entomologist. Worked with South Australia Museum in Adelaide. Best remembered for mapping tribal groupings of Aboriginal Australians. Author of *Aboriginal Tribes of Australia* (1974).

Tuchman, Barbara Wertheim (1912–1989). Pulitzer-prize-winning historian and author; books include *The Zimmerman Telegram* (1958) and *The Guns of August* (1962).

Tucson Mountain Park. Large county park west of Tucson, Arizona.

Tucson Pressed Brick Company (TPBCo). Early Tucson brickyard, established by Quintus Montier, later owned by the Steinfeld family, acquired in 1948 by contractor John Sundt.

Turner, Raymond M. Botanist with the U.S. Geological Survey, now retired, who worked extensively in the Pinacate. With J. Rodney Hastings, authored a classic book of repeat photography, *The Changing Mile* (1965), updated with Robert H. Webb and Janice E. Bowers as *The Changing Mile Revisited* (2003).

Turney, Omar Asa. City engineer for Phoenix, Arizona; produced notable map of Hohokam canals in Salt River Valley (1929) and supported preservation of Pueblo Grande.

Udall, Morris King "Mo" (1922–1998). Congressional representative from southern Arizona (1961–1991). Author of *Too Funny to Be President* (1987).

Udall, Stewart Lee "Stew" (1920–2010). Congressional representative from southern Arizona (1955–1961) and secretary of interior (1961–1969) under presidents Kennedy and Johnson. Author of *The Quiet Crisis* (1963) and largely responsible for Wilderness Act (1964) and Endangered Species Act (1966).

Underhill, Ruth Murray (1884–1984). Anthropologist; much of her career was with Bureau of Indian Affairs. Author of several books, including *Singing for Power* (1938) and *Social Organization of the Papago Indians* (1939).

University Indian Ruins. Important Hohokam village along Rillito River, Tucson. See Hayden (1957).

Valley of Fire. Nevada's oldest state park (1935), fifty miles northeast of Las Vegas.

Van Bergen, Charles. A wealthy enthusiast from New York who sponsored archaeology expeditions and research, such as the Van Bergen–Los Angeles Museum Expeditions in California, Arizona, and Nevada during 1929–1932.

Ventana Cave. A very important Papaguería archaeology site west of Sells, Arizona. See Haury, *The Stratigraphy and Archaeology of Ventana Cave*.

Walker, Lewis Wayne "Lew" (1906–1971). Author, photographer, avid ornithologist, and Baja California explorer; associate director of the Arizona-Sonora Desert Museum for seventeen years.

Warnock, Barton H. (1911–1998). Botanist, authority on flora of Trans-Pecos, and professor at Sul Ross State University in Alpine, Texas.

Warren, Claude N. Archaeologist and professor at University of Nevada, Las Vegas. Studied San Dieguito culture and Harris Site, and human prehistory in Mojave Desert.

Waters, Michael R. Professor of anthropology and geography at Center for Study of the First Americans, Texas A&M University. Author of *Principles of Geoarchaeology: A North American Perspective* (1992) and co-author of major pre-Clovis papers: Waters and Stafford, Jr., "Redefining the Age of Clovis: Implications for the Peopling of the Americas," and Goebel, Waters, and O'Rourke, "The Late Pleistocene Dispersal of Modern Humans in the Americas."

Webb, Delbert E. "Del" (1899–1974). Contractor and real estate developer. Founded Del Webb Corporation, which had a construction contract at Yuma Army Airfield during World War II; later became widely known for developing retirement communities.

Webb, George (b. 1893). Pima Indian born at Gila Crossing, south of Phoenix, Arizona. Author of *A Pima Remembers* (1959).

Wegener, Alfred (1880–1930). Interdisciplinary scientist who proposed theory of continental drift and plate tectonics in *The Origins of Continents and Oceans* (1915).

Wetherill, John "Hosteen John" (1866–1944). Early trader, settler, and explorer in Four Corners region; archaeological enthusiast and guide for researchers. His wife, Louisa Wade Wetherill, was an accomplished ethnographer. See Blackburn, *The Wetherills: Friends of Mesa Verde,* and Gillmor, *Traders to the Navajos.*

Wetherill, Milton "Milt" (1898–1978). Ranger at Navajo National Monument, 1934–1938; long associated with the Museum of Northern Arizona; nephew to John Wetherill.

White Tanks. Natural waterholes and major archaeological site in the Tank Mountains between Gila Bend and Yuma. (Not to be confused with White Tanks in White Tank Mountains west of Phoenix.)

Whiting, Nancy Pinkley (1910–1979). Daughter of Frank "Boss" Pinkley. She served as a lab technician at Snaketown I; her primary career was as a Red Cross nurse.

Wilbur, Antonio. Pima medicine man.

Wilder, Carleton Stafford (1911–1986). Anthropologist, author of *Yaqui Deer Dance* (1963). Married to Judith C. Wilder (1910–1995).

Wilder, Joseph C. Son of Carleton and Judith Wilder; director of the University of Arizona's Southwest Center.

Wirkus, Faustin. U.S. Marine assigned to administer the affairs of La Gonâve, an island off Haiti, in 1920. The reigning queen, Ti Memmene, pronounced him king. He published his story as *The White King of La Gonave* (1931).

Woodin, Ann. Author of *Home Is the Desert* (1964).

Woodin, William "Bill". Naturalist. Former director of Arizona-Sonora Desert Museum.

Woodward, Arthur "Art" (1898–1986). Archaeologist; curator of history and anthropology at the Natural History Museum of Los Angeles County, California, 1928–1953. Particularly known for his work at the Grewe Site, Arizona.

Wormington, H. (Hannah) Marie (1914–1994). Anthropologist affiliated with the Denver Museum of Natural History, known particularly for her work on Early Man. Author of *Ancient Man in North America* (1939) and *Prehistoric Indians of the Southwest* (1959).

Wright, Frank Lloyd (1867–1959). Prominent architect. Taliesin West, located in Scottsdale, Arizona, served as his winter home as well as a school, and is now the headquarters for the Frank Lloyd Wright Foundation.

Xavier, Juan (1897–1975). Tohono O'odham leader and medicine man, once married to Gwyneth Harrington.

Yazzi, Nakai. Born at Fort Sumner, New Mexico; a half-Navajo, half-Mexican man who later lived near Keet Seel in northern Arizona.

Young, William S. "Bill" (1902–1990). Mule packer for the 1933–1934 Keet Seel stabilization project. Worked as a trader in several trading posts throughout the Navajo Reservation, most notably at the Hubbell Trading Post in Ganado, Arizona.

Yuha Man. Possible pre-Clovis culture as indicated by human remains and artifacts found by W. Morlin Childers in 1976 at Yuha Pinto Wash in southeastern California.

Bibliography

WORKS BY JULIAN HAYDEN
Published Works

c. 1930a   (with C. A. "Biz" Bisbee) *Bunk House Bunk: The Real Story of Bouldoover Dam*. Boulder City: privately printed.

c. 1930b   (with C. A. "Biz" Bisbee) *Bunk House Bunk: Denizens of the Dam*. Boulder City: privately printed.

1937   (with Charlie R. Steen) "The Vikita Ceremony of the Papago." In *Supplement, Southwestern Monuments Monthly Report for April, 1937*, 263–283. Coolidge: National Park Service.

1942a   "Seri Indians on Tiburon Island." *Arizona Highways* 18, no. 1 (January): 22–29, 40–41.

1942b   "Plaster Mixing Bowls." *American Antiquity* 7, no. 4: 405–407.

1943   "Objects to 'Three Babies' Version. . . ." *Desert Magazine* 6, no. 8 (June): 26.

1945   "Salt Erosion." *American Antiquity* 10, no. 4: 373–378.

1956a   "Notes on the Archaeology of the Central Coast of Sonora, Mexico." *Kiva* 21, nos. 3–4: 19–22.

1956b   *The Facts of Life with Septic Tanks*. Tucson: Hayden Excavation Service.

1956–1978   "Hayden Says." A weekly editorial-advertising paragraph in the *Arizona Daily Star* and *Tucson Citizen*, Tucson.

1957   *Excavations, 1940, at University Indian Ruin*. Southwestern Monuments Technical Series 5. Globe: Southwestern Monuments Association.

1958   Introduction to "San Dieguito Implements from the Terraces of the Rincon-Pantano and Rillito Drainage System" by Malcolm J. Rogers. *Kiva* 24, no. 1: 1–2.

1959   "Notes on Pima Pottery Making." *Kiva* 24, no. 3: 272–306.

1961   "Malcolm Jennings Rogers, 1890–1960." *American Anthropologist* 63, no. 6: 1323–1324.

1965   "Fragile-Pattern Areas." *American Antiquity* 31, no. 2: 272–276.

1966a   "Restoration of the San Dieguito Type Site to Its Proper Place in the San Dieguito Sequence." *American Antiquity* 31, no. 3, part 1: 439–440.

1966b   Comments on "Kino's Exploration of the Pinacate Region" by Ronald L. Ives. *Journal of Arizona History* 7, no. 4: 196–200.

1967   "A Summary Prehistory and History of the Sierra Pinacate, Sonora." *American Antiquity* 32, no. 3: 335–344.

1969   "Gyratory Crushers of the Sierra Pinacate, Sonora." *American Antiquity* 34, no. 2: 154–161.

1970a   "Recovery of Jawbones of Extinct Horses and C-14 Samples from Ventana Cave, Arizona." In Current Research, *American Antiquity* 35, no. 4: 508–509.

1970b   "Of Hohokam Origins and Other Matters." *American Antiquity* 35, no. 1: 87–93.

1972   "Hohokam Petroglyphs of the Sierra Pinacate, Sonora and the Hohokam Shell Expeditions." *Kiva* 37, no. 2: 74–83.

1974   (with Jon Nathan Young) Review of *Yuman Pottery Making* and *Early Lithic Industries of the Lower Basin of the Colorado River and Adjacent Desert Areas* by Malcolm J. Rogers. *Journal of Arizona History* 15, no. 2: 195–197.

1975a   (with V. K. Pheriba Stacy) *Saguaro National Monument: An Archeological Overview.* Tucson: Arizona Archeological Center.

1975b   (with Emil W. Haury) Preface to *The Stratigraphy and Archaeology of Ventana Cave* by Emil W. Haury, v–vi. 2nd printing. Tucson: University of Arizona Press.

1976a   "Changing Climate in the Sierra Pinacate of Sonora, Mexico." In *Desertification: Process, Problems, Perspectives,* edited by Patricia Paylore and Richard A. Haney Jr., 70–86. Tucson: University of Arizona Arid/Semi-Arid Natural Resources Program.

1976b   "Pre-altithermal Archaeology in the Sierra Pinacate, Sonora, Mexico." *American Antiquity* 41, no. 3: 274–289.

1976c,d c: "Resumen de la Arqueología del Distrito de los Ríos Sonoita y Altar," 261–265. d: "La Arqueología de la Sierra del Pinacate, Sonora, México," 281–304. In *Sonora, Antropología del Desierto,* edited by Beatriz Braniff C. and Richard S. Felger. Colección Científica 27. Mexico: Instituto Nacional de Antropología e Historia.

1977   "Wihom-ki." *Kiva* 43, no. 1: 31–35.

1978a   "Kiet Siel." *Kiva* 43, nos. 3–4: 161–166.

1978b   Introduction to "Indian Night Stories" by Malcolm J. Rogers. *Kiva* 44, no. 1: 51.

1980a,b a: "A Camp at Kiet Siel," 96–102. b: "Sierra Pinacate, 145–152. In *Camera, Spade and Pen: An Inside View of Southwestern Archaeology,* edited by Marnie Gaede with photographs by Marc Gaede. Tucson: University of Arizona Press.

1980c   "Comments on Calico." *Journal of Field Archaeology* 7, no. 3: 379.

1981   "C-14 Ages of Foodshell from Occupied Dunes of the Bay of Adair, Sonora, Mexico." In Current Research, *American Antiquity* 46, no. 4: 933.

1982   "Ground Figures of the Sierra Pinacate, Sonora, Mexico." In *Hohokam and Patayan: Prehistory of Southwest Arizona,* edited by Randall H. McGuire and Michael B. Schiffer, 581–588. New York: Academic Press.

1984a   *Sierra de El Pinacate, Sonora, Mexico.* Hermosillo: SYGMA Gráfica for State of Sonora.

1984b   "Comments on Spaulding's Report on Overkill." *Quaternary Research* 22: 140–141.

1984c   Review of *Camp-Fires on Desert and Lava* by William T. Hornaday. *Journal of Arizona History* 24, no. 3: 326–328.

1985   "Food Animal Cremations of the Sierra Pinacate, Sonora, Mexico." *Kiva* 50, no. 4: 237–248.

1987a   "Notes on the Apparent Course of San Dieguito Development." In *San Dieguito–La Jolla: Chronology and Controversy,* edited by Dennis Gallegos, 43–47. San Diego County Archaeological Society Research Papers No. 1. San Diego: San Diego County Archaeological Society.

1987b   "Early Man in Southwest North America [Abstract]." In *Abstracts,* edited by A. L. Bryan. Mainz: Commission on the Peopling of the Americas, International Union for Pre and Protohistoric Sciences, XI Congress.

1987c   "Talking with the Beasts." *City Magazine* 2, no. 6: 47–49.

1987d   "Talking with the Animals: Pinacate Reminiscences." *Journal of the Southwest* 29, no. 2: 222–227.

1987e   "The Vikita Ceremony of the Papago." *Journal of the Southwest* 29, no. 3: 273–324.

1987f   "Adobe and Salt Erosion = Solution." *Earth and Sun* 49: 27, with reprint of "Salt Erosion" (1945), 35–38. Las Cruces: Solar Earthbuilder International.

1987g   Review of *Death Valley and the Amargosa: A Land of Illusion,* by Richard E. Lingenfelter. *Journal of Arizona History* 28, no. 2: 201–202.

1988a "History of the Puerto Peñasco Area: Part 1: Prehistory, the Pinacateños and Areneros/ Historia de la Región de Puerto Peñasco: Parte 1: Prehistoria, los Pinacateños y los Areneros." *CEDO News* 1, no. 2: 12–13.

1988b "History of the Puerto Peñasco Area: Part 2: Prehistory, the Hohokam and Estero Morúa/ Historia de la Región de Puerto Peñasco: Parte 2: Los Hohokam y Estero Morúa. *CEDO News* 1, no. 3: 10–11.

1988c "The Sierra del Pinacate." In *Simposio de Investigación sobre la Zona Ecológica de El Pinacate, Memoria*, edited by Fernando Lizárraga, 52–56. Hermosillo: Comité de Ecología y Medio Ambiente.

1989a "Borderlands: Views of a Region by Julian Hayden. Photographs catalogued and selected by Mary Bernard-Shaw and Chet Shaw." *Journal of the Southwest* 31, no. 4: 453–470.

1989b Review of *Hoover Dam: An American Adventure*, by Joseph E. Stevens. *Journal of Arizona History* 30, no. 3: 357–359.

1993a Foreword to *Archaeology of the Pueblo Grande Platform Mound and Surrounding Features*, vol. 1: *Introduction to the Archival Project and History of Archaeological Research*, edited by Christian E. Downum and Todd W. Bostwick, xii–xvi. Pueblo Grande Museum Anthropological Papers 1 (1). Phoenix: Pueblo Grande Museum.

1993b,c b: "La Arqueología de la Sierra de Pinacate, Sonora, México," 145–153. c: "Resumen de la Arqueología del Distrito de los Ríos Sonoita y Altar," 137–138. *Noroeste de México* 12. Reprinted from 1976.

1994a (with Christian E. Downum, David A. Gregory, Todd W. Bostwick, and Stephen H. Savage) "Pithouses and Other Structures." In *Archaeology of the Pueblo Grande Platform Mound and Surrounding Features*, vol. 2: *Features in the Central Precinct of the Pueblo Grande Community*, edited by Todd W. Bostwick and Christian E. Downum, 47–130. Pueblo Grande Museum Anthropological Papers 1 (2). Phoenix: Pueblo Grande Museum.

1994b (with Donald Bahr, Juan Smith, and William Allison Smith) *The Short Swift Time of Gods on Earth: The Hohokam Chronicles*. Berkeley: University of California Press.

1994c "The Sierra Pinacate, the Legacy of Malcolm Rogers, and the Archaeology of the Lower Colorado River." In *Recent Research along the Lower Colorado River*, edited by Joseph A. Ezzo, 121–125. Statistical Research Technical Series 51. Tucson: Statistical Research.

1997a "Changing Place-Names in the Pinacate." *Journal of the Southwest* 39, nos. 3–4: 697–702. Reprinted 2007, 80–84 in *Dry Borders: Great Natural Reserves of the Sonoran Desert*, edited by Richard Stephen Felger and Bill Broyles. Salt Lake City: University of Utah Press.

1997b "A Trip to Laguna Prieta." *Journal of the Southwest* 39, no. 3–4: 321–329. Reprinted 2007, 577–580 in *Dry Borders: Great Natural Reserves of the Sonoran Desert*, edited by Richard Stephen Felger and Bill Broyles. Salt Lake City: University of Utah Press.

1998a "The Compound Wall." In *Archaeology of the Pueblo Grande Platform Mound and Surrounding Features*, vol. 4: *The Pueblo Grande Platform Mound Compound*, edited by Christian E. Downum and Todd W. Bostwick, 27–146. Pueblo Grande Museum Anthropological Papers 1 (4). Phoenix: Pueblo Grande Museum.

1998b (with Christian E. Downum) "Rooms, Courts, and Other Features of the Northwest Compound." In *Archaeology of the Pueblo Grande Platform Mound and Surrounding Features*, vol. 4: *The Pueblo Grande Platform Mound Compound*, edited by Christian E. Downum and Todd W. Bostwick, 27–146. Pueblo Grande Museum Anthropological Papers 1 (4). Phoenix: Pueblo Grande Museum.

1998c *The Sierra Pinacate*. Tucson: University of Arizona Press and Southwest Center.

Unpublished Works

1982   Julian D. Hayden and Antonio A. Andretta. The San Dieguito complex and the Trans-Pecos, Texas. Unpublished paper submitted for inclusion in *Stone Tool Analysis: Essays in Honor of Don E. Crabtree*. Albuquerque: University of New Mexico Press.

1987   Early Man in the Far Southwestern United States and Adjacent Sonora, Mexico. Submitted to The International Union for Pre-and Proto-historic Sciences, Commission for the Peopling of the Americas, XI Congress, Mainz, West Germany 1987, revised for publication January 1988.

Published Interviews

1988   Dolzani, Michael. "A Bridge over Time, Interview with Julian Hayden." In *Mammoth Trumpet* 4, no. 4: 1, 4–6. Orono: Center for the Study of Early Man, University of Maine.

1993   (with Gary Paul Nabhan, Bill Broyles, Anita Williams, and Caroline Wilson) "Sheep Cremations and Massacres." In *Counting Sheep: Twenty Ways of Seeing Desert Bighorn*, edited by Gary Paul Nabhan, 27–36. Tucson: University of Arizona Press.

Unpublished Interviews

Unless otherwise noted, Diane Boyer (DB) and Bill Broyles (BB) conducted the interview.

April 19, 1989. Peter Booth only. (1 tape)

January 15, 1990. (1 tape)

January 25, 1990. (1 tape)

February 2, 1990. DB only. On Malcolm Rogers's photo album. (1 tape)

February 8, 1990. (1 tape)

March 7, 1990. (1 tape)

March 14, 1990. (1 tape)

March 21, 1990. (1 tape)

April 26, 1990. (1 tape)

May 16, 1990. (1 tape)

May 24, 1990. (1 tape)

June 6, 1990. (2 tapes)

June 21, 1990. (2 tapes)

July 12, 1990. BB only. (1 tape)

September 29, 1991. (1 tape)

December 29, 1991. (1 tape)

June 20, 1992. (1 tape)

September 20, 1992. (1 tape)

December 24, 1992. (2 tapes)

June 20, 1993. (1 tape)

July 11, 1993. Including Charles Bowden. (2 tapes)

October 9, 1994. BB only. (1 tape)

November 5, 1995. (2 tapes)

SELECTED READINGS

Adams, Jenny L.
1993   *Pinto Beans and Prehistoric Pots: The Legacy of Al and Alice Lancaster.* Tucson: Arizona State Museum Archaeology Series, 183.

Bancroft, Griffing
1932   *Lower California: A Cruise. The Flight of the Least Petrel.* New York: G. P. Putnam's Sons.

Blackburn, Fred M.
2006   *The Wetherills: Friends of Mesa Verde.* Durango, CO: Durango Herald Small Press.

Blaine, Peter, as told to Michael S. Adams
1981   *Papagos and Politics.* Tucson: Arizona Historical Society.

Bolen, Jean Shinoda
1979   *The Tao of Psychology: Synchronicity and the Self.* New York: Harper & Row.

Bonnichsen, Robson, Bradley T. Lepper, Dennis Stanford, and Michael R. Waters, editors
2005   *Paleoamerican Origins: Beyond Clovis.* College Station: Center for the Study of the First Americans (Texas A&M University Press).

Bostwick, Todd W.
2006   *Byron Cummings: Dean of Southwest Archaeology.* Tucson: University of Arizona Press.

Bowen, Thomas
2000   *Unknown Island: Seri Indians, Europeans, and San Esteban Island of the Gulf of California.* Albuquerque: University of New Mexico Press.

Broyles, Bill
1988   "Desert Archaeology: An Interview with Paul H. Ezell, 1913–1988." *Journal of the Southwest* 20, no. 3: 398–449.
2008   "Paul Ezell in the Papaguería." In *Fragile Patterns: The Archaeology of Western Papaguería,* edited by Jeffrey H. Altschul and Adrianne G. Rankin, 41–62.

Bryan, Kirk
1925   *The Papago Country, Arizona: A Geographic, Geologic, and Hydrologic Reconnaissance with a Guide to Desert Watering Places.* U.S. Geological Survey Water-Supply Paper No. 499. Washington, DC: U.S. Government Printing Office.

Cabell, James Branch
1919   *Jurgen, A Comedy of Justice.* New York: R. M. McBride.

Carter, George F.
1980   *Earlier Than You Think: A Personal View of Man in America.* College Station: Texas A&M University Press.

Cather, Willa
1927   *Death Comes for the Archbishop.* New York: A. A. Knopf.

Chamberlin, C. Thomas, and Rollin D. Salisbury
1904   *Geology.* New York: Henry Holt and Co.
1921   *Introductory Geology: A Textbook for Colleges.* New York: Henry Holt and Co.

Coolidge, Dane, and Mary Roberts Coolidge
1939   *The Last of the Seris.* New York: E. P. Dutton.

Courbin, Paul
1988   *What Is Archaeology? An Essay on the Nature of Archaeological Research.* Chicago: University of Chicago Press.

Crabtree, Don E.
1972   *An Introduction to Flintworking.* Occasional Papers of the Idaho State University Museum, no. 8. Pocatello: Idaho State University Museum.

Davis, Emma Lou, and Sylvia Winslow
1965   "Giant Ground Figures of the Prehistoric Deserts." *Proceedings of the American Philosophical Society* 109, no. 1: 8–21.

Davis, Emma Lou, and Christopher Raven, editors
1986   *Environmental and Paleoenvironmental Studies in Panamint Valley.* Contributions of the Great Basin Foundation, No. 2. San Diego: Great Basin Foundation.

Dillehay, Thomas D.
2000   *The Settlement of the Americas: A New Prehistory.* New York: Basic Books.

Downum, Christian E., and Todd W. Bostwick, editors
1993   *Archaeology of the Pueblo Grande Platform Mound and Surrounding Features. Volume 1: Introduction to the Archival Project and History of Archaeological Research.* Pueblo Grande Museum Anthropological Papers, No. 1. Phoenix: City of Phoenix.

Eckhart, George Boland
1961   *Missions of Sonora.* Tucson: self-published.

Eiseley, Loren C.
1958   *Darwin's Century: Evolution and the Men Who Discovered It.* Garden City, NY: Doubleday.
1975   *All the Strange Hours: The Excavation of a Life.* New York: Scribner.

Ezell, Paul H.
1954   "An Archeological Survey in Northwestern Papagueria." *Kiva* 19, nos. 2–4: 1–26.
1955   "The Archaeological Delineation of a Cultural Boundary in Papaguería." *American Antiquity* 20, no. 4: 367–374.

Felger, Richard Stephen
2000   *Flora of the Gran Desierto and Río Colorado of Northwestern Mexico.* Tucson: University of Arizona Press.

Felger, Richard Stephen, and Mary Beck Moser
1985   *People of the Desert and Sea: Ethnobotany of the Seri Indians.* Tucson: University of Arizona Press.

Fell, Barry
1976   *America, B.C.: Ancient Settlers in the New World.* New York: Quadrangle/New York Times Book Co.
1980   *Saga America.* New York: Times Books.

Flaccus, Elmer W.
1981   "Arizona's Last Great Indian War: The Saga of Pia Machita." *Journal of Arizona History* 22, no. 1: 1–22.

Fontana, Bernard L.
1981   *Of Earth and Little Rain: The Papago Indians.* Flagstaff: Northland Press.
1994   *Entrada: The Legacy of Spain and Mexico in the United States.* Tucson: Southwest Parks and Monuments Association.
2010   *A Gift of Angels: The Art of Mission San Xavier del Bac.* Tucson: University of Arizona Press.

Forman, Harrison
1935   *Through Forbidden Tibet: An Adventure into the Unknown.* New York: Longmans, Green, and Co.

Gaede, Marc, and Marnie Gaede
1980   *Camera, Spade and Pen: An Inside View of Southwestern Archaeology.* Tucson: University of Arizona Press.

Gillmor, Frances, and Louisa Wade Wetherill
1934   *Traders to the Navajos.* Boston: Houghton Mifflin.

Goebel, Ted, Michael R. Waters, and Dennis H. O'Rourke
2008   "The Late Pleistocene Dispersal of Modern Humans in the Americas." *Science* 319, no. 5869: 1497–1502.

Greenberg, Joseph H.
1966   *Language Universals with Special Reference to Feature Hierarchies.* The Hague: Mouton.

Greenway, John
1972   *Down among the Wild Men: A Narrative Journal of Fifteen Years Pursuing the Old Stone Age Aborigines of Australia's Western Desert.* Boston: Little, Brown.

Gregory, Herbert E.
1917   *Geology of the Navajo Country, a Reconnaissance of Parts of Arizona, New Mexico and Utah.* U. S. Geological Survey Professional Paper, 93. Washington, DC: U.S. Government Printing Office.

Gutmann, James T.
2007   "Geological Studies in the Pinacate Volcanic Field." *Journal of the Southwest* 49, no. 2 (Summer): 189–243.

Harrington, Alan
1987   "Juan and Jack: Memories of a Desert Town, 1949." *City Magazine* 2, no. 5 (May): 39–41.

Harrington, Marie
1985   *On the Trail of Forgotten People: A Personal Account of the Life and Career of Mark Raymond Harrington.* Reno: Great Basin Press.

Hastings, James Rodney, and Raymond M. Turner
1965   *The Changing Mile: An Ecological Study of Vegetation Change with Time in the Lower Mile of an Arid and Semiarid Region.* Tucson: University of Arizona Press.

Haury, Emil W.
1950   *The Stratigraphy and Archaeology of Ventana Cave.* Tucson: University of Arizona Press.
1976   *Hohokam Desert Farmers and Craftsmen: Excavations at Snaketown 1964–1965.* Tucson: University of Arizona Press.

Hayden, Irwin
1930   *Mesa House.* Southwest Museum Papers, 4. Los Angeles: Southwest Museum.

Hornaday, William T.
1908   *Camp-Fires on Desert and Lava.* New York: Scribner.

Hrdlička, Aleš
1919   *Physical Anthropology: Its Scope and Aims, Its History and Present Status in the United States.* Philadelphia: Wistar Institute of Anatomy and Biology.

Huckell, Bruce B., Darrell C. Creel, and G. Michael Jacobs
1997   "E. B. 'Ted' Sayles, Pioneer Southwestern Archaeologist." *Kiva* 63, no. 1: 69–85.

Hudson, W. H.
1904   *Green Mansions: A Romance of the Tropical Forest.* London: Duckworth and Co.

Ives, Ronald L.
1962   "In Memory: Alberto Celaya." *Explorers Journal* 40, no. 2: 91–92.
1963   "Alberto Celaya, 1885–1962." *Kiva* 28, no. 4: 21–22.
1989   *Land of Lava, Ash and Sand: The Pinacate Region of Northwestern Mexico.* Tucson: Arizona Historical Society.

Jennings, Jesse D.
1994   *Accidental Archaeologist: The Memoirs of Jesse D. Jennings.* Salt Lake City: University of Utah Press.

Jennings, Jesse D., and Edward Norbeck, editors
1964   *Prehistoric Man in the New World.* Chicago: University of Chicago Press for Rice University.

Kimmelman, Alex Jay
2002   *Harold Ashton: Reflections of a Proud Family Patriarch, Gentleman, and Master Builder.* Tucson: Ashton Co.

Lister, Florence C., and Robert H. Lister
1968   *Earl Morris & Southwestern Archaeology.* Albuquerque: University of New Mexico Press.

Longacre, William A.
1999   "Why Did the BAE Hire an Architect?" *Journal of the Southwest* 41, no. 3: 359–369.

Lumholtz, Carl
1912   *New Trails in Mexico.* New York: Charles Scribner's Sons.

Martin, Paul S., and Richard G. Klein, editors
1984   *Quaternary Extinctions: A Prehistoric Revolution.* Tucson: University of Arizona Press.

McGee, W J
1898   *The Seri Indians of Bahia Kino and Sonora, Mexico.* Bureau of American Ethnology, vol. 17. Washington, DC: Smithsonian Institution.
2000   *Trails to Tiburón: The 1894 and 1895 Field Diaries of W J McGee.* Transcribed by Hazel McFeely Fontana; annotated and with an introduction by Bernard L. Fontana. Tucson: University of Arizona Press.

Meltzer, David J.
1989   "Why Don't We Know When the First People Came to North America?" *American Antiquity* 54, no. 3: 471–490.
1993   *Search for the First Americans.* Washington, DC: Smithsonian Books.
2006   *Folsom: New Archaeological Investigations of a Classic Bison Kill.* Berkeley: University of California Press.

Morell, Virginia
1990   "Confusion in Earliest America." *Science* 248, no. 4954: 439–441.

Morris, Ann Axtell
1931   *Digging in Yucatan.* Garden City, NY: Doubleday, Doran and Co.
1933   *Digging in the Southwest.* Garden City, NY: Doubleday, Doran and Co.

Morris, Earl H.
1939   *Archaeological Studies in the La Plata District, Southwestern Colorado and Northwestern New Mexico.* Washington, DC: Carnegie Institution of Washington.

Morris, Elizabeth Ann
1981   "Obituary: Alan Peter Olson, 1926–1978." *American Antiquity* 46, no. 2: 342–345.

Mulvaney, Derek J., and John H. Calaby
1985   *"So Much That Is New": Baldwin Spencer, 1860–1929, a Biography.* Carlton, Victoria: University of Melbourne at the University Press.

Nichols, Tad
1999   *Glen Canyon: Images of a Lost World.* Santa Fe: Museum of New Mexico Press.

Olsen, Stanley J.
1979   *Osteology for the Archaeologist.* Papers of the Peabody Museum of Archaeology and Ethnology, vol. 56, nos. 3–5. Cambridge, MA: Peabody Museum.

Payen, Louis A., Carol H. Rector, Eric Ritter, R. E. Taylor, and J. E. Ericson
1978   "Comments on the Pleistocene Age Assignment and Associations of a Human Burial from the Yuha Desert, California." *American Antiquity* 43, no. 3: 448–453.

Pinkley, Edna Townsend
1927   *Casa Grande: The Greatest Valley Pueblo of Arizona.*

Plew, Mark G., James C. Woods, and Max G. Pavesic, editors
1985   *Stone Tool Analysis: Essays in Honor of Don E. Crabtree.* Albuquerque: University of New Mexico Press.

Potter, Russell M., and George R. Rossman
1977   "Desert Varnish: The Importance of Clay Minerals." *Science* 196, no. 4297: 1446–1448.
Pumpelly, Raphael
1870   *Across America and Asia*. New York: Leypoldt and Holt.
1918   *Reminiscences*. New York: Henry Holt and Co.
Rabelais, François
1928   *Gargantua*. New York: Modern Library.
Riddell, Francis A., editor
1968   "Current Research." *American Antiquity* 33, no. 3: 409–425.
Rogers, Malcolm J.
1929   "The Stone Art of the San Dieguito Plateau." *American Anthropologist* 31, no. 3: 454–467.
1939   *Early Lithic Industries of the Lower Basin of the Colorado River and Adjacent Desert Areas*. San Diego Museum papers, no. 3. San Diego: San Diego Museum.
1958   "San Dieguito Implements from the Terraces of the Rincon-Pantano and Rillito Drainage System." *Kiva* 24, no. 1: 1–23.
1966   *Ancient Hunters of the Far West*. A Copley Book. San Diego: Union-Tribune Publishing Co.
Russell, Frank
1975   *The Pima Indians*. Tucson: University of Arizona Press.
Sandoz, Mari
1939   *Old Jules*. Boston: Little, Brown, and Co.
Schroeder, Albert H.
1975   *The Hohokam, Sinagua, and the Hakataya*. El Centro, CA: I.V.C. Museum Society.
Seymour, Deni
1989   "The Dynamics of Sobaipuri Settlement in the Eastern Pimeria Alta." *Journal of the Southwest* 31, no. 2: 205–222.
Shreve, Forrest, and Ira L. Wiggins
1964   *Vegetation and Flora of the Sonoran Desert*. Stanford, CA: Stanford University Press.
Spicer, Edward H.
1954   *Potam: A Yaqui Village in Sonora*. Menasha, WI: American Anthropological Association, vol. 56, no. 4, pt. 2. Memoirs of the American Anthropology Association, no. 77.
1962   *Cycles of Conquest*. Tucson: University of Arizona Press.
Stanley, Henry M.
1890   *In Darkest Africa, or the Quest, Rescue, and Retreat of Emin, Governor of Equatoria*. London: S. Low, Marston, Searle, and Rivington Ltd.
Taylor, R. E., and Clement W. Meighan, editors
1978   *Chronologies in New World Archaeology*. New York: Academic Press.
Tindale, Norman B.
1974   *Aboriginal Tribes of Australia: Their Terrain, Environmental Controls, Distribution, Limits, and Proper Names*. Berkeley: University of California Press.
Tuchman, Barbara W.
1958   *The Zimmerman Telegram*. New York: Viking Press.
1962   *The Guns of August*. New York: Macmillan.
Turner, Raymond M., Robert H. Webb, Janice E. Bowers, and J. Rodney Hastings
2003   *The Changing Mile Revisited: An Ecological Study of Vegetation Change with Time in the Lower Mile of an Arid and Semiarid Region*. Tucson: University of Arizona Press.
Turney, Omar A.
1924   *The Land of the Stone Hoe*. Phoenix: Arizona Republican Print Shop.

Udall, Morris K.
1987   *Too Funny to Be President.* New York: H. Holt.

Udall, Stewart L.
1963   *The Quiet Crisis.* New York: Holt, Rinehart and Winston.

Underhill, Ruth Murray
1938   *Singing for Power: The Song Magic of the Papago Indians of Southern Arizona.* Berkeley: University of California Press.
1939   *Social Organization of the Papago Indians.* New York: Columbia University Press.

Waters, Michael R.
1992   *Principles of Geoarchaeology: A North American Perspective.* Tucson: University of Arizona Press.

Waters, Michael R., and Thomas W. Stafford Jr.
2007   "Redefining the Age of Clovis: Implications for the Peopling of the Americas." *Science* 315, no. 5815: 1122–1126.

Webb, George
1959   *A Pima Remembers.* Tucson: University of Arizona Press.

Wegener, Alfred
1924   *The Origin of Continents and Oceans.* Translated by J. G. A. Skerl. New York: Dutton.

Wilder, Carleton S.
1963   *The Yaqui Deer Dance: A Study in Cultural Change.* Smithsonian Institution/Bureau of American Ethnology Bulletin 186, No. 67. Washington, DC: U.S. Government Printing Office.

Wirkus, Faustin, and Taney Dudley
1931   *The White King of La Gonave.* Garden City, NY: Doubleday, Doran, and Co.

Woodbury, Richard B.
1960   "Nels C. Nelson and Chronological Archaeology." *American Antiquity* 25, no. 3: 400–401.
1993   *Sixty Years of Southwestern Archaeology: A History of the Pecos Conference.* Albuquerque: University of New Mexico Press.

Woodin, Ann
1964   *Home Is the Desert.* New York: Macmillan.

Woodward, Arthur
1930   "Cremation-Pit 'Shrine Area,' and Other 'Rubbish-Heap History': Revelations of the Oldest-Known Culture of the Gila Valley, Arizona." *Illustrated London News,* July 26, pp. 156–159, 184.

Wormington, H. Marie
1939   *Ancient Man in North America.* Denver: Denver Museum of Natural History.
1947   *Prehistoric Indians of the Southwest.* Denver: Denver Museum of Natural History.

Index

About the Author

Although he held no degree or faculty position, Julian Hayden (1911–1998) worked with a number of renowned archaeologists and acquired a wide-ranging array of friends who studied, built, shaped, and loved what we know as the Southwest. This is more than a personal history of one man—it is also an intellectual history spanning the Southwest in the twentieth century.

He was a keen observer and listener, as well as a spellbinding storyteller and published scholar. He ran an excavation company by day and wrote about ancient peoples by night. He was a close friend of such noted scholars as archaeologist Emil Haury, field historian Bernard Fontana, geologist James Gutmann, and ethnologist Anita Alvarez Williams, and he encouraged a host of students and scholars who are now famous in their own right, such as archaeologist Christian Downum and paleoarchaeologist Michael Waters. Julian himself was a blue-collar scholar.

He helped excavate famous archaeological sites at Mesa House, Keet Seel, Pueblo Grande, Ventana Cave, and University Ruins. He ran a CCC crew. He formed the theory of "fragile-pattern areas" and was a proponent of pre-Clovis cultures in North America. He became the expert on human prehistory in the Sierra Pinacate of Mexico. He stands alongside Malcolm Rogers and Paul Ezell as a founder of North American desert archaeology, and he was proud to work in the dust where ancient people had lived, walked, and laughed. He never used a computer or GPS, but he excavated, puzzled, and argued with the best of scholars. He was, foremost, a field man.

About the Editors

Bill Broyles is a research associate at the University of Arizona's Southwest Center. He majored in philosophy, taught English and physical education in the public high school classroom for thirty-one years, and now studies the Sonoran Desert and its people. His bookwork includes writing *Sunshot* and *Our Sonoran Desert*, and co-editing *Dry Borders* and *Desert Duty: On the Line with the U.S. Border Patrol.* Thirty-some years ago he knocked on Julian Hayden's door to ask a question about Sierra Pinacate, and he returned frequently for Julian's patient answers.

Diane Boyer began exploring the Pinacate as a child on family camping trips led by her grandfather, Glenton Sykes. Through him, she met Julian Hayden, Bill Broyles, and a host of other desert rats. For the past twenty years, she has primarily worked as a photo archivist, including stints at the Arizona Historical Society, Northern Arizona University Cline Library, and the U.S. Geological Survey. She is a co-author of *Damming Grand Canyon: The 1923 USGS Colorado River Expedition* and a co-editor of *Repeat Photography: Methods and Applications in the Natural Sciences.*

THE SOUTHWEST CENTER SERIES

Joseph C. Wilder, Editor

Bill Broyles and Michael Berman, *Sunshot: Peril and Wonder in the Gran Desierto*

David W. Lazaroff, Philip C. Rosen, and Charles H. Lowe Jr., *Amphibians, Reptiles, and Their Habitats at Sabino Canyon*

David Yetman, *The Organ Pipe Cactus*

Gloria Fraser Giffords, *Sanctuaries of Earth, Stone, and Light: The Churches of Northern New Spain, 1530–1821*

David Yetman, *The Great Cacti: Ethnobotany and Biogeography*

John Messina, *Álamos, Sonora: Architecture and Urbanism in the Dry Tropics*

Laura L. Cummings, *Pachucas and Pachucos in Tucson: Situated Border Lives*

Bernard L. Fontana and Edward McCain, *A Gift of Angels: The Art of Mission San Xavier del Bac*

David A. Yetman, *The Ópatas: In Search of a Sonoran People*

Julian D. Hayden, *Field Man: Life as a Desert Archaeologist*, edited by Bill Broyles and Diane Boyer